COMPARATIVE REVOLUTIONARY MOVEMENTS

Search for Theory and Justice

second edition

THOMAS H. GREENE
University of Southern California

PRENTICE-HALL, INC., ENGLEWOOD CLIFFS, N.J. 07632

P9-DUU-779

Library of Congress Cataloging in Publication Data
Greene, Thomas H., (date)
   Comparative revolutionary movements.

   Bibliography: p. 225
   Includes index.
   1. Revolutions.   2. Comparative government.   I. Title.
JC491.G67 1984   322.4'2   83-9776
ISBN 0-13-154203-6

Editorial/production supervision and
   interior design: Virginia M. Livsey
Cover design: Wanda Lubelska
Manufacturing buyer: Ronald Chapman

Prentice-Hall
Contemporary Comparative Politics Series
JOSEPH LaPALOMBARA, Editor

Printed in the United States of America

10 9 8 7 6 5 4 3 2 1

ISBN 0-13-154203-6

Prentice-Hall International, Inc., *London*
Prentice-Hall of Australia Pty. Limited, *Sydney*
Editora Prentice-Hall do Brasil, Ltda., *Rio de Janeiro*
Prentice-Hall Canada Inc., *Toronto*
Prentice-Hall of India Private Limited, *New Delhi*
Prentice-Hall of Japan, Inc., *Tokyo*
Prentice-Hall of Southeast Asia Pte. Ltd., *Singapore*
Whitehall Books Limited, *Wellington, New Zealand*

"All is change; all yields its place and goes."

Euripides

"A little rebellion, now and then, is a good thing, and as necessary in the political world as storms in the physical."

Thomas Jefferson

"What is the hardest task in the world? To think."

Ralph Waldo Emerson

DEDICATION

Hasty explanations of the sources of individuality in modern society include the following.

You are what you eat.
Clothes make the man (and, presumably, the woman).
You get what you pay for.

I am pleased to propose another, one that is less hasty and more appropriate to scholarly endeavor.

You are what you are taught.

The more worldly will want to amend this to read: You are what you think you are taught.

I have known for a long time that I have been blessed with more than my fair share of good teachers, from the elementary grades through graduate school and beyond. More than a few of these may qualify as great teachers. They were intelligent, yes; but they also were sensitive to the needs and interests of their students, informed about their subject matter, creative in their methods of instruction, and dedicated to giving more of themselves than what was formally required by their positions of authority and trust. To a substantial degree, I am what they have taught me.

Thus what I have written here and what I have written elsewhere is, in part, a measure of their accomplishment, however indirect and remote their influence and however badly I have expressed it. But it is a great satisfaction for me, here and now, to be able to honor them in this small way.

Ann Wood	Pier-maria Pasinetti	Joseph LaPalombara
Eugen Weber	Steven Muller	Thomas Jenkin
Vena Stanger	Dwaine Marvick	Andrew Hacker
Currin Shields	Evelyn McCormick	Mario Einaudi
Harold Schwartz	Theodore Lowi	Arch Dotson

T.H.G.

CONTENTS

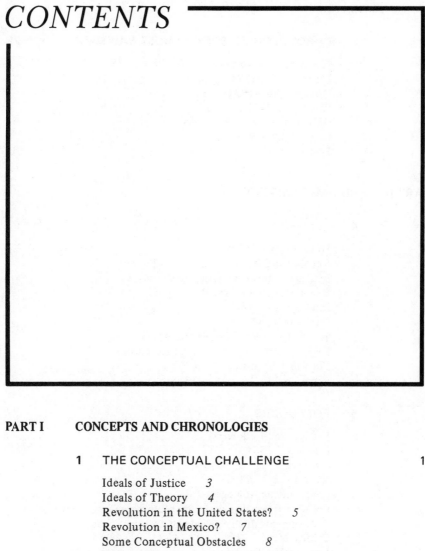

THE
CONCEPTUAL
CHALLENGE

IDEALS OF JUSTICE

Revolution begins in the mind. It is an expression of high ideals, great expectations, an unqualified confidence in the capabilities of human nature and in the creative potential of a part or all of mankind. It is a tribute to the irrepressible optimism of the human spirit. It sustains and renews the memory, myth, or dream of a Golden Age in which all men and women live harmoniously with each other and each person identifies his or her interest with the interest of all. Revolution begins in the mind because its inspiration is an idea of justice.

Revolution begins in the mind, but our idea of justice is focused by the real world of political, economic, and social relationships. Committed to building a new way of life, the revolutionary seeks to destroy the old way of life. Meaningful reform of existing society is considered impossible, and the revolutionary who is true to his or her convictions is intolerant of compromise. Thus people and institutions that stand in the way of justice also must be destroyed. There is either justice or injustice, there is nothing halfway and nothing in-between.

It is in this way, too, that the revolutionary is an extremist. The uncompromising pursuit of justice is not for the uncertain, not for those who are given to moderation, not for those who rank a genial consensus higher than absolute truth. Absolute truth and perfect justice are the ends that serve to justify the revolutionary's extremism of thought and action. And so there is nothing in political life that is more breathtaking and more audacious than a revolutionary act that is inspired by a vision of perfect justice. Many will regard it as worthy of celebration, others as a lamentable defect of the human condition.

IDEALS OF THEORY

Revolution begins in the mind, but its object is to change the world. The impulse to understand the nature and meaning of revolution also begins in the mind, but the mind must probe the world in order to satisfy the urge to understand.

It may be easier to carry out a revolution, however, than it is to understand it. Just as a revolutionary act demands ideological commitment and physical courage, writing a book about revolution demands intellectual audacity. And the social scientist, aware of the gaps, contradictions, and ambiguities of his or her data is likely to feel more apprehensive about writing the book than the revolutionary does about assaulting the battlements of injustice.

Why? Because the social scientist is skeptical of claims to certain knowledge in the interpretation of historical events and social relationships. This is especially true as those events and relationships are more complex and extended in time. The revolutionary, on the other hand, is likely to be a model of self-confidence and optimism. Only the religious dogmatist's faith in service to a divine will can rival the revolutionary's conviction of absolute righteousness in the pursuit of perfect justice. The arrogance and presumption of the revolutionary is ironic counterpoint to the apprehension and skepticism of the scholar—especially of the modern scholar—who studies revolution.

Why? Because a review of the abundant literature on revolution shows that attempts to explain *the success* of a revolutionary movement may include reference to any and all facets of a society's politics, culture, economics, sociology, or social psychology. The same is true of efforts to explain *the failure* of revolution: inadequate leadership, weak organization, a remote ideology, the narrowness of the movement's membership base, inappropriate economic and social conditions, the legitimacy and effectiveness of the existing government—all may be cited to explain why the revolutionaries' defeat was inevitable. Our perspective and interpretations are almost invariably shaped by the fate of the movement, and our generalizations can perhaps never rise above the shortcomings of analysis after the fact.

REVOLUTION
IN THE UNITED STATES?

Consider the following as an illustration of the above.

There were many apostles of absolute truth and perfect justice who were persuaded that, in the early and mid-1970s, the United States already had traveled far down the road toward revolution. The argument was not without some dramatic support.

The International Association of Chiefs of Police reported that 1971 was the worst year in American history for incidents of domestic bombing. More than 2,500 explosive and fire bombs injured 207 persons and killed eighteen others. The apparent motivation in most of these incidents was political, frequently related to racial conflict. Government officials also noted a marked increase in politically motivated crimes after 1968 and the escalation of American military involvement in Southeast Asia.

That not all of the bombings or criminal activity could be attributed to the random acts of individuals was suggested by a U.S. State Department report released in late 1970. The report linked responsibility for much of the urban and campus violence in the United States to the more than 1,000 Americans who had received training in revolutionary techniques in Cuba since 1959. In fact, the *communiqué* left by the revolutionaries who bombed the University of Wisconsin math center in 1970 explicitly associated their actions with the Cuban revolution, the Tupamaro guerrillas in Uruguay, and the Viet Cong in South Vietnam.

Many public officials agreed with the self-proclaimed revolutionaries— including Mark Rudd, Bernardine Dohrn, Jerry Rubin, and Timothy Leary, all of whom predicted escalating revolutionary activity in the United States. In October 1970 William C. Sullivan, a high level assistant to the director of the FBI, stated that the Weathermen and other American radicals were organizing underground guerrilla units in order to carry out acts of sabotage, bombing, kidnapping, and assassination. Other government officials alledged that in various American cities Black Panther organizations, inspired by the teachings of Mao Tse-tung, were recruiting and training militants in the techniques of guerrilla warfare. Subsequent events seemed to support these allegations and apprehensions.

Police chiefs in Los Angeles and New York expressed alarm over the increasing incidence of armed attacks on uniformed police carrying out their normal duties. In New York City in January 1973, Police Commissioner Patrick V. Murphy attributed two incidents of ambush occurring within a seventy-two hour period to the activities of the Black Liberation Army. Hoping to arouse the poor against the rich and the oppressed against their rulers, the Symbionese Liberation Army plotted means to galvanize public attention. SLA guerrillas assassinated the superintendent of schools of Oakland, California, and on February 4, 1974 they kidnapped newspaper heiress Patricia Hearst. The media sensation provoked by Patty Hearst's kidnapping helped to spread the fever of revolution to other American guerrillas. Within the next several weeks a group calling itself Americans for Justice bombed two California facilities of the Shell Oil Company and the women's unit of the Weather Underground detonated a pipe-bomb at the San Francisco offices of the Department of Health, Education and Welfare.

These and other examples of American society coming apart at the seams often were explained as part of a more general malaise that affected a broad segment of the American people. In December 1971 the Los Angeles County Tax Assessor cited widespread cynicism regarding the operations of local government and flatly predicted a revolution unless significant tax relief for citizens was soon implemented. From a more general perspective, William P. Bundy, a former high official in the U.S. State Department, referred to "the disillusionment of Americans" and predicted for the foreseeable future "a sea of troubles." He cited findings from a national opinion survey by Potomac Associates in Washington, D.C., which reported substantial loss of public confidence in business and government leaders and the widespread sentiment that the American system was heading for a major breakdown.[1]

National opinion surveys over the next several years dramatically underlined the point. A Louis Harris poll in late 1975 found that, over the previous decade, public confidence in business had fallen from 55 percent to 18 percent; public confidence in the presidency had fallen from 41 percent to 14 percent; public confidence in the Congress had fallen from 42 percent to 14 percent;[2] and while in 1966 only about one-third of the American public agreed with the statement, "What you think doesn't count much anymore," two-thirds agreed with the statement in 1976. And a startling 86 percent of Americans subscribed to the view that, "Most government leaders are afraid to treat the public as adults and tell them the hard truth about inflation, energy and other subjects."[3]

And yet, from the vantage point of the 1980s, it was obvious that all the indicators and prophesies of an approaching American revolution in the 1970s had been refuted by the realities of current events. The political, social, and economic systems of the United States remained intact, and the most notable characteristic of the American way of life was its continuity with a past already remarkable for its stability. In short, more of the same.

Clearly, then, the prophets of an American revolution in the 1970s were false prophets who misled themselves as they misled their disciples. Apparently it is not very easy to predict correctly a society's potential for revolution.

There is more at issue here than just the errors that derive from wishful thinking. And if the thoughtful reader already has in mind some explanation for the failure of revolution to materialize in the United States in the 1970s, he or she may be better tested by reflection on the following.

REVOLUTION IN MEXICO?

Looking beyond the borders of the United States helps to impart (especially to American students) a more objective view of the revolutionary potential of a given society at a given point in time. In this regard, consider Mexico in the early 1980s.

There is no doubt that Mexican society is very different from society in the United States. Most United States citizens live in an urban environment; most Mexican citizens live in rural villages. The economy of the United States is highly industrialized and solidly launched into the postindustrial phase of high technology; the Mexican economy, even well after the discovery of immense deposits of oil in 1977, remains primarily agricultural. Literacy and school attendance are much higher in the United States than they are in Mexico. So are per capita income and the possession of the necessary luxuries of modernity, including telephones, televisions, and automobiles. The alert reader will already have recognized some useful categories for probing the characteristics of two or more societies—in order to understand better the differences in their patterns of politics (including their revolutionary potential).

In both the United States and Mexico there was substantial student unrest in the 1960s, and in the 1970s there were dramatic increases in terrorism and in the activities of urban and rural guerrillas. But the extent of organized political violence in Mexico was and is much greater than it is or has been in the United States. And, in the early 1980s, Mexico seemed headed for a revolutionary con-flagration that needed only an incendiary spark. What were the facts that sup-ported this generalization?

Various groups of urban and rural guerrillas, including the Communist League of September 23, were well organized and securely placed, especially in Mexico's southern states and in the more impoverished districts surrounding Mexico City. These groups capitalized on the realities and consequences of the following: Mexico's recent population explosion; high rates of unemployment and underemployment; galloping inflation; rampant corruption in government, business, and in the trade unions; the undernourishment of the large majority of the rural population; the land hunger of some four million landless peasants; and the unfulfilled promises made by Mexico's ruling elites—promises that could be traced back to the Mexican Revolution that began in 1910.

Mexico's revolutionaries of the 1980s also strengthened their support by attacking the monopoly of power exercised by the ruling political party, by exposing the rigged elections and the government controlled press, by appealing to an increasingly demoralized middle class, by pointing to the economic development that followed the discovery of oil and that benefited mainly those few who already were rich, and by documenting the impact on Mexico's faltering economy of banking and investment interests located in the United States.

Was Mexico in the early 1980s ripe for revolution? Perhaps the spark to light Mexico's new conflagration would come from the revolutionary fires already burning to the south, in Nicaragua, El Salvador, and Guatemala.

But then to what extent could a prediction be anything better than a reasonably informed guess?

SOME CONCEPTUAL OBSTACLES

How might we take the guesswork out of the study of revolution?

It no doubt is beginning to dawn on the student who is newly recruited to the study of revolution that he or she stands before some towering walls. First is the wall of definition, followed by the wall of classification, which in turn is followed by a maze of high-walled alleyways—many of them blind—that are related to data collection. There then looms the most formidable wall of all, that which is labeled "theory" and which promises from its towering height a clear view of the whole horizon of revolution. Climbing this last wall is more difficult, more challenging, and more dangerous than climbing all the walls that came before.

The revolutionary searches for justice. In the study of revolution we search for theory. It may be that each of us will come away from our quest empty-handed, or with precious little to hold onto. It is almost certain that our sense of frustration will be greater than our sense of satisfaction.

This, too, is part of the human condition, because the stronger our commitment to justice, the sharper our sense of injustice. *And* the more meaningful the question, the more uncertain the answer.

NOTES

[1] William P. Bundy, "The Missing Center," *Newsweek*, October 4, 1971, p. 46.

[2] As reported in the *Los Angeles Times*, November 23, 1975.

[3] Ibid., November 21, 1976.

*CHAPTER
TWO*

KEY
CONCEPTS

ADMITTING OUR LIMITATIONS

Students who major in physics, chemistry, biology, or in any of the natural sciences are likely to take for granted the scientific precision of their field of study. There is so much to learn that already is demonstrated fact and theory that there is little or no interest in pondering the philosophical assumptions that define the facts and the theories.

In the social sciences, however, a continuing concern for the appropriate approach, method, model, or theory makes clear—by itself—how severely limited is the theoretical potential of the social sciences. Especially political science. Those who talk the most about the nature of theory are likely to be working in those fields of research that are the least susceptible to theory development. Why is this the case?

In the natural sciences there is virtually unanimous agreement on,

1. the *definitions* that are appropriate to the phenomena under study;
2. the *classification schemes* that are appropriate for organizing the data, thereby imparting logical coherence to research and analysis;

3. the *methods* that are appropriate for carrying out the research and for testing the hypotheses that are both the inspiration and the result of the research.

It also is true that, in the natural sciences,

1. the phenomena studied are subject to direct or indirect *observation* by one or more of our five senses;
2. the observations that are made often can be expressed in terms of *quantitative measurement;*
3. the validity of findings can usually be confirmed (or disconfirmed) by *reproducing prior experiments;*
4. *controlled experiments* make possible the precise measurement of selected variables in a given context.

These same generalizations describe succinctly what the study of revolution is not and does not have.[1]

REVOLUTION:
HOW NORMAL AND HOW FREQUENT?

Even if we postpone defining *revolution* until we have uncovered its "meaning in the use," we still are confronted by immediate and unsettling controversy. For example, should we consider revolution and the events that often precede it normal or abnormal characteristics of social and political development?

Those who subscribe to an equilibrium model of the social system, including Chalmers Johnson, at least implicitly view revolution and political violence as a deviation from the norms of social process and change.[2] Another leading student of revolution, Harry Eckstein, also regards the violence and other characteristics of *internal war* as fundamentally opposed to the more typical and nonviolent manifestations of social process and organization.[3] Crane Brinton, perhaps the best-known writer on revolution, dramatizes his analysis of the stages of revolution with analogies to fever in the human body, citing "delirium," "convalescence," "relapse," and, subsequently, even "immunization" as metaphors appropriate to the more advanced and recuperative stages of the revolutionary process.[4] Brinton clearly means to say that revolution is not a characteristic of the healthy body politic.

Karl Marx also approved of metaphors in social scientific discourse (his favorite one was childbirth). But Marx saw revolutions and their underlying class conflicts as an inherent part of societies based on an unequal distribution of the ownership of the means of production. Two centuries before Marx, Thomas Hobbes held much the same point of view, although his basic unit of social analysis was the individual instead of economic class. More recently, and in part as an updated revision of Marx's thought, Ralf Dahrendorf has argued that all industrial societies are best understood in terms of "the coercion theory of social structure," and that group conflict is an abiding characteristic of social organization.[5]

Another leading German sociologist, Georg Simmel, wrote in the first decade of the twentieth century that social conflict is not only universal and unlikely to disappear, but that it plays a positive and functional role in social organization.[6] And from Pitirim A. Sorokin's massive study of internal disturbances in eleven political communities, from Greece in the seventh and Rome in the sixth centuries B.C. to Western Europe and Russia in 1933, it is difficult to conclude that revolution and violent domestic conflict are an atypical manifestation of social organization and change. Of the 1,622 disturbances studied, Sorokin found that 70 percent "involved violence and bloodshed on a considerable scale," and that for every five years of relative tranquillity there was one year of "significant social disturbance."[7]

Although Sorokin concluded his studies before the Second World War, his observation that the twentieth century was "the bloodiest and the most turbulent period" in history has been dramatically confirmed by subsequent events. Between the end of the war and 1969, forty of the approximately 100 states in Asia, Africa, and Latin America experienced at least one successful military seizure of power.[8] Between 1948 and 1967, almost all the countries of Latin America, two-thirds of the countries of Asia, and one-half of those African countries independent by 1962 recorded one or more successful or unsuccessful attempts to change their governments by unconstitutional means.[9] In Africa alone, and looking back from the 1980s to the launching of African independence in Ghana in 1957, there were more than fifty successful coups d'état, perhaps three times as many unsuccessful coups d'état, and at least a dozen African chiefs of state had been assassinated.[10] Over a shorter time span (1946 to 1959), but including a wider range of types of political instability, Eckstein cites the *New York Times* as reporting more than 1,200 clear cases of internal war, including "civil wars, guerrilla wars, localized rioting, widely dispersed turmoil, organized and apparently unorganized terrorism, mutinies, and coups d'état."[11] The prospect of a worldwide depression provoked by unstable economies and by crippling shortages of energy and food, coupled with the political instability that already troubles so much of the contemporary world, also suggests that the future is no cause for optimism. The point seems to be that political violence is not peculiar to either the past, the present, or the future.

DEFINING REVOLUTION

But to say "political violence" is not to say precisely "revolution." And the alert reader will already have observed the proliferation of terms that seem relevant to a study of revolutionary movements: revolution, internal war, internal disturbance, civil war, anticolonial war, wars of independence, guerrilla warfare, rebellion, revolt, insurrection, riot, coup d'état, palace revolution, *jacquerie* or peasant revolt (peasant rebellion?), general strike, turmoil, uprising, mutiny, terrorism. The consequent opportunity for conceptual confusion is bound to be appreciated by those who argue that social science cannot be really scientific.

The same event, for example, often receives a different label: the 1956 Hungarian "Revolution" for one author[12] is the Hungarian "Revolt" for another, because (by definition) "revolutions" succeed while "revolts" fail.[13] Even when authors agree on the appropriate criteria for distinguishing revolutions from other types of political violence they may disagree on the way in which a particular event should be classified. For example, both Barrington Moore, Jr. and Samuel P. Huntington argue that the social and economic changes that accompanied the American colonies' separation from Great Britain after 1776 make inappropriate the term *revolution*.[14] But J. Franklin Jameson's historical research (which was available to Moore and Huntington) suggested to him that it was indeed a revolution. The American Revolution, Jameson argued, substantially reduced the prominence, role, and wealth of the colonial upper classes and accelerated the rise of a middle-class gentry which greatly benefited from the confiscation of Tory estates, the emigration to Canada of British Loyalists, the removal of the Crown's restrictions on land colonization, and the abolition of primogeniture.[15]

As already noted, Harry Eckstein has introduced the term *internal war,* which must be acknowledged as a commendable effort to minimize confusion. But Eckstein specifically exempts from his definition of internal war cases "where political violence is endemic and expected,"[16] which (as we have seen above) presumably excludes from analysis the majority of countries in Latin America, Asia, Africa, and the Middle East, in both the recent past and the foreseeable future. It must also be of some embarrassment that William Kornhauser, one of the prominent contributors to Eckstein's study, refused to adopt the term *internal war* and instead identified *rebellion* as the genus, while the species included "revolutions, civil wars, military insurrections, coups d'état, colonial revolts, and riots and strikes against the state."[17] And, as we will see in a subsequent chapter, one of the frequently critical variables in the success or failure of revolutionary movements is the extent to which the particular movement receives *external* support from foreign states and sympathizers.

Any embarrassment over definitional wrangles should be short-lived, however, especially in the social sciences. It often is the case that the definition of concepts fundamental to research and theory is endlessly disputed, but this does not seem to impede continuing research or even the development of theory. In a classic case, two leading anthropologists summarized in a 223-page paper 164 definitions of *culture,* and mercifully refused to add their own.[18] In their study of revolution, Carl Leiden and Karl M. Schmitt reviewed more than a dozen definitions of revolution and concluded that "we are content to leave the question open-ended."[19]

However tempting, it would be unfair to the accomplishments of the many students of revolution to let the matter rest here. It is well established that the term *revolution* derives from astronomy, that it was initially used by philosophers to imply a cyclical process in human events, and that it entered common political parlance only after the French Revolution of 1789.[20]

It is the almost unanimous opinion of writers on the subject that *revolution* also means an alteration in the personnel, structure, supporting myth, and functions of government by methods that are not sanctioned by the prevailing constitution. These methods almost invariably involve violence or the threat of violence against political elites, citizens, or both. And it is the opinion of a majority of scholars that *revolution* means a relatively abrupt and significant change in the distribution of wealth and social status.[21]

Some students of revolution also have restricted the term according to the characteristics of "modernization." They thus exclude from the truly revolutionary those movements that are primarily religious in inspiration, that lack coherent organizational structures, and whose interests and demands are poorly articulated or not expressed at all.[22] But very few scholars appear to agree with Hannah Arendt's argument that *revolution* should be applied only to those relatively infrequent and modern movements that have extended the scope of human freedom.[23] This seems to be an overly restrictive definition, even though based on an understandable prejudice against the traumas generated by communism and fascism in the twentieth century.

REVOLUTION AS A PROCESS

The dispute over the meaning of *revolution* is at least in part a result of confusing the *ends* of revolutionary movements with their particular *techniques*. Revolutionaries, by definition, seek a major alteration in the prevailing distribution of wealth, status, and power. But their *techniques* may range from terrorism through peasant guerrilla warfare and general strikes to a coup d'état. These may be executed sequentially, but it is more likely that various techniques will overlap in the course of revolutionary mobilization. In fact the more useful typologies of revolutionary movements focus on means rather than ends, and an important task for theory development in the field is to determine the relationship between specific techniques and the more objective circumstances in which the movement operates.[24]

This is also to say that "revolution" should be conceived of more as process than event. In the detailed studies of specific revolutionary movements, it is often observed that the "revolutionaries" initiated their acts without revolu-

tionary intent. Only in the context of the regime's response to the first manifestations of resistance or violence, and only with the movement's mobilization of
unexpected resources, are the revolutionary objective and the movement itself
given explicit definition.[25]

There is both logical and empirical support, then, for the contention that
revolution should be understood as part of a continuum of patterns of collective
behavior that deviate from prevailing norms. The same circumstances that are
associated with increasing rates of suicide, criminal violence, religious revivalism,
labor unrest, and constitutional movements for political or social reform are
often associated with those types of political violence that eventually find
expression as revolutionary movements.[26]

This is also to emphasize a critical oversight in much of the literature on
revolution. Earlier studies focused on the so-called "great revolutions" of the
modern world, including the Puritan, American, French, and Russian. Later
studies have broadened the frame of reference to include the Mexican, Chinese,
Cuban, and other revolutions of the postwar period. But to understand the
characteristics of revolution and the circumstances of its development we must
also study those revolutionary movements that have failed to capture power. No
hypothesis or theory of revolution can claim credibility if it has been derived
exclusively from the study of successful revolutionary movements.

Admitting the theoretical importance of unsuccessful revolutionary movements inevitably commits us to a conception of revolution in terms of *process*.
James A. Geschwender writes that "conditions which produce a revolution are
no different in principle from those that produce a smaller or even an unsuccessful protest movement."[27] And Carleton Beals refers to radical student, black,
and peace movements in the United States as "far from constituting a bona fide
revolution, though they are typical preludes to revolution."[28]

These arguments are supported by the observation that the incidence of
suicide and ordinary criminality frequently declines during periods of revolutionary unrest.[29] They also are supported by statistical research on the relationships
between the various forms of political violence. R. J. Rummel's factor analysis
for 113 countries between 1946 and 1959 identifies a close relationship between
the variables of two dimensions of domestic conflict behavior. According to
Rummel's categories, the variables of the first dimension are coups, plots, internal warfare, mutiny, and large-scale terrorism, and for the second dimension,
riots, small-scale terrorism, quasi-private violence, and turmoil.[30]

Douglas Bwy's study of social conflict and political instability in Latin
America finds an even closer relationship between the various categories of
"turmoil" (strikes, demonstrations, riots) and "internal war" (terrorism, guerrilla
warfare, civil war, revolutionary invasion). While these continua are not meant
to imply a necessary progression from one form of political violence to another,
they are closely related in terms of contributing factors, including the degree

of the regime's legitimacy and the nature of the government's response to instability.[31]

Thus by imposing a dogmatic definition of revolution upon the complexity of the data we both distort and oversimplify the subject matter of our research. Definitional categories ask questions that are answered by "yes" or "no," and the data consequently are treated in terms of "either-or." But revolution and probably most political phenomena require categories that can be answered with "more" or "less," helping to clarify our research problems in terms of degree instead of clouding them with the illusion of finality.

WHERE WE STAND

"More" or "less."

We are concerned, then, with a society's *potential* for revolution.[32] We observe the society's changing rates of political violence, for example, without feeling compelled to give a definitive "yes" or "no" to the question that asks whether revolution in the society is inevitable or impossible. It is enough that we are able to study the ups and downs of a society's revolutionary potential without pretending to predict the broad outlines of its political future.

This means that our attempt to understand the revolutionary process is not confined to the study of only those societies that have been buffeted by the winds of revolution. If our conceptualization of the revolutionary process and a society's revolutionary potential is sufficiently general, we may learn something useful about revolution even by studying political phenomena that are not directly associated with revolution. Thus we toil in many fields of research in order to harvest something substantial to feed our appetite for understanding.

It bears repeating that the quality of our understanding of the revolutionary process also turns on our commitment to study revolutionary movements that have failed as well as those that have succeeded. In the same way, we better understand what it takes to succeed in business if we study companies that have gone bankrupt as well as those that have prospered. Bankruptcy and prosperity, revolutionary failure and success, high and low revolutionary potential, are at opposing ends of the same scales.

The reader also deserves to know the author's strategy for developing systematically the reader's understanding of the revolutionary process. The next chapter deals with revolution on a *country-by-country* basis according to a strict chronology of events. But the narrative that is structured by the chronology is designed more to stimulate the reader's conceptual curiosity than to answer any probing questions about the nature of revolution.

In Parts II and III of the book, however, the focus is *cross-national* and topically defined. We identify particular variables that are associated with the revolutionary process and we test their relationships with other variables in a variety of contexts. Historical narrative provides information; the cross-national testing of hypotheses provides understanding.

In this way we also test the field's potential for theory development. Here we should understand that, in this book, *theory* does not mean "philosophy" or "speculation." It means one generalization, or a set of logically related generalizations, that implies or imply a series of testable hypotheses. Theories are not tested directly; only hypotheses can be tested. Thus we build theory on top of hypotheses, and hypotheses may be deduced from theory. In either case, we are concerned with generalizations that are based on fact (or on what seems to be fact). We hope to test the field's potential for theory development, then, by generating and testing hypotheses on the basis of a cross-national study of variable relationships that are associated with the process of revolution.

This still leaves a lot unsaid. Even if we agree that the study of the revolutionary process is best divided into the study of the *characteristics* of revolutionary movements (Part II of this book), and the study of the *setting* in which the movements take place (Part III of this book), we still must decide on a classification scheme for breaking down "characteristics" and "setting." The classification scheme adopted for this book is simple, and is revealed in the table of contents (for Chapters 4 through 11) and in the various topic headings of each chapter.

But the reader is invited first to try to invent his or her own classification scheme. What are the characteristics of revolutionary movements, whether they end in triumph or tragedy? And what are the characteristics of the setting that, for any society at any point in time, will provide us with a measure of the society's revolutionary potential? The materials of the following chapter include a useful sampling of revolutionary movements that have succeeded and failed, from the ideological left, center, and right, and of societies whose revolutionary potential has fluctuated significantly over time.

Thus the subject matter of Chapter 3 constitutes a do-it-yourself kit for the aspiring student of revolution. It is often the case that more is learned by a conceptual effort that leads to blunders than by being told from the outset what is supposed to be right. Read on, then, and pay close attention to how your mind works—as it strives to move from the particular to the general in order to transform information into understanding.

NOTES

[1] Here the student might ponder a concept fundamental to political science and central to revolution: *power*. How should it be defined, how should its various manifestations be classified, how might it be observed *and* measured, and to what extent can the variables associated with it be experimentally controlled and the findings of one researcher replicated by another?

[2] C. Johnson, 1966.

[3] Eckstein, 1964; Eckstein, 1965.

[4] Brinton, 1965, pp. 16-17.

[5] Dahrendorf, 1959, p. 237.

[6] Simmel, 1955, especially p. 41 where Simmel summarizes his argument on the relationship between ideology and social conflict.

[7] Sorokin, 1970, pp. 126-27 and 130.

[8] von der Mehden, 1969, p. 92.

[9] Taylor, 1970, p. 6.

[10] A country's government-controlled news media may fail to report an unsuccessful coup attempt, in part to maintain the government's myth of unquestioned legitimacy, but also to protect the government's credit rating in the international banking and business community.

[11] Eckstein, 1964, p. 3.

[12] C. Johnson, 1966, p. 102.

[13] Kecskemeti, 1961, p. 2. But see the complete title of Kecskemeti's book, cited in the Bibliography.

[14] Moore, 1966, p. 112; Huntington, 1968, p. 304.

[15] Jameson, 1956, p. 16-20 and 32-35.

[16] Eckstein, 1964, p. 14.

[17] Kornhauser, 1964, p. 142.

[18] Kroeber and Kluckhohn, 1952.

[19] Leiden and Schmitt, 1968, p. 9.

[20] Arendt, 1965, pp. 35-36; Schrecker, 1966, p. 34; Kamenka, 1966, p. 125.

[21] Definitions of revolution that include the qualifications cited here may be found in Stone, 1966, pp. 159-64; Hunter, 1940, p. x; Neumann, 1949, pp. 333-34.

[22] Hobsbawm, 1959, Chap. 1; Huntington, 1968, p. 264.

[23] Arendt, 1965, Introduction.

[24] Janos, 1964, classifies revolutionary movements according to seven techniques. Smelser, 1963, p. 315, also suggests the utility of classifying a revolutionary movement "according to the tactics it employs—terrorism, street fighting, guerrilla warfare, coup d'état, etc." Typologies emphasizing the circumstances of revolution may be found in Kornhauser, 1964, and Rosenau, 1964. Stone, 1966, reviews several typologies of revolutionary movements.

[25] Gusfield, 1968, p. 447. Lemarchand, 1968 (p. 37), in describing revolution in Rwanda between 1959 and 1962, nicely captures the shifting goals and complex process typical of most revolutionary movements.

[26] Smelser, 1963, pp. 49, 120-21, 227, 271, and 317; Parsons, 1951, p. 72; Iglitzin, 1972, p. 29; Leiden and Schmitt, 1968, p. 44; Gurr, 1970, pp. 5 and 334. Geschwender, 1968, pp. 129-30, summarizes Durkheim's analysis of the circumstances associated with fluctuations in the rate of suicides.

[27] Geschwender, 1968, p. 128.

[28] Beals, 1970, p. 12.

[29] Brinton, 1965, p. 174.

[30] Rummel, 1966.

[31] Bwy, 1968. Midlarsky and Tanter, 1967, report a correlation coefficient of .63 between the various forms of political violence and revolution in Latin America. In a broader study, the same authors exclude only "the palace revolution from the concept of a continuum" (Tanter and Midlarsky, 1967, p. 279). Other statistical studies of the relationships between types of political violence are summarized in Feierabend and Feierabend, 1966.

[32] Both Gurr, 1970 (pp. ix-x, 8), and Feldman, 1964 (pp. 115-21), recognize the close relationship between the various forms of political violence, and consequently suggest the utility of measuring revolutionary potential rather than the actual incidence of revolutionary movements.

CHAPTER
THREE

CHRONOLOGIES
Some almost Raw Data

THE AMERICAN COLONIES, 1660-1781

1660

Parliament confirms its constitutional right to legislate for England's colonies by passing the First Navigation Act. This and subsequent Navigation Acts require the colonies to sell specified agricultural products (including cotton and tobacco) only to England. Colonial merchants, traders, and shipping interests are thereby prohibited from dealing in other (foreign) markets where profits might be higher than they are in England. A parliamentary act of 1663 requires that all foreign goods imported by the colonies must be shipped through English ports—thereby raising the cost of goods imported by colonists in America. The Navigation Acts also impose restrictions on the development of manufacturing and trade in the colonies—to the advantage of manufacturing interests in England.

1733

Parliament passes the Molasses Act, which forces the colonists to import their sugar from Britain's colonies in the West Indies. Previously, America's sugar came from the French West Indies and was less expensive than the sugar imported from the British West Indies. An extensive smuggling trade develops in the colonies over the next several decades. Britain's attempt to eliminate the smuggling, sometimes by seizing ships owned by American merchants, raises hostility for British colonial control.

1763

The Treaty of Paris formally ends the French and Indian Wars, which date back to 1689. French control in parts of Canada is ended, Great Britain is the dominant imperial power in North America, and the Indian threat to the colonists' western outposts is substantially reduced. Less dependent for their security and protection on Great Britain, however, the American colonists now are all the more eager to cultivate a spirit of insularity and independence.

1765

A new administration in Great Britain has been attempting to implement policies that will (1) raise revenue from the colonies so that (2) the cost of defending and governing the colonies might be paid for by the colonists themselves. Additional taxes on molasses and sugar already have been imposed, but colonial merchants are especially alarmed by the British government's promise to enforce the tax laws vigorously. And in 1765, Parliament passes the Stamp Act, the first direct tax imposed on citizens of the American colonies. All newspapers, advertisements, pamphlets, legal documents, and other papers issued in the colonies must carry a stamp—and the money to purchase the stamps goes to Great Britain. The new law is loudly denounced by many of the more educated and wealthy colonists—those most directly affected by the stamp tax, including merchants, lawyers, publishers, and journalists. Groups of prominent colonists are formed with the express purpose of organizing opposition to the Stamp Act. These groups call themselves the Sons of Liberty and they maintain contact with each other through "committees of correspondence." A Stamp Act Congress is convened in New York City in October with delegates present from nine of the thirteen colonies. The Congress adopts a Declaration of Rights and Grievances, which argues that Parliament has no right to tax the colonists without their direct consent as expressed through colonial representatives in Parliament ("no taxation without representation"). Business interests in the colonies, supported by the Sons of Liberty, threaten a boycott of all British imports.

1766

Parliament repeals the Stamp Act, but important precedents, both ideological and organizational, already have been established in the colonies for resisting British authority. And Parliament formally reasserts its legal right to tax the colonies. (Members of Parliament are the "virtual representatives" of all British subjects, whether or not those subjects send a directly elected representative to Parliament.)

1767

Parliament passes the Townshend Acts, which impose duties on specified manufactured goods imported by the colonists, including tea, paper, lead, and glass. Samuel Adams, John Dickinson, and other prominent colonists lead the protests against the new taxes. Merchants in Boston organize a boycott of English imports.

1768

Attempting to enforce the Townshend Acts, British authorities seize a ship (the *Liberty*) owned by John Hancock, Boston's most prominent businessman and merchant. A riot ensues, and the ship eventually is burned. The Massachusetts Assembly is dissolved by the British colonial government because the Assembly has circulated a letter to other colonial legislatures explaining the colony's difficulties and asking for support.

1770

British troops have been garrisoned in Boston to maintain order and to enforce the collection of customs duties authorized by the Townshend Acts. The troops frequently are exposed to the physical threats and verbal taunts of gangs of Boston residents. On March 5 a riot is suppressed only after British troops fire into the crowd. Three men are killed and two die later from their wounds (the "Boston Massacre"). A funeral for the five martyrs turns into an anti-British demonstration (or, depending on one's point of view, a patriotic rally).

1773

Parliament has repealed the Townshend Acts (in 1770) but has signified its right to tax the colonies by retaining the tax on tea. (The tax also is designed to aid Britain's financially troubled East India Company.) Leading colonists have organized a successful boycott of tea, but British authorities in Boston refuse to allow three loaded tea ships to leave Boston harbor until the tea duty is paid. Paul Revere, Samuel Adams, and others disguise themselves as Indians, board the loaded tea ships on the night of December 16, and throw the cases of tea into the harbor (the "Boston Tea Party").

1774

Parliament passes the Quebec Act, which is intended to strengthen Britain's control of Canada, especially in Quebec province. To ensure the loyalties of French Canadians, the Quebec Act reconfirms the authority of the French civil law in Quebec and guarantees religious freedom. This concession to Roman Catholicism angers Protestants in the American colonies. But the colonists are especially angered by the Act's extension of Quebec's provincial boundaries south to the Ohio River and west to the Mississippi. Thus, many of the western territorial claims of the colonies are nullified, and a substantial part of the frontier is closed to American expansion. Colonial opposition to the Quebec Act, and to other actions of Parliament (referred to as the "Intolerable Acts") that are designed to punish the colonists for resisting British authority, results in the convening of the First Continental Congress in Philadelphia in September and October. Twelve of the thirteen colonies are represented. The Congress's delegates draw up petitions of grievances, which are sent to the king, and agree to boycott British imports and to prohibit colonial exports. Only a few delegates favor more radical measures.

1775

Units of the Massachusetts' colonial militia (the "minutemen") have built up a supply of military stores at Concord. The British commander in Boston intends to deny the colonists the means of armed rebellion and on April 19 sends a column of royal infantry to Concord to seize the colonists' military depot. Paul Revere is one of several colonial patriots who spread the alarm that warns of the British advance. A forward detachment of British troops is met at Lexington by a group of minutemen. Shots are exchanged, several minutemen are killed, the colonists withdraw, and the British continue their march. At Concord there is another exchange of musket fire, and some of the colonists' military supplies are destroyed. There are some 200 casualties among the British troops after their troubled withdrawal back to Boston. On May 10 Fort Ticonderoga (in northeastern New York) is captured from the British by armed colonials commanded by Ethan Allen and Benedict Arnold. On the same day the Second Continental Congress convenes in Philadelphia, but the delegates are badly divided on the issue of whether or not to push for a final break with Great Britain. Nevertheless, the Congress creates a Continental army and, on June 15, appoints George Washington as the army's commander in chief. On June 17 the British siege of Boston is climaxed by a costly British victory in the battle of Bunker Hill. In August the Congress sends troops to Quebec in order to protect the colonies' northern borders and to raise anti-British sentiment among the Canadians.

1776

The pro-British opinion of Loyalists is a strong force for reconciliation in almost all the colonies, especially among large landowners, businessmen, professionals, Anglicans, those who have been born in Great Britain, and those who are officials in the British colonial administration. Perhaps a third of the population is apathetic or neutral on the issue of separation from Great Britain. But the vocal minority that favors revolution is strengthened in its convictions by the pamphlet *Common Sense,* written by Thomas Paine and published in January. The volunteer soldiers of the Continental army need more than conviction, however. The army's campaign in Quebec is a disaster, and the soldiers are poorly trained and badly equipped. The Continental Congress has virtually no authority over the separate governments of the colonies and is hard pressed to raise the money essential to the conduct of the war. Nevertheless, the majority of delegates to the Congress eventually are persuaded by John Adams, John Hancock, Samuel Adams, and others to take the decisive step. The final draft of a Declaration of Independence (first drafted by Thomas Jefferson) is adopted by the Congress on July 4. In August, a combination of British land and naval forces induces Washington to fight a series of losing battles as he evacuates his troops from Long Island and lower New York.

1777

During the winter of 1776-1777 Washington's troops win some minor victories, mainly against German mercenaries employed by the British. Later in the year the British win major battles at Brandywine and Germantown, and they occupy Philadelphia. But the British plan to split the colonies along the Hudson River valley fails and, on October 17, one of Britain's expeditionary armies is outnumbered, outmaneuvered, and is forced to surrender at Saratoga (in New York).

1778-1781

The battle of Saratoga proves to be the turning point of the war. The American victory confirms in the eyes of the French the legitimacy of the revolutionaries' cause, and it is the military aid provided by France that eventually proves decisive. Although many battles remain to be fought, although the theaters of military operations eventually extend from north to south and from the Atlantic to the frontier, and although Washington's troops must still confront many hardships, the American colonies are now successfully launched on their way to becoming the United States of America. The end of Great Britain's military opposition to American independence comes with General Cornwallis' surrender at Yorktown (in Virginia) to a Franco-American force on October 19, 1781.

FRANCE, 1776–1794

1776

Turgot has been France's Controller General of Finance since 1774. He has attempted to introduce major economic reforms, including free trade, taxation of all landowners, and the elimination of France's remaining feudal restraints on agriculture and commerce. Turgot thus has antagonized France's powerful nobility. No less influential than the nobility is the clergy, and Turgot has antagonized the clergy by favoring the toleration of Protestants—a group that has been an important source of business enterprise and economic modernization in France. Pressured by the nobility and the clergy, King Louis XVI forces Turgot to resign his office in May 1776.

1787

France is faced with a large public debt that threatens the government with bankruptcy. The government's economic crisis derives in part from its support of the American War of Independence—a manifestation of France's long-standing opposition to British interests in Europe and the New World. Charles Calonne, France's Controller General of Finance since 1783, hopes to solve the government's economic problems by imposing a direct tax on land, by introducing a stamp tax, and by reducing the economic privileges of the nobility and the clergy. In order to secure adoption of these reforms, Calonne persuades the king to convene an Assembly of Notables. The Assembly refuses to consider Calonne's proposals and persuades the king to dismiss Calonne. De Brienne, one of Calonne's opponents in the Assembly, is appointed by the king to succeed Calonne as Controller General of Finance. De Brienne then adopts Calonne's proposal for a direct tax on land. Other government officials argue that such a program can be approved only by the Estates-General. De Brienne persuades the king to convene the Estates-General for the first time since 1615.

1789

May 1 The Estates-General convenes in Versailles. It consists of three separate estates or chambers: the first estate includes representatives of the clergy; the second estate includes representatives of the nobility; and the representatives of the third estate, the commons, are drawn from France's untitled but prosperous citizens. The king has ordered each province to draw up lists (*cahiers*) of grievances, and these are to serve as the agenda of the Estates-General's proceedings. Public opinion seems convinced that major change is about to take place.

June 17 Voting in the Estates-General is according to estate. Thus an actual majority (seated in the commons) is unable to change government policy. But some of the nobility seated in the Estates-General, and many of the clergy representing the first estate, agree with the third estate on the necessity of introducing fundamental reform. These members of the Estates-General form an alliance and declare themselves the National Assembly. The National Assembly, they argue, is representative of the entire French nation.

June 20 The king has ordered the meeting hall of the National Assembly closed. But members reconvene in a building on the grounds of the Versailles palace which houses an indoor tennis court. In the "Oath of the Tennis Court" the members of the National Assembly swear not to adjourn until a new constitution has been written.

June 27 The king unwillingly accepts the National Assembly's assumption of parliamentary authority. The Estates-General is effectively dissolved. But the king orders his troops to surround Versailles.

July 11 The queen, Marie Antoinette, leads a faction of the court nobility that is resolutely opposed to any reform. She prevails upon the king to dismiss Jacques Necker, Director General of Finance and Minister of State. Necker favors fundamental reform and is identified with the interests represented by the third estate. His dismissal signifies the monarchy's refusal to alter the economic and political relationships between France's major social classes.

July 14 A mob storms the Paris Bastille in search of weapons. The Bastille is a fortress, a prison, and a symbol of royal absolutism and political oppression. The storming of the Bastille marks the first mobilization of the Paris masses in the French Revolution. The king reappoints Necker, who is supported by the Paris populace, to his former position in the government. The king also approves the organization of the Commune of Paris as the city's new form of government. A National Guard is organized under the command of the Marquis de Lafayette (on July 15). Lafayette, a delegate to the Estates-General from the second estate, also is elected vice president of the National Assembly.

July-August Labor unrest breaks out in most of the cities and towns of France. Peasants pillage and burn many of the manors of the nobility.

August 4 Members of the National Assembly, including representatives from the clergy and nobility, give up their economic privileges and, in a single legislative session, abolish what remains of France's feudal system. Groups of radical citizens, organized as political clubs, gain numbers and influence, especially in Paris. Chief among these clubs is the Jacobins, named for the Jacobin friars' convent, their meeting place in Paris. Composed mainly of commoners and citizens of the bourgeoisie, the Jacobins establish ties with similar groups organized in many cities and towns throughout France.

August 26 The Assembly (now calling itself the Constituent Assembly) adopts a "Declaration of the Rights of Man and Citizen." The principal author of the Declaration is the Abbé Sieyès, one of the lower clergy but elected to the Estates-General as a representative of the third estate. Influenced by the American Declaration of Independence, the Declaration of the Rights of Man and Citizen proclaims the "inalienable rights" of the individual to "liberty, property, security, and resistance to oppression." It also declares that all men are equal (intended to deny aristocratic privilege) and vests sovereignty (authority to rule) in the people.

October 5 There are food shortages, and the lower classes also are hard hit by economic depression. And there are rumors that the king plans to send his troops to attack and disperse the Assembly. A mob of angry Parisians marches to Versailles. The king and queen, their lives threatened, are escorted by Lafayette to the Tuileries palace in Paris, where they become virtual prisoners of the Paris Commune. The Assembly also moves to Paris, and its members begin to draft a new constitution that will limit the power of the monarchy.

1790

The property of the Roman Catholic Church in France had been nationalized by the Assembly in 1789. In 1790 the Assembly extends it attack on France's religious institutions. In July the Assembly orders all clergy to take an oath of loyalty to the state. There is widespread resistance by the clergy who are supported by the more religious sectors of the population. Violence breaks out in many of the clerically dominated rural districts of France.

1791

The Assembly completes its draft of a constitution that calls for a limited monarchy responsible to a one-chamber parliament. The right to vote is restricted to citizens who own substantial amounts of property. The king and queen decide to join the nobility that have fled abroad and to raise foreign support in order to restore royal authority. They flee Paris but are arrested at Varennes in northeastern France on June 21. They are forcefully returned to Paris, where the king accepts the new constitution. But among royalist supporters abroad and in France there is growing sentiment for war to restore the French monarchy to its earlier position of absolute authority. On October 1 a newly elected Assembly convenes in Paris. It is eventually dominated by the Girondists, a political organization that is made up mainly of lawyers, journalists, and merchants who represent the educated middle classes of the provinces.

1792

April 20 The Assembly, under the control of the Girondists, declares war on Austria. The Austrian monarchy has affirmed its willingness to join with other European states in restoring to France its *ancien régime* (former or previous government). Austria allies with Prussia; their armies invade France and march toward Paris.

June 20 The military failures of the disorganized French armies and rumors of the king's treason mobilize the Paris masses. An attempted insurrection fails.

August Another insurrection of the Paris masses overthrows the Paris Commune. Prominent in the new commune is Georges Danton, a Paris lawyer and persuasive orator who enjoys widespread popular support. Under pressure from the Paris Commune, the king is "suspended" by the Assembly and the royal family is imprisoned. Elections are scheduled for a new national legislative body, which is to be called the National Convention.

September Mass arrests of real and alleged supporters of the monarchy have been carried out. On the night of September 2, antiroyalist mobs invade jails throughout France and hundreds of royalists and royalist sympathizers are killed (the "September massacres"). On September 20 the French revolutionary armies defeat the invading Austrian-Prussian armies at Valmy: one of the French commanders is General Dumouriez, and the victory is partly the result of massed artillery that lays a killing barrage upon the invaders. On September 21 the newly elected National Convention assembles in Paris. The Convention abolishes the monarchy, proclaims the First French Republic, and initiates judicial proceedings against the king who is charged with treason.

November French armies under Dumouriez advance on the Austrian Netherlands (Belgium) and defeat the Austrians at the Battle of Jemappes on November 6. Another French army captures Mainz (Germany) and moves toward Frankfurt.

1793

January King Louis XVI is convicted of treason by the National Convention (by an absolute majority of one vote). He is executed on January 21. The execution of the king, a proclamation by the Convention that offers France's assistance to all those who rebel against tyranny, and France's military and commercial maneuvers in the Austrian Netherlands, provokes the formation of an anti-French alliance of European powers. Joining with Austria and Prussia in declaring war on revolutionary France are Great Britain, Spain, and Holland.

March Dumouriez is defeated by the Austrians and defects to the royalists on March 18. Revolt against the National Convention begins in the west of France, in the Vendée. Eventually supported by an army of 50,000 men, the counterrevolutionaries march north, defeating government forces in the provinces of Brittany, Maine, and Normandy.

June The moderate Girondists lose power in the National Convention and are replaced by the radical Jacobins.

July-August The second or "Great" Committee of Public Safety is established by the Convention. Prominent leaders of the Committee are Robespierre, Saint-Just, and Carnot. The "Reign of Terror" is instituted: a collective dictatorship struggles with the economic, social, and political crises associated with war and counterrevolution. Supported by the Parisian lower classes, the Committee regulates the national economy, imprisons and executes counterrevolutionaries, raises new armies to fight the battles of Republican France. Several thousand real or alleged counterrevolutionaries, including the queen, are guillotined and many more are imprisoned. Carnot reorganizes the Republic's armies, which now are based on universal military conscription.

October-December The counterrevolutionary forces of the Vendée are defeated by the Republic's armies. Reprisals are carried out against the rebels, including mass execution by drowning in the river Loire (at Nantes). Between three and five thousand people are killed. By the end of 1793 the Republic's armies have defeated the foreign invaders and France, in early 1794, moves to the offensive beyond her borders.

1794

March Jacques Hébert and other revolutionary extremists prepare a popular insurrection of the Paris masses. But Hébert and his collaborators are arrested and executed.

April   Danton and others who advocate a relaxation of the extreme measures taken by the Committee of Public Safety are arrested and executed.

July   The membership of the National Convention, now more moderate than the members of the Committee of Public Safety, arrests Robespierre. (The date according to the revolutionary calendar is 9 Thermidor.) Robespierre is guillotined on July 28, bringing to an end the Reign of Terror. Those who now come to power are drawn from the old bourgeoisie and the newly enriched who have profited from speculation and inflation. The period is described as the "Thermidorian reaction."

MEXICO, 1808–1934

1808

Napoleon's armies occupy parts of Spain. Napoleon installs his brother, Joseph Bonaparte, as the Spanish king. Mexico has been Spain's colonial possession since the early 1500s, and Napoleon's victories in Spain, as well as the American and French revolutions, raise hopes in Mexico for national independence.

1810

A Mexican priest, Father Hidalgo, whose parish is the village of Dolores, launches the rebellion against Spain by issuing a revolutionary proclamation, the *Grito de Dolores* (Cry of Dolores/Cry of Pains). The *Grito* calls for independence and major social change, including equality between Mexico's three racial communities: whites (those of Spanish descent), native Indians, and mestizos (mixed white and Indian). Most of the country's wealth, land, and political power are controlled by the whites. A growing laboring class of Indians and mestizos works under depressed conditions on the land, in the mines, and in the textile mills. The whites themselves are divided between those born in Spain (*gachupines*) and those born in Mexico (*criollos*, or creoles). Government officials often are corrupt, and much of the country's national wealth has been transferred to Spain according to the mercantilist policies of Spanish colonialism. The *Grito* also demands basic land reform in the interests of Mexico's impoverished peasantry.

1815

After initial successes, the rebel armies (consisting mostly of Indians and lower-class mestizos) are defeated by royalist forces. In Europe, Napoleon is defeated at the Battle of Waterloo. The tide of liberalism and national independence that was announced by the American Revolution has been reversed to the advantage of established power. In Mexico, this means the Church, the higher echelons of the military, and the landowners (with whites predominating in each category).

1821

Fearing that an eventual independence movement might also lead to a change in the distribution of status and power, Mexican conservatives succeed in negotiating Mexico's independence from Spain. Independence has been achieved without liberalizing reform. Augustín de Iturbide, leader of the conservatives, is head of the new government, which soon becomes a dictatorship. In 1822, Iturbide has his soldiers proclaim him emperor.

1823

Iturbide is forced to abdicate, and a republic is established. Mexico's first president is Guadalupe Victoria, but the dominating figure in Mexican politics for most of the next three decades is General Antonio de Santa Anna. Mexico's competing elites are drawn largely from the army; the highest officers gather groups of loyal supporters whose only program is personal enrichment. Government is corrupt and inefficient, and turnover at the top is high. There are no attempts to remedy the many inequities of Mexican society.

1846-1848

War with the United States ends with Mexico's loss of two-fifths of its territory. The Mexican war effort has been handicapped by political instability and by the refusal of some of Mexico's states to cooperate with the national government.

1855

Santa Anna has been ruling as "perpetual dictator," but he is overthrown by a revolution led by a group of liberal reformers. Among the revolutionary leaders is Benito Juárez. Juárez is Indian, a lawyer, former governor of the state of Oaxaca; he was imprisoned in 1853 by Santa Anna for his opposition to Santa Anna's dictatorship.

1857

A new federal constitution is adopted. The property of the Church is brought under the state's control and the power of the army is curtailed. Political power passes from Mexico's creoles to the mestizos. A sense of social consciousness and national identity begins to develop among Mexico's lower classes.

1858

Intense opposition by conservatives to the constitution and reforms of 1857 results in civil war (referred to as the War of Reform). Juárez and his government are forced to flee to Guanajuato, Guadalajara, and then to Veracruz before the conservative armies finally are defeated (in 1861).

1864

The conservatives have succeeded in winning foreign support for their counterrevolution. In France, Louis-Napoleon (Napoleon III) seeks a colonial empire and sends French troops to support the anti-Juárez forces. The Juárez government is evacuated from the capital and, eventually, is moved to El Paso del Norte (later Ciudad Juárez). Military intervention by the United States is forestalled only by the U.S. government's preoccupation with the American Civil War. In Mexico, the empire is established under Maximilian, a prince of the Austrian Hapsburgs who is heavily dependent on the French for support. Maximilian's rule alienates most of Mexico's native elite, including both conservatives and liberals.

1867

The withdrawal of French troops has fatally weakened the empire. Maximilian assumes personal command of his remaining forces, but they are defeated after a siege at Querétaro. Maximilian is captured and executed. Juárez, strongly supported by most of the Mexican population, is reelected president.

1871

Juárez is reelected again to the presidency. His ambitious program of reform, however, has been frustrated by political division among the liberals. The defeated presidential candidate, Porfirio Díaz, attempts to overthrow the Juárez government. Díaz, a mestizo, has been formerly identified with the liberals.

1872

The government succeeds in suppressing the rebellion led by Porfirio Díaz. But Benito Juárez dies.

1876

Díaz again is defeated in an election for the presidency, and again he leads a rebellion against the government. This time he succeeds. With the exception of the period 1880–1884, Díaz rules Mexico as its president until 1911. Political power is vested in the hands of Díaz and his supporting oligarchy, despite the façade of democratic institutions. Economic development is accelerated. Transportation and communications facilities are expanded. But Mexico's wealth, especially its mineral resources, is exploited mainly by foreign-owned companies. The profits returned to Mexicans are pocketed almost exclusively by the ruling elite. Millions of acres of land are sold to Díaz' supporters: the land becomes part of a vast system of ranching estates (*haciendas*). Mexico's peasants are increasingly dispossessed: 80-90 percent of the rural population own no land at all. Many of the common lands (*ejidos*) of the peasants, which represent a communal tradition that can be traced back to the Aztecs, also are absorbed into the hacienda system of private property. Half of Mexico's rural population is enslaved by indebtedness and bound to peonage. (Peons are legally free but in fact are forced to provide labor to the large landowners.)

1900-1910

Power continues to be concentrated in a narrow oligarchy, there is increasing prosperity for a few, but discontent among the general population intensifies.

1908

President Díaz announces that Mexico is ready for true democracy. Popular expectations of major reform are raised. In response to Díaz' announcement and his promise not to run for reelection in 1910, Francisco Madero publishes a book that is critical of the Díaz regime. Madero is the son of a wealthy landowner, and he argues for democratic and social reforms that will improve the conditions of peasant life. His book brings him national prominence. He declares himself a candidate for the presidency, and he calls for honest elections and a presidential term of office that is nonrenewable.

1910

Despite his earlier promise, Díaz again runs for president. Madero, his opponent, is imprisoned and Díaz easily engineers another election victory. Nor is there any indication after the election that Díaz intends to introduce democratic reforms. Madero is eventually released, and he flees to Texas where he announces for revolution in Mexico. Returning to Mexico, Madero is supported by several groups of armed rebels, including those in the north that are led by Francisco "Pancho" Villa.

1911

Ciudad Juárez is captured by the rebels on May 9. In the south, a rebel army under the command of Emiliano Zapata seizes hacienda lands for distribution to the peasants. The revolution gains momentum throughout Mexico. Díaz resigns on May 25 and flees the country. Madero is elected president and takes office in November.

1912

The Madero government is attacked by conservatives for favoring reform and by revolutionaries for not implementing radical reform (including returning the land to the Indians). And the government is constantly pressured by the United States (through its ambassador, Henry Lane Wilson) on behalf of American business interests in Mexico. Madero also proves to be a poor administrator. Armed insurrection breaks out across the country. The guiding principles of some rebel groups do not rise above simple lawlessness and banditry.

1913

Victoriano Huerta, one of Díaz' former generals and now commander of the government's army, secretly joins with rebel forces in the capital and plots Madero's downfall. The conspiracy is supported by the U.S. ambassador. Huerta kills Madero's brother, seizes power, and imprisons Madero. Madero is shot while allegedly trying to escape. A military dictatorship is established that is marked by corruption and by the assassination and imprisonment of the government's opponents. Opposition to Huerta's rule takes the form of armed insurrection in various parts of the country. The major insurgent leaders are Villa, Zapata, and Venustiano Carranza. President Woodrow Wilson in the United States also is hostile to the Huerta government and threatens military intervention.

1914

Confronted with increasing military pressure, Huerta resigns in July and flees the country. Carranza becomes president but Villa and Zapata refuse to recognize his government as legitimate. Civil war ensues.

1915

By the end of 1915, Carranza has established his government's control over most of the country. His military commander is Alvaro Obregón. Obregón was an early supporter of Francisco Madero and is one of the revolution's most liberally oriented generals.

1917

Pressured by General Obregón, President Carranza promulgates a new constitution: Mexico's mineral resources, until now largely controlled by foreign (mainly U.S.) interests, are nationalized; church and state are separated; educational and labor reforms are prescribed; debt peonage is abolished; and provision is made for restoring the *ejido* (communal) land system to Mexico's Indian population. Opposed to the reforms prescribed by the 1917 Constitution, however, Carranza refuses to implement them. To further strengthen his position, Carranza has Zapata murdered in 1919.

1920

Carranza attempts to prevent Obregón from becoming president. Obregón leads an insurrection that forces Carranza to flee the capital; he is later ambushed and killed. Obregón becomes president, and, during his administration (1920-1924), schools are built and some land is redistributed to the peasantry.

1923

Obregón is allied with another political and military leader, Plutarco Calles, and together they suppress an armed insurrection against the government.

1924

Calles is elected president and continues Obregón's educational and agrarian programs. But there are many outbreaks of violence in the country and there is increasing conflict between the government and militant Catholics (who oppose the Church's loss of privileges and the separation of church and state).

1928

Obregón is reelected president, but he is assassinated by a Catholic militant before taking office. Calles remains Mexico's most important political figure until 1934. In 1929, Calles organizes the National Revolutionary party—renamed the Institutional Revolutionary party (PRI) in 1946. The party enjoys a virtual monopoly on political power. Calles' early reformist spirit fades as he acquires land and wealth. His government becomes a conservative dictatorship.

1934

Lázaro Cárdenas is elected president. The Cárdenas government (1934-1940) accelerates the pace of liberal reform in Mexico. The *ejido* system is enlarged, the Mexican labor movement is strengthened, legislation is passed aimed at fully integrating Indians into Mexico's social structure, educational and medical facilities are extended, relations with the Church are stabilized, the railroads and oil resources are brought under the national government's control, and many other reforms are introduced that work toward fulfilling the promises and expectations associated with the Revolution of 1910. But the pace of reform slows under subsequent presidents. Power and wealth are concentrated in the hands of an oligarchy, and the ruling elite within the PRI is self-perpetuating.

RUSSIA, 1861-1920

1861

Tsar Alexander II abolishes serfdom in Russia. The tsar hopes to launch Russia on the road of modernization that has already been traveled by the more developed countries of Western Europe. The abolition of serfdom in Russia, however, works mainly to the advantage of the already wealthy nobility. A small minority of Russia's vast peasant population also is able to acquire land and to improve its economic position. But the great majority of Russia's peasants continue to live under impoverished circumstances, too poor to be able to buy the land they farm, exploited by landowners and money lenders, politically impotent, religious, superstitious, and far behind the more culturally developed laboring classes of Western Europe.

1881-1894

Tsar Alexander III continues the modernizing policies of his father. The autocracy encourages the development of industry, which is heavily financed by foreign investment. Russia's new factories are concentrated in a few large cities, notably in St. Petersburg (the capital of tsarist Russia) and in Moscow. Large working-class populations live in the industrial districts of these cities. While carrying on his father's modernizing policies, however, Alexander III reverses the tentative liberalizing trends that his father had initiated. Russia is to be developed economically without weakening the authority of the autocratic state. The powers of the police over the people are extended, censorship and control of education are tightened, and the authority of provincial rural governments (*zemstvos*) and the judiciary is limited—to the advantage of the centralizing autocracy. Persecution of religious and cultural minorities, especially Russian Jews, is intensified. Nicholas II succeeds his father as tsar in 1894 and continues his father's repressive policies. Conspiratorial organizations committed to violence and revolution grow rapidly.

1898

The Russian Social Democratic Labor party is organized and holds its first congress (in secret) in the Russian city of Minsk. The party's program is based on the writings of Marx and Engels, as introduced to Russia's intellectuals by Georgi Plekhanov. Following Marx, Plekhanov opposes terrorism as a means of political change and argues that Russia must first undergo capitalist development before it will be possible to establish democracy and socialism in Russia.

1903

The Second Congress of the Russian Social Democratic Labor party is convened, first in Brussels and then in London. In London, the party is split between two factions—Bolsheviks (meaning those of the majority) and Mensheviks (meaning those of the minority). The Bolsheviks favor the organization of a conspiratorial party led by professional revolutionaries who are not necessarily constrained to wait for capitalist development in Russia before launching a socialist revolution. Lenin, the Bolsheviks' leader, has been exiled twice to Siberia for subversive activities against the tsarist state and, since 1900, has been living in Western Europe among the many émigrés and intellectuals who have fled tsarist repression.

1904-1905

Russia declares war on Japan in February, 1904. The tsar hopes to advance Russian imperialism in Manchuria and Korea, to defeat Japanese imperialist ambitions in the same areas, and to defuse the revolutionary time bomb that is ticking in Russia (there are many manifestations of conspiracy and opposition to the tsarist state). Expecting an easy victory over an Asian enemy, Russia's leaders instead are confronted by a series of military disasters (climaxed in May 1905 by the destruction of the Russian fleet at Tsushima). Even the first reported reversals of the war, however, lead to an outbreak of peasant revolts and labor strikes. On January 9, 1905, a peaceful demonstration of workers assembles before the tsar's Winter Palace in St. Petersburg and is fired on by tsarist troops. (The demonstration is led by a priest, Father Gapon, and its suppression is referred to as "Bloody Sunday.") Strikes, riots, assassinations, naval mutinies, and peasant violence quickly follow and are soon intensified by Russia's military defeat and surrender to Japan in mid-1905. A general strike takes place in October, and soviets (or "councils") of workers are organized in the factories to coordinate the activities of the strikers. Led by Leon Trotsky, previously an associate of Lenin's, the St. Petersburg soviet plays a prominent role in preparing a workers' insurrection. The insurrection takes place in December but is suppressed, and members of the soviet are arrested. (Trotsky is exiled to Siberia but soon escapes.) The tsar's army has remained loyal to the government, and the tsar promises reforms leading to representative government and basic civil liberties. Revolutionary agitation subsides.

1906-1907

The First Duma (parliament) is elected on the basis of limited suffrage. A majority of the Duma's deputies, however, opposes the tsar's policies and government. The tsar dissolves the Duma and calls for new elections. Deputies elected to the Second Duma are even more hostile to the tsar and his government. The tsar dissolves the Second Duma and orders changes in the electoral law. Deputies elected to the Third Duma readily subordinate themselves to the demands of the tsar and his appointed ministers.

1907-1911

The tsar's prime minister and minister of the interior is Piotr Stolypin. Stolypin combines repression of continued revolutionary activity and peasant violence with basic economic reform. The Stolypin land reforms are designed to create a landowning peasantry (a reasonably self-sufficient peasant middle class), but without compromising the domination of Russia's landed nobility. Among the principal effects of the reforms, however, is the disruption of the village commune (the *mir*), which has provided Russia's peasants with a rudimentary system of social welfare and equality.

1912

The Bolsheviks, with most of their leaders living in European exile, formally cut their ties with the Menshevik wing and other factions of the Social Democrats. The Bolsheviks now constitute themselves as a separate and independent revolutionary party.

1914-1916

Russia enters the First World War in August 1914. At first, only the Bolsheviks oppose participation in the war—which the Bolsheviks regard as a struggle between European imperialist powers that conceals the exploitation of Europe's working classes. Repeated defeat on the battle fronts, however, the administrative imcompetence of the tsar's government, severe food shortages, inflation, and popular hostility for the tsar's court and cabinet eventually reduce the supporters of the autocracy to a small minority.

1917

March By early March (or the middle of February according to the Old Style Russian calendar), most workers in Petrograd and Moscow are on strike and demanding higher food rations. The tsar's troops refuse to restore order. Mutiny spreads among the military garrisons of the capital. The Duma urges the tsar to compromise, but on March 11 he orders the Duma dissolved. The Duma's deputies refuse to disband. On March 12 workers and soldiers take control of Petrograd. Their activities are coordinated in part by the newly formed Soviet of Soldiers' and Workers' Deputies. The tsar, who has assumed personal command of his armies at the front, abdicates on March 15 in favor of the Grand Duke

Mikhail. Mikhail refuses to become tsar. The Duma appoints a Provisional Government of political moderates, headed by Prince Lvov and including the Socialist leader Alexander Kerensky. The program of the Provisional Government calls for liberal reforms and the election of a Constituent Assembly that is based on universal manhood suffrage. But the Provisional Government also presses for a continuation of the war and promises but refuses to implement basic land reform.

April The Petrograd Soviet, at first dominated by Social Revolutionaries and Mensheviks, functions as a rival government to the Provisional Government. The Soviet controls transport, communications, and the movement of troops. It calls for an immediate end to the war and distribution of land to the peasantry. The Petrograd Soviet extends its influence by establishing soviets among soldiers, including those at the front, among workers and intellectuals in other cities, and among the peasantry. The German government, hoping to sabotage or to end the Russian war effort, enables Lenin to travel by train from Switzerland to Sweden, where he continues on to Petrograd.

May Trotsky arrives in Petrograd, having sailed from New York after learning of the February Revolution. He does not declare himself a Bolshevik, but he joins with Lenin in arguing that the February Revolution and the program of the Provisional Government represent the bourgeois revolution in Russia. Trotsky and the Bolsheviks call on workers, soldiers, and peasants to seize power through the developing system of soviets. Bolshevik organizers and agitators popularize Lenin's program with the slogans "end the war," "all land to the peasants," and "all power to the soviets."

June The First All-Russian Congress of Soviets is convened in Petrograd with delegates representing workers, soldiers, and peasants. Of the more than 600 delegates, the Bolsheviks count only 105 supporters, but they gain increasing strength from the ranks of the Mensheviks and Social Revolutionaries.

July Continuing to prosecute the war, the Provisional Government launches a major military offensive. The offensive fails. Defections of soldiers from the front, many of them gathering in Petrograd, and general disorder encourage the Bolsheviks to attempt an uprising. The uprising fails and Lenin takes refuge across the border in Finland. Trotsky and other Bolshevik leaders are imprisoned. Prince Lvov resigns as prime minister. He is replaced by Kerensky, whose coalition government is based on a socialist majority in the Duma. The government prosecutes the imprisoned Bolsheviks on charges of conspiracy and espionage for Germany.

August-September Conservatives and some moderates rally behind General Kornilov, military commander-in-chief, who is resolutely opposed to the revolution. Kornilov sends troops toward Petrograd with the objective of reconstructing the Provisional Government along less radical lines. In order to defend the government and the revolution, Kerensky calls on Bolsheviks and Socialists (many of those in prison, including Trotsky, are released) to help defeat the Kornilov offensive. Kornilov's troops fail to reach Petrograd, and Kornilov is arrested. (He subsequently escapes and is one of the White generals during the Civil War.) Food shortages prompt the government, in late August, to double the price of grain. The Bolsheviks now control a majority of deputies in the soviets of both Petrograd and Moscow.

October Bolshevik influence spreads throughout the system of soviets, among workers, peasants, and soldiers. Armed soldiers returning from the front help to radicalize peasants in the countryside, where rebellion already is widespread. Peasants raid estates and seize the land of the nobility. The number of industrial strikes and the extent of worker participation in the strikes increase.

November-December Lenin returns to Petrograd and supports Trotsky's initiative in organizing an insurrection. Under Trotsky's command, the Military Revolutionary Committee of the Petrograd Soviet occupies government buildings, communications and transportation facilities, and the tsar's Winter Palace on the night of November 7 (October 25 according to the Old Style calendar). Kerensky flees, and other members of the Provisional Government are arrested. The Bolsheviks establish a Council (*soviet*) of People's Commissars with Lenin as chairman and Trotsky as commissar for foreign affairs. A Second All-Russian Congress of Soviets is convened, which abolishes private property and gives all private and church lands to village soviets for redistribution to the peasants. Moscow also is forcefully taken by the Bolsheviks. Local soviets soon take control of most of the cities of Russia and declare their support for the Bolsheviks.

1918-1920

The long-promised Constituent Assembly convenes in January 1918. But the Bolsheviks are a minority, and soldiers force the Assembly to disband in the evening of its first day of meetings. The Bolsheviks formally change their name to the Russian Communist party. Fear of continued German aggression prompts the new Soviet government to move the country's capital from Petrograd to Moscow. In March 1918 Trotsky and Lenin force the other party and government leaders to accept the Treaty of Brest-Litovsk, negotiated with Germany and Austria-Hungary to the extreme detriment of Russia, but finally ending Russia's involvement in the war. The Soviet government is saved from having to honor the harsh terms of the treaty by the victory of the Allies over the Central

Powers in November 1918. Between late 1918 and 1920 the Soviet government is engaged in a destructive civil war in which the Red armies, organized and led by Trotsky, fight the counterrevolutionary White armies. The military operations of the Whites are first centered in the south among troops commanded by General Kornilov. At various times during the struggle, Red armies also are engaged in the west by Polish troops, in the east by the Japanese and by Whites supported by the Czech Legion, and in the north by Whites supported by British, French, and United States military personnel. U.S. troops also intervene in the Far East, but they do not participate in the actual fighting. By 1920 the Soviet government succeeds in consolidating its control over most of Russia, in part because of Trotsky's leadership, and also because of the failure of the several White armies to coordinate their military operations. And the Whites fail to win the support of the peasants, who fear a return to tsarist autocracy and the loss of land they have acquired because of the revolution.

GERMANY, 1918-1934

1918

March The Treaty of Brest-Litovsk ends the war between Soviet Russia and the Central Powers. Germany now is able to concentrate its entire war effort on the western front.

April A unified military command is established for the Allied armies. Germany and its allies are confronted by the combined military strength of France, Great Britain, and the United States.

July-August A major German offensive, the second battle of the Marne, is halted near Paris. The Allies counterattack and force the German armies into a general retreat. The Germans sustain heavy losses.

September The Allies invade Bulgaria, one of the Central Powers. The Bulgarian government capitulates.

October Turkey, also one of the central Powers, negotiates an armistice with the Allies.

November 3-4 Austria-Hungary, Germany's principal ally, surrenders to the Allies following the Italian victory at Vittorio Veneto. Germany continues to sustain heavy losses on the western front, and its military and economic resources are virtually exhausted. The collapse of German morale is dramatized by a mutiny of sailors in Kiel, Germany's principal naval base.

November 7   King Louis III of Bavaria is deposed following a popular uprising in Munich. A republic is proclaimed. The premier of the new Bavarian government is Kurt Eisner. Eisner is a revolutionary socialist who was recently convicted of treason for inciting munitions workers to strike.

November 8   Popular revolt spreads and royalist autocrats are dethroned in the German states of Baden, Württemberg, Thuringia, and Saxony.

November 9   Prince Maximilian of Baden, Germany's chancellor since October, forces Kaiser Wilhelm II to abdicate. On the recommendation of the German military high command, Maximilian already has begun negotiations with the Allies for an armistice to end the war. (U.S. President Woodrow Wilson has made the kaiser's abdication a precondition for peace negotiations.) Having secured the kaiser's abdication, Maximilian resigns as chancellor.

November 10   Germany's new chancellor is Friedrich Ebert, a Social Democrat and trade union leader.

November 11   The Socialist government of Friedrich Ebert concludes an armistice with the Allies, bringing an end to the First World War. The Treaty of Brest-Litovsk is declared void, and Germany is required to evacuate all territory west of the Rhine. Germany's surrender to the Allies, without a decisive military defeat in the field, will become a basis for nationalist claims that the war was lost, not by the army, but by the traitorous (and Socialist) politicians.

December   A national conference of the Spartacus League, a group of revolutionary German socialists founded in 1916, changes the League's name to the German Communist party (the KPD). The party is led by Rosa Luxemburg and Karl Liebknecht. Supported by the more radical elements of the German working class, the KPD calls for the establishment of a dictatorship of the proletariat. Rosa Luxemburg argues that proletarian dictatorship is most likely to result from a largely spontaneous eruption of the masses that is climaxed by a general strike.

1919

January   On January 5, the KPD initiates political violence and mass action in Berlin and in other major German cities. The party's objective is to overthrow the government and establish a socialist workers' state. In Berlin on January 6, a large demonstration of workers is organized, but the great majority of participants is unwilling to attempt a revolution. The demonstration is controlled by police and the military. The KPD's leaders, Karl Liebknecht and Rosa

Luxemburg, are arrested. They are murdered by soldiers while being transported to prison.

February–March   A wave of industrial strikes sweeps across Germany. An attempted general strike in Berlin is suppressed by the military. On February 21, the Bavarian premier, the socialist Kurt Eisner, is assassinated.

April   Bavarian Communists attempt a revolution, but the revolt is suppressed by the German army. The Bavarian government ends its formal independence and joins the German Weimar Republic.

June   The Treaty of Versailles is signed after long and bitter negotiations among the victorious Allies. The treaty formally ends the war; it also charges Germany and the other Central Powers with responsibility for starting the war, imposes heavy reparations payments on Germany, and limits the size of the German army and navy. All of Germany's former colonies are ceded to the mandate authority of the newly organized League of Nations. Germany also loses Alsace-Lorraine to France and most of West Prussia to Poland. The Versailles Treaty orders plebiscites to be held in territories that Germany eventually will lose to Belgium, Poland, and Denmark. In the west, Germany cedes the Saar Territory to France for fifteen years while the Rhineland is to be occupied by the Allies for the same period. The terms of the Versailles peace settlement help to undermine the legitimacy of the Weimar Republic and contribute to the growth of nationalism and militarism.

July   The first democratic German constitution is adopted in the town of Weimar by members of the German National Assembly (elected in January). The constitution provides for universal suffrage, including women, and for elections that are based on proportional representation (PR). The PR electoral system helps to reduce the Weimar Republic's potential for stability by contributing to the development of a multiparty system and a series of coalition governments, especially ineffective after 1929. The democratic center also is eventually weakened, to the advantage of extremist parties on the left and right—which greatly benefit from the electoral law.

1920

February   Adolf Hitler gains control of a small party of extremists, the German Workers' party, which is based in Munich and was previously led by Gottfried Feder. Hitler changes the party's name to the National Socialist German Workers' party (N.S.D.A.P., or "Nazi" from the German pronunciation of the first two syllables of the word "National"). The Nazis are one of the many extremist groups that profit from the widespread discontent of German citizens following the war. The Nazi program combines socialist economics with militant nationalism and a strong bias for authoritarian organization. Hitler adds to his following by violently attacking Jews and Communists and by capitalizing on German nationalist resentment of the Versailles Treaty. The socialist content of the party's program eventually is minimized and the emphasis is on order, national greatness, and racial purity.

March Wolfgang Kapp, an extreme right-wing politician, leads an armed revolt of monarchists and army officers who seize power in Berlin. The "Kapp *putsch*" is defeated only by a general strike of Berlin workers. The Weimar government's weakness is obvious to all. The government also is unable to suppress the political violence that is engineered by the private armies of anti-democratic organizations.

1923

In January, French and Belgian troops occupy the industrial centers of the Ruhr. The occupation is designed to enforce the reparations provisions of the Versailles Treaty. German nationalist sentiment intensifies. Workers and employees respond to the occupation with passive resistance and a series of general strikes that are supported by the government. To ensure the workers' economic welfare in the face of foreign occupation and industrial collapse, the government prints large quantities of paper money. This immensely aggravates the inflation that already is characteristic of the postwar period. By the end of 1923, one U.S. dollar equals more than four trillion German marks. Personal savings and debts are wiped out. Germany's middle classes are especially hard hit; many citizens are bankrupt and most are demoralized. There is increased support for Germany's extremist groups, including the Nazis. On November 8, the Nazis' paramilitary "Storm Troopers" invade a meeting of Bavarian government officials that is convened in a Munich beer hall. Hitler's "beer hall *putsch*" is intended to bring Germany under the control of the nationalists and the army. After swearing loyalty to the "revolution," however, the freed Bavarian officials suppress the *putsch* with the aid of the army. Hitler flees, is soon arrested and is sentenced to five years in prison. The Bavarian government is nevertheless sympathetic to the cause of the extreme nationalists, and Hilter serves only nine months of his sentence. While in prison, he writes *Mein Kampf,* which describes his plans for Germany's revenge and eventual world domination.

1924-1929

In an effort to settle Germany's reparations problem and to rehabilitate the German economy, the Dawes Plan is adopted in 1924. The plan is named for Charles Dawes, an American banker who heads the international reparations committee. Under the terms of the plan, French and Belgian troops evacuate the

Ruhr in 1925 and the amount of German reparations is reduced. The way is opened for foreign investment in German industry, much of it provided by private capital from the United States. Over the next several years the German economy stabilizes and rapid growth in construction and industrial development leads to a measure of prosperity for German citizens. The fortunes of the Nazis and other extremist groups decline. But Germany's dependency on foreign loans makes the country particularly vulnerable to the worldwide economic depression that begins in late 1929.

1930-1932

The depression brings widespread business failure and massive unemployment. Mounting discontent in Germany is reflected in the polarization of voting support between the Communist and the Nazi parties. The Nazis are the largest single party in the Reichstag following the elections of July 1932. The Weimar government is hard pressed to put together a democratic majority in the legislature. The government effectively ceases to function.

1933

January   The aged president of the republic, General von Hindenburg, is confronted by the threat of both civil war and public exposure of government corruption. His only apparent alternative to appointing Hitler chancellor is to put the government in the hands of General von Schleicher. But von Schleicher openly advocates a military dictatorship. And von Hindenburg is persuaded by his advisers that Hitler and the Nazis can be kept under control. Von Hindenburg appoints Hitler chancellor on January 30. Hitler calls for new national elections, scheduled for March.

February   On February 27, a week before the elections, the Nazis arrange for the burning of the building that houses the Reichstag. The Nazis attribute the fire to Communist revolutionaries. Declaring a national emergency and alleging a Communist plot to seize power, Hitler's government suspends freedom of speech and the press. The Nazi Brownshirts march through the streets of German cities and towns, intimidating the opposition and mobilizing support for Hitler and his allies.

March   Allied with the right-wing Nationalist party, the Nazis emerge from the elections of March 5 with a bare parliamentary majority (based on 44 percent of the popular vote). The Communist deputies are excluded from the Reichstag, and on March 23 the Reichstag passes legislation that gives Hitler dictatorial power.

1934

The Nazis are declared the only legal party in Germany. Open opposition is suppressed by the Gestapo. The powers of the state governments are abolished. The more leftist factions within the Nazi party are liquidated in the "Blood Purge" of June—thereby helping Hitler to establish his control over the army's right-wing officer corps. With the death of President von Hindenburg, the chancellorship and the presidency are united in the person of Hitler, who is proclaimed the sole leader, or *führer*, of Germany. Hitler's government strengthens Germany's economy and begins to mobilize the nation for war.

CHINA, 1839-1949

1839-1842

Great Britain attacks several Chinese coastal cities. According to the British, the "Opium War" is in retaliation for the destruction in Canton of opium supplies belonging to British merchants. The British also are opposed to China's restrictions on foreign trade.

1842-1860

Military operations along China's coast by Great Britain and other imperialist powers force the Chinese government to grant extensive commercial and territorial concessions to foreign interests.

1848-1865

Marked by extreme violence, the Taiping Rebellion mobilizes many of China's impoverished masses against the ruling Manchu Ch'ing dynasty. The rebels demand the adoption of new religious values and fundamental changes in China's political and socioeconomic organization. They extend their control from the eastern Yangtze valley to Nanking, which is captured in 1853. Fearing the collapse of foreign trade, the Western powers intervene and assist the Manchus in suppressing the rebellion.

1894-1895

China loses more territory, this time to Japan following Japan's victories in the First Chinese-Japanese War.

1899

John Hay, U.S. Secretary of State, attempts to secure the agreement of other Western powers to an "open door" policy in China. The U.S. initiative is intended to guarantee American commercial access to China in the face of a growing monopoly by Japan and the European powers over Chinese territory and trade.

1900

The Boxer Rebellion, encouraged by a war faction in the Manchu court led by the dowager empress, attacks foreigners and Chinese Christians. The rebels occupy Peking (the capital) for eight weeks in June and July. In August, the rebellion is suppressed by military contingents from Great Britain, France, Germany, Russia, Japan, and the United States. The Chinese government is compelled to pay an indemnity of $333 million, to permit the stationing of foreign troops in the capital, and to alter existing commercial treaties to the even greater advantage of foreign powers.

1905

The "Revolutionary Alliance" is organized among Chinese who are living in Japan. The leader of the Alliance is Sun Yat-sen. Sun is a doctor who has received part of his education in the west. He has traveled throughout the world raising funds and support for revolution in China. He identifies his guiding principles as nationalism, socialism, and democracy.

1911

Supporters of Sun Yat-sen launch their revolution. A republic is proclaimed in territory occupied by the rebels. In December, Sun Yat-sen is elected president of the republic.

1912

Yüan Shih-kai, China's most powerful warlord, advises the emperor to abdicate. The emperor abdicates on February 12, ending the monarchical system of government that has ruled China since the third century B.C. Sun Yat-sen resigns the presidency of the republic in favor of Yüan. Yüan proceeds to establish a military dictatorship. Sun transforms his Revolutionary Alliance into the Kuomintang (KMT, the National People's Party).

1913–1915

There are sporadic and unsuccessful revolts by followers of Sun Yat-sen and by others who oppose Yüan's dictatorship. Yüan suppresses the KMT; it holds a majority of seats in the First National Assembly. Yüan dissolves the assembly in 1914, and in 1915 he declares himself emperor.

1916

Yüan Shih-kai dies and the republic is restored. China, however, is divided by the struggles between the semi-independent warlords and by the commercial and territorial concessions controlled by foreign states.

1917

Civil war breaks out between the KMT, which is based in the south, and the national government with its supporting coalition of warlords, which are based in the north.

1921

Leaders of the KMT's armies occupy Canton and proclaim a national government. Sun Yat-sen is elected president. Heavily influenced and largely controlled by Moscow and the Communist International, the Chinese Communist party (CCP) is founded by Chen Tu-hsiu and Li Ta-chao, professors at Peking University.

1923-1925

The CCP is formally allied with Sun's KMT. Communists hold many responsible positions in the KMT's organization. Sun Yat-sen dies in 1925. The leadership of the KMT passes to Chiang Kai-shek, one of Sun's principal aides.

1926

Chiang Kai-shek leads the KMT's armies against the warlords in the north and captures Hankow, Shanghai, and Nanking. In March, Chiang purges most of the Communists from the KMT's hierarchy. But the CCP, obedient to the demands of Soviet advisers, continues its alliance with Chiang and the KMT.

1927

In April, Chiang expels the Communists from their major urban stronghold, Shanghai. Thousands of Communist leaders and cadres are liquidated. In August, Mao Tse-tung leads peasants of Hunan province in an uprising. The uprising is suppressed by KMT forces with heavy losses for the Communists and their supporters. Chiang's march to the north is resumed, but the KMT's armies are prevented from reaching Peking by the military intervention of the Japanese. Japan has occupied a part of Chinese territory since defeating Russia in the Russo-Japanese War of 1904-1905. The Japanese government now is dominated by militarists who are committed to Japan's economic and territorial expansion. They adopt an aggressive policy toward China.

1928

Chiang Kai-shek establishes a national government in Nanking that is formally recognized by most major foreign powers.

1928-1931

The commune government established by the Communists in Canton in December 1927 is defeated by KMT forces. The CCP begins to shift its mobilization strategy away from China's small urban proletariat to China's vast peasant population. Rural soviets are organized in central and south China, in the provinces of Kiangsi, Hunan, Anhwei, and Hupei. The Communists introduce major land reform programs in the areas under their control. They gain increasing support from the peasants. The Red army, led by Mao Tse-tung and Chu Teh, is recruited from the peasantry of Kiangsi province, the center of Communist control.

1934-1935

After several military campaigns, the KMT's armies force the Communists to abandon their bases in the center and south. Under the leadership of Mao Tse-tung, Chu Teh, Chou En-lai, and Lin Piao, some 90,000 men and women begin the "Long March," first to the east and then to the north. By October 1935, and with less than half of the original marchers remaining, the Communists establish a new base in northern Shensi province near the city of Yenan. The Communists again introduce major agrarian reform in the areas under their control. They also build factories, strengthen the party's organization, and continue the civil war with Chiang Kai-shek.

1935-1937

The Japanese extend their military occupation of China into Chahar and Hopeh provinces. The Communists seek an end to the civil war and propose an alliance with the KMT against Japanese aggression. In 1937, after being kidnapped by one of his generals, Chiang Kai-shek agrees to a truce with the Communists. Full scale war between China and Japan begins. But the Japanese extend their occupation to the northern cities of Peking and Tientsin.

1938

Japanese armies capture Soochow, Amoy, Hankow, Canton, Shanghai, and the Nationalist's capital (Nanking). Chiang evacuates his government deep into central China, to the city of Chungking.

1939-1940

The always shaky truce between the CCP and the KMT breaks down completely in 1939. Communist guerrillas are the only effective military force resisting Japanese aggression in the north. By 1940, Chiang's best troops are deployed against the Communists instead of against the Japanese.

1941-1945

Following the entry of the United States into the war against Japan, Chiang's government and armies receive substantial support from both the United States and Great Britain. By the time of Japan's defeat in 1945, the Chinese Communists control large areas of rural China in the center and in the north, including an area of some 400,000 square miles with a population of 100 million. The Communists also have built an army of 900,000 and a people's militia of 2 million. Entering the war against Japan in 1945, the Soviet Union occupies Manchuria in July. But Stalin gives his support to Chiang instead of to the Communists—in exchange for Soviet shipping rights at Ports Arthur and Darien and joint control of the Manchurian railroads.

1946-1949

The Chinese Communists occupy Manchuria after the Soviet Union's withdrawal from China in May 1946. The CCP's membership grows rapidly. The KMT government is troubled by bureaucratic inefficiency, widespread corruption, and runaway inflation. But the Nationalists are largely successful in their continuing war with the Communists through 1947, in part because of important military and economic aid from the United States. Beginning in 1948, however, Communist armies gain momentum and advance through urban and rural areas into the south. By the end of 1949, the Communists control almost all the mainland of China. Chiang Kai-shek and his supporters flee the mainland and occupy the island of Taiwan—which both Nationalists and Communists claim as a province of China.

POSTSCRIPT TO PART I

"Chronologies: Some *almost* Raw Data." Thus does the title of Chapter 3 mislead the gullible, dupe the innocent, and confirm the devious nature of the author.

There is not a single entry in any of the preceding chronologies that is not clearly relevant to the fate and fortunes of the designated revolutionary movement (or movements).

And yet for each of the six countries surveyed, an infinite number and an unlimited variety of events might have been entered for each time period. The writing of "chronologies of revolution," then, entails a rigorous screening out of what is considered irrelevant and extraneous material.

Where do the criteria for making such decisions come from? And from where do we derive the classification categories that are already implicit in our minds and that facilitate our selection of data? Apparently we already have in our minds some idea of what is relevant and what is irrelevant to the study of revolution, no matter how advanced or preliminary our familiarity with the subject matter. Presumably, the greater our familiarity with the subject matter, the more comprehensive and conceptually useful our strategies for research and analysis.

Here we also may lay to rest some nagging concerns traditional to the study of revolution. In reading through the chronologies included in Chapter 3, was the reader tempted to "periodize" the events of the revolutionary process, to arrange them conceptually into stages and so to discover some general law or pattern of revolutionary development? In studies where this has been attempted, it has resulted in an unnecessarily artificial arrangement of data invariably reflecting a small sample of revolutionary movements.

The most obvious example is Crane Brinton's understanding of the stages of revolution, which is drawn from his earlier study of the French Revolution, but which he also applies to the Russian, American, and Puritan revolutions. Brinton identifies "the rule of the moderates" as the first stage of (successful) revolution, followed by "the accession of the extremists," the "reign of terror," and then "Thermidor" or a partial return to prerevolutionary conditions.[1]

Aside from its teleological implications, Brinton's construct invites endless dispute over the criteria and utility of periodizing history. Brinton himself is unable to fit it to the American case and to revolutions of the fascist variety.[2] And with explicit reference to Brinton, Leiden and Schmitt conclude from their study of the Mexican Revolution that stages involving extremism, terror, military dictatorship, and counterrevolutionary reaction do not apply to the Mexican case.[3] Nor do they apply to most of the cases that provide data for this book.[4]

Because of considerations of space and not of significance, this book also has little to say about the *consequences* of revolutionary movements. Whether in triumph or defeat, the socioeconomic and political effects of any part of the revolutionary process obviously deserve close attention. Much remains to be done in this area of study, especially from the perspective of social science. Only by looking at the long-range consequences of a successful revolution can we attempt a summary judgment of the revolutionaries' success or failure in implementing their dreams of justice. It is the subject matter of another book, or an entire library, but a few of the major points on the issue may be noted here.

A large majority of western scholars who have reflected on revolution admit its occasional inevitability but lament its inevitable shortcomings. And it is true that one of the characteristics of revolutionary movements is a utopian ideology that overemphasizes existing injustice while oversimplifying the possibilities of fundamental change. Revolutionary leaders typically view the cause of the evils they attack in the objective characteristics of the social order. They assume that a restructuring of authority and economic relationships will significantly affect human behavior. They consequently forget the extent to which the patterns of culture and the habits of thought and behavior are characterized more by continuity than by change. The point is underlined by the perversions of revolutionary regimes that invoked the names of Rousseau or Marx, or that pretended to serve the ideals of liberty, equality, fraternity, freedom, social order, or national independence.[5]

But it also is true that even revolutions that apparently fail have their positive effects. Despite the English Restoration, the Puritan Revolution raised the standard of parliamentary supremacy over monarchical authority, a principle that was soon to become the hallmark of British constitutionalism. Despite the distortions worked by the United States Constitution of 1789, the ideals of the Declaration of Independence of 1776 have continued to serve as an inspiration for political and social reform and probably have found their clearest expression in the twentieth century. Despite the Thermidorian Reaction and its aftermath, the French Revolution so enfeebled aristocratic privilege that the foundations were laid for a society based more on achievement than on hereditary rank. Despite the horrors of enforced collectivization, millions of peasants in Asia and Europe have material and educational opportunities long denied them by more benign dictatorships.

The question of the consequences of revolution is obviously answered according to our own personal values and the particular perspective we choose to fix on history. But perhaps the best answer is that provided by Trotsky, one of history's greatest revolutionaries: "Do the consequences of a revolution justify in general the sacrifices it involves . . . ? It would be as well to ask in face of the difficulties and griefs of personal existence: Is it worth while to be born?"[6]

NOTES

[1] Brinton, 1965, Chaps. 5-8.

[2] Brinton, 1965, pp. 175, 236, 254, and 262.

[3] Leiden and Schmitt, 1968, p. 135.

[4] For a conception of the stages of revolution that differs from Brinton's paradigm, see Hopper, 1950. But also see Elton, 1923 (pp. 1-3), for a historian's criticism of the arbitrariness of all periodization.

[5] A largely negative view of the results of revolution may be found in Brogan, 1966, pp. 266-68; Hopper, 1950, pp. 278-79; Brinton, 1965, pp. 235-36, 266, and Chap. 9; also see Huntington, 1968, pp. 308-9.

[6] Trotsky, 1957, Vol. III, p. 348.

CHAPTER
FOUR

LEADERS

SOCIAL CLASS

The population of every large society is differentiated according to status, wealth, and power, and the great majority of any given population may be thought of as the broad base of a steep pyramid. If we define social class as the measure of one's position along the vertical slope of the pyramid, we can then say that the higher the class-standing of any individual, the smaller the percentage of the population that belongs to his social class. This is a more precise way of saying that the poor and humble are many while the rich and powerful are few.

It obviously follows that the political elites of established governments are not sociologically representative of the citizens they rule. The great majority of citizens are farmers, factory workers, office workers, artisans, shopkeepers, salaried employees, or small businessmen, while the great majority of political elites are lawyers, doctors, large landowners, industrialists, business executives, publishers, bankers, or professional politicians whose fathers can claim the distinctions of these or other high-status professions.[1]

What is at issue here is the extent to which the leaders of revolutionary movements are more representative of the social base of their society than are the political elites they seek to displace. In most cases, they are not. And although it requires some careful amending (which follows), one of the best-documented ironies of revolutionary movements is that the social class of revolutionary leaders approximates that of political elites more closely than it does the social class of those the revolutionaries claim to lead toward greater social justice.

REVOLUTIONARIES
ON THE LEFT

This is especially true of revolutionary leaders who advocate greater equality in the political, social, or economic relationships of their society. In fact, it is frequently the case that as revolutionary leadership is more leftist or egalitarian-oriented, it is increasingly unrepresentative, in sociological terms, of its mass base, actual or potential.

Marx, Lenin, Kautsky, and other supporters of *proletarian* revolution argued that if the working class is left to its own devices, its political vision will never pierce through the veil of trade-union consciousness. And Mao Tse-tung, Ho Chi Minh, Che Guevara, and other supporters of *peasant* revolution have argued that a successful agrarian movement also depends on the skills of leaders who are not drawn from its sociological base.

These justifications for elitism in leftist revolutionary movements reflect the actual differences in social class between leftist revolutionary leaders and their followers. And there are some obvious examples of upper-class revolutionary leaders who have focused their appeals for greater equality on the lowest social categories of their societies.

Francisco Madero, who first raised the standard of revolution in Mexico in 1910, came from a wealthy landowning family and was himself an industrialist engaged in mining and smelting. Lenin's mother was the daughter of a physician; his father was a respected administrator of a provincial school district who had been elevated to the minor Russian nobility. Ch'en Tu-hsiu, the founder of the Chinese Communist party in 1921, was born of a wealthy Mandarin family and was a professor and college dean at the University of Peking. The father of Fidel and Raul Castro was a rich plantation farmer and a member of prerevolutionary Cuba's provincial upper class. Fidel graduated from the University of Havana and practiced law before 1953. Che Guevara was a medical doctor and son of an Argentine architect. The anarchist uprisings in southern Italy in the nineteenth century were led by intellectuals, including the nobleman Errico Malatesta who urged the peasantry to expropriate the land it worked but did not own.[2]

Nor are these isolated examples. The higher leadership cadres of most revolutionary movements on the left collectively share the same characteristics describing the very top leaders themselves. The twelve Tupamaro guerrilla leaders captured between 1968 and 1971 were all from Uruguay's upper social classes and were qualified in professions such as engineering and contracting. Among the top leaders of the Sandinista National Liberation Front, which overthrew the Somoza dictatorship in Nicaragua in 1979, were men whose fathers were wealthy lawyers and businessmen and whose high social standing had derived in part from the patronage and support of the Somoza family. Several of the Sandinista leaders themselves were successful businessmen and prominent in the professions and in higher academic affairs. And most of the top leadership of the Sandinista movement was university-educated. The Malayan Communist insurgency after the Second World War was oriented toward the lowest categories of Malayan peasants and workers, but its leadership was drawn almost exclusively from the ranks of the intelligentsia and the urban professions. These last characterizations also apply to the National Liberation Front in South Vietnam.[3] A study initiated after the Second World War by the Vietnamese Communist party of 1,855 of its leading cadres found that 74 percent were intellectuals or of bourgeois origin, 19 percent were from peasant families, and only 7 percent were from the Vietnamese working class.[4] Referring to the boat that landed Castro and his men in Cuba in 1956, Guevara wrote that "none of the first group who came in the 'Granma' . . . had workers' or peasants' backgrounds."[5]

David Lane's research on Bolsheviks and Mensheviks in the Russian Social Democratic party finds that the top leadership of both factions was "drawn from the upper social status groups."[6] Robert C. North and Ithiel de Sola Pool find from their study of the Chinese Communist Central Executive Committee (CEC) in 1945 that 40 percent of the members had fathers with upper-class occupations while only 23 percent had fathers who were lower-class peasants or workers. The authors add that the lower-class social ethic of Chinese Communism probably induced the CEC's cadres to understate the extent of their upper-class origins.[7]

BOURGEOIS REVOLUTIONARIES

Compared with leftist revolutionary leaders, bourgeois revolutionaries seek only to extend equality to the middle classes of their society. Their social class is consequently much closer to the social class of their particular clienteles than in the case of leftist revolutionary leaders.

Historically, bourgeois revolutionaries typically do battle with monarchical authority and aristocratic institutions, or assault only the battlements of upper-class privilege. They do not threaten the upper classes by promising to elevate the status of the lower classes. They want only to enlarge the society's dominant minority by including themselves within it. And in part because of their *relative* moderation, there is greater sociological similarity and personnel overlap between bourgeois revolutionaries and the existing political elites than there is between political elites and leftist revolutionaries.

Like many of his Puritan allies and Royalist adversaries, Oliver Cromwell was a country gentleman. But Barrington Moore's study of the 522 members of the Long Parliament (between 1640 and 1642) finds that the Puritan elites were drawn primarily from those constituencies which had the most to gain from a dissolution of aristocratic privilege: areas where manufacturing and new business interests were further developed and where the enclosures of common land had laid a more firm base for competitive market agriculture.[8] It was no coincidence that the poorer peasants of England supported the king in his struggle with the Puritan Parliamentarians.

Crane Brinton has found that the Puritan and American revolutionary leaders were strikingly similar in terms of social class—men of property and, in most instances, respected leaders of their communities. Even the more radical Samuel Adams came from a successful merchant family of Boston and was graduated from Harvard. The extremists and lower social status representatives of the French Revolution, including Marat and Babeuf, were exceptions to the general rule: most of the leaders of the French Revolution also came from the middle classes and were "substantially of the same social standing as the rank and file" who supported them.[9] Members of the French aristocracy who joined the revolution, including the Duke of Orléans, Mirabeau, and Lafayette, also were exceptions to the general rule of professional and middle-class predominance.[10]

Especially prominent in the French Revolution were men of the legal profession, and lawyers constituted the majority of the Third Estate's representatives in the Estates-General of 1789. Lawyers, in fact, are the most overrepresented professional category in virtually every political system of the western world, and their prominence in modern revolutionary movements only confirms the continuity between the social classes of old and new regimes, a continuity that is especially obvious in the case of bourgeois revolutions.

But we also have noted the occasional role of lawyers in leftist revolutionary movements: Castro and, in the Bolshevik Politburo of 1917, Lenin and Krestinsky are examples that come quickly to mind. We might hypothesize, then, that lawyers are more prominent in leftist revolutionary movements when the classes they typically represent are weak or nonexistent.[11] This appears to apply especially to those societies where a relatively small middle class is dominated by foreign capital, which was the case for both prerevolutionary Cuba and Russia.

The major tendency, however, is for lawyers to represent best those citizens who have the most. As a social class they consequently are able to overlap with old political elites and to identify with emergent new wealth. In this sense, they help to typify the characteristics of bourgeois revolutionary leaders who are more sociologically representative of their clienteles than are revolutionaries on the left.

This generalization also may be illustrated by the characteristics of Kuomintang (KMT) leaders in revolutionary China. Their nationalist commitment reflected the interests of the landowning and merchant classes, and the KMT leaders themselves derived precisely from these same groups.[12] The leadership of the urban-based and middle-class oriented movement against Castro in 1961 was drawn from urban intellectuals and the white-collar classes, which also had provided Castro with substantial support during the earlier and more ideologically ambiguous stages of his revolutionary activity.[13] The point, again, seems clear: bourgeois revolutionaries are, sociologically, more closely identified with their followers than are leftist revolutionaries. And this in turn helps to explain the less coherent ideologies and weaker revolutionary organizations that distinguish bourgeois from leftist revolutionary movements.

REVOLUTIONARIES ON THE RIGHT

Revolutionaries on the right define social justice in terms of social order. They preach authority instead of equality. Especially in the case of fascist movements, the only equality their leaders have in mind is the equal subordination of followers to the authority of the leadership. There may be the illusion of participation in politics, but for the great majority it is not participation in policymaking. Exclusion from the decision-making process in fact characterizes the rank-and-file of almost all revolutionary movements, regardless of ideological orientation, especially as the revolutionary struggle is extended in time. But rightist elites are explicit about the political inequality of their movement, even as they try to create an aura of comradeship, and they regard the exalted position of leadership as more of a permanent virtue than a temporary necessity.

Rightist movements typically receive an important part of their impetus from the actual or threatened extension of equality throughout the social order. In this respect the leaders of rightist revolutionary movements are more sociologically representative of their supporting clienteles than are leftist revolutionaries, but in comparison to bourgeois revolutionaries they also are characterized by less overlap with established political elites. At the same time, rightist revolutionaries frequently enjoy the tacit or overt support of these same political elites. For example, both the German Nazis and the Italian Fascists received assistance and encouragement from bureaucratic, military, and police personnel in the hierarchies of their established political systems. Even without personnel that overlap between revolutionary leaders and political elites, rightist revolutionaries enjoy more access to established policy-makers than do the revolutionary leaders of leftist movements. The importance of this relationship will be elaborated in the last section of this chapter.

The sociological similarity between rightist leaders and their followers is illustrated by the characteristics of the counterrevolutionaries seeking to reestablish the traditional order in France after 1789: their leadership was drawn from the nobility and the higher clerical orders. And where substantial numbers of peasants did mobilize for counterrevolution, as in the Vendée, it was precisely where the authority of the local clergy with whom the peasants closely identified was attacked by the revolutionary government in Paris. In Spain, too, it was the local priests living in the same circumstances as their peasant parishioners who organized the guerrilla resistance to Napoleon's invading armies.[14]

Nor was it coincidental that the appeal of German Nazism and Italian Fascism to the demobilized soldiers of the First World War reflected the personal experience of the movements' leadership, including that of Hitler and Mussolini. The Nazis' initial focus on the German middle and lower-middle classes also reflected the sociological composition of the Nazi elite: two of every three persons sampled in the 1934 *Fuehrerlexikon* reported military service in the war, and only 4.5 percent had fathers with high social status, while 5.6 percent had fathers with low social status.[15] S. L. Andreski confirms the anti-upper-class bias of both the Nazi leadership and its ideological appeal with his finding that "the top party elite contained practically no members of the old establishment." And of those young aristocrats who eventually joined the Nazi party, "none of them reached top positions."[16]

The less doctrinaire orientation of Italian Fascism (in comparison to German National Socialism) coincided with the greater sociological mix of its leadership. But like the Nazis, the Italian Fascists were also predominantly middle and lower-middle class in origin. Of the sixty-six provincial party secretaries appointed to their posts before the Ethiopian War, only three were from the working class, four were from the aristocracy, nine belonged to the "plutocracy" (nonaristocratic but with high income), and fifty were of the "lesser bourgeoisie."[17]

However, the social origins of both Hitler and Mussolini make especially clear the middle and lower-middle class orientation of fascism. Emphasis here on the top leaders' own status is justified by the critical role and symbolic importance of charismatic authority in rightist political movements. The lower social class origin of fascist leaders (Hitler's father was a customs official and Mussolini's a blacksmith) not only coincides with the sociological focus of their doctrinal appeal, but it also is in marked contrast to the higher social class origins of bourgeois and leftist revolutionary leaders. And the more progressive orientation of the latter suggests the more educated and humanistic outlook characteristic of intellectuals and the higher social classes.

INTELLECTUALS

"Intellectuals" may be defined as those "who are predisposed—through temperament, family, education, occupation, etc.—to manipulate the symbolic rather than the material environment."[18] Intellectuals deal in ideas, and their ideas are meant to form a logically consistent view of man's role in society and the relationship between man, society, nature, and history. Intellectuals also tend to be skeptical of established norms and are willing to speculate on alterations in the social environment that presumably would correspond better to the nature of man.

There is more than a little ambiguity, then, in Crane Brinton's famous hypothesis that it is the "transfer of the allegiance of the intellectuals" from the established regime that signals the approach of revolution.[19] Had Brinton studied revolutionary movements that failed, as well as the role of intellectuals in nonrevolutionary circumstances, he would have discovered that the allegiance of intellectuals, except to their own ideas, is almost always in doubt.

But it is true that intellectuals play a prominent role in the history of revolution. This is especially the case for leftist revolutionary movements in underdeveloped societies. And it is well established that leftist revolutionary leaders in underdeveloped societies are not only likely to be intellectuals, but that they also are likely to have been exposed to the progressive norms of more modern societies in the course of their intellectual development. They thus become more acutely aware of the apparent backwardness of their own government. All the more so if their government is the handmaiden of foreign interests.

For example, Sun Yat-sen, the father of the Chinese Revolution, was a physician who received part of his education in an Anglican college in Hawaii, and he had traveled throughout the western world raising money and support for revolution in China. Mao Tse-tung was university-educated and the son of a prosperous peasant family in Hunan province where the penetration of western missionary and economic influence was especially strong. In one of his interviews with Edgar Snow, Mao reported receiving high-school instruction in a nontraditional curriculum where "I could study natural science and new subjects of Western learning."[20] In noting the similarities of Kuomintang and Chinese Communist elites ("sons of landlords, merchants, scholars, or officials"), North and Pool also observe that most of them received at least a part of their education abroad.[21]

Most of the leaders of the Vietnamese rebellion against French colonialism after the Second World War, including Ho Chi Minh and Vo Nguyen Giap, came from the French-educated intelligentsia of the Mandarin and gentry classes. Giap received the highest academic degree that was available in French Indochina, a doctorate in law. Both Ho and Giap originated from the provinces of north-central Vietnam, an area of traditional rebellion against central authority and especially impacted by French industrial development (including textile factories and railway maintenance yards).

Many Muslims prominent in the Algerian rebellion against the French after 1954 were educated in French schools and universities, and many of these already had received a westernizing orientation from their military service in the French army during the Second World War. Almost all the leaders of the Angolan liberation movement that, in 1974, triumphed over factional rivals and

Portuguese colonialism were intellectuals and students who previously had studied outside of Africa. Their first government in exile was established in Paris in the early 1960s, and the movement only later moved its headquarters to Africa (to the Congo) in anticipation of launching a guerrilla insurgency inside Angola. In the cases of both Algeria and Angola, the initial impetus for anti-colonial revolt came from the few who were younger, better educated, and more widely traveled than the many who were the object of liberation. In this way do the few who are exposed to new ideas alter the lives of the many who live and think in ways that are bound by tradition and place. In fact, Kautsky's study of 32 revolutionary leaders in 30 countries, all of which were countries with under-developed economies at the times of their respective revolutions, shows the following: 59 percent of the revolutionary leaders had lived or traveled in indus-trialized countries; 78 percent had received higher education, in their native country or abroad; and 88 percent had received "an education appropriate to an industrialized country." [22]

Military officers in parts of the Arab world, Asia, and Latin America are often the only coherent force working for modernization in their respective societies. Their usually greater exposure to the norms of western societies, their higher educational attainment, and their awareness of the dependency of mili-tary power on economic development all coincide with the frequency of military coups d'état in these areas of the world. [23] In fact, the Decembrist Revolt in Russia in 1825 was also led by army officers who had encountered the ideas of Western Europe, in this case through their campaigns against Napoleon's armies and the liberalizing thrust of the French Revolution.

The intellectual's commitment to revolutionary change appears to be dramatically reinforced when he experiences at firsthand the repressive power of autocratic government. The Mau Mau revolt (1952–1956) against British rule in Kenya has been attributed in part to the imprisonment by British authorities of more than 100,000 Kenyan citizens for an average of seven years—a fate which befell the principal Mau Mau leader, Jomo Kenyatta. Fidel and Raul Castro were sentenced to fourteen years' imprisonment under the Batista regime following their unsuccessful attack on the Moncada army barracks in 1953; they served two years and fled to Mexico after release under the terms of a general amnesty in 1955. [24] Trotsky reported that of the 175 Bolshevik delegates to the Sixth Party Congress of July 1917, 171 answered questionnaires showing that 110 of the delegates had spent a total of 245 years in prison, 150 had recorded a total of 549 arrests, and 55 had been exiled to remote provinces for a total of 127 years. [25]

It is not difficult to conclude from these and similar biographical data that a man or woman predisposed toward intellectual reflection on his or her own fate and the fate of others, in an underdeveloped society but exposed to the im-pact of modernization, and with personal experience of the repressive force of the state, is very likely to develop a leftist revolutionary orientation. Under these circumstances, the intellectual's middle or upper social class origins only lay the basis for his or her greater receptivity to revolutionary ideas.

STUDENTS

Close to the category of intellectuals, and with many of the same predispositions, are students at the higher educational levels of their society. Like intellectuals, they tend to be skeptical of conventional norms, and they are especially sensitive to the discrepancy between the regime's social ideals and the social realities of citizen life. Even more so than in the case of intellectuals, students also lack the social ties to professional and occupational groups that tend to moderate the individual's values and ideological perspective.[26]

The prominence of both students and intellectuals in the higher echelons of revolutionary leadership helps to explain another unanimous finding of scholars writing on revolution. Revolutionary leaders are below the mean age level of their society and are typically in their late twenties and seldom older than forty.[27] And they almost always are male and not constrained in their revolutionary activity by family responsibilities.

While students themselves seldom emerge as the leaders of sustained revolutionary movements, their universities are frequently the seedbed for revolutionary ferment and the germination site for those young intellectuals who eventually become revolutionary leaders. Thus the geographic location of the university can be a major factor in determining the vitality of the revolutionary movement, its impact on other social classes in the society, and the very life of the regime that is under attack. Students in the political capitals of Paris, Havana, Budapest, Bangkok, Seoul, Guatemala City, San Salvador, Cairo, Prague, Warsaw, Tehran, Mexico City, and Madrid can and have played central roles in the political ferment of their particular societies in the postwar period. But students in Bordeaux, Munich, Bologna, Cambridge, Berkeley, Ann Arbor, New Haven, or San Diego are very unlikely to enjoy the political leverage that makes their activities critical to the functioning of government.

As in the case of intellectuals, students also tend to have a leftist orientation. In fact, rightist student organizations seldom develop except in the context of already strong and extreme-left student organizations. This leftist tendency among student activists again confirms the sociological irony of leftist revolutionaries of bourgeois origins advancing the interests of lower-class groups.

The irony is even more apparent when we differentiate the characteristics of student activists from those of student nonactivists. Using data collected from university campuses in the United States during the 1960s, Richard Flacks and Leonard Baird concluded that the typical student activist, compared with the nonactivist, is more academic and intellectually oriented, has a higher grade-point average, and is the son or daughter of a high-income family in which both parents are college-educated.[28]

In his study of the revolutionary events of May–June 1968 in France, Jacques Ellul found that the more violent student demonstrators were from "relatively well-off backgrounds," and that the student leaders were "the sons of bankers, doctors, lawyers, university professors and high officials (even of government ministers)." Ellul also found that the French student activists were most likely to be students of philosophy, sociology, and psychology, and least likely to be majoring in science or medicine. Students of law, economics, and political science were closer to the nonactivists of science and mathematics than to the *"provocateurs"* of the first three academic disciplines.[29]

We might generalize from these findings that those students who are more predisposed toward radical politics and revolutionary activity are not only from higher social class backgrounds, but also tend to be concentrated in areas of study that heighten their sensitivity to the dehumanizing characteristics of technocratic society. In this way, students in both developed and under-developed societies can play the role of "spark" to the fires of revolution.

And this is precisely the role credited to students in the study of many revolutionary conflagrations. Their actions are seen as the catalyst that mobilizes broader sectors of the public for an assault on the ramparts of government—from the Paris revolution of 1848 to more recent events in more modern circum-stances. In the 1956 Hungarian revolt, for example, it was the university stu-dents of Budapest who first demonstrated against the regime and then carried in their wake whole sectors of the population. Their actions were instrumental in mobilizing popular revolutionary sentiment in Budapest, especially in the early stages of the fighting. And in the provinces, wherever there was a college or uni-versity, it was the students who took the initiative in organizing the revolt.[30]

But however much intellectuals and students are predisposed toward revolutionary action, they almost never constitute, by themselves, the decisive forces of revolution. These typically are peasants and workers. And the inherent suspicions of peasants and workers for students and intellectuals make very difficult the building of a revolutionary alliance that unites one group with another. This in turn raises the issue of the roles of revolutionary leaders.

THE ROLES
OF REVOLUTIONARY LEADERS

Most students of revolutionary movements agree that revolutionary leaders do not make revolutions. At best, they select the means of revolutionary action, they determine the movement's tactics and the timing of their implementation, and they may deflect the course of the movement a few degrees this way or that, but the movement's ends, strategy, and general direction are largely beyond their control. It is in this sense that the genius of Lenin and Mao was in adapting the long-range objectives of communist revolution to the immediate demands of urban and rural masses in Russia and China.

Part of the revolutionary leader's role, then, is to focus on issues that can effect cross-cutting alliances between peasants, workers, students, and intellectuals, and between the urban and rural sectors of the society. But these issues cannot be manufactured in the cerebral cortex of the revolutionary leader. As we shall see in later chapters, they derive from major events that affect a large cross-section of the population. These events may include defeat in war, economic crisis, the threat of a foreign enemy, or any combination of these and other circumstances that can be used to mobilize part or all of the population. Thus the accomplishment of Ho Chi Minh was in building a powerful grass-roots organization that united the anti-French passions of the Vietnamese with the commitment of the peasantry to agrarian reform. And Castro's success was in his ability to mobilize broad support from among diverse sectors of the Cuban population that were at least as much anti-Batista as they were pro-Castro.[31]

The successful revolutionary leader, by definition, is able to interpret these greater events and more general conditions into terms that have meaning for the everyday life of rank-and-file citizens. He does not implant new ideas as much as he summarizes them in an especially coherent and appealing way; he simplifies complexity. While more objective conditions lay the basis for revolutionary action, it is in the consciousness of the revolutionary leader (as Marx argued) that revolutionary action begins. He must then be able to communicate his own insights and understanding of events to others, convincing and converting them very much like the religious reformers of an earlier age. His interpretive role is especially important when the revolutionary movement seeks to mobilize illiterate peasants, weighed down by traditions of oppression but unaware of the revolutionary options available to them and suspicious of all forms of collective organization.

There is, in fact, a close relationship between the importance of leadership, the militancy of the ideology, the cohesion and power of the revolutionary organization, and the amount of time necessary for the revolutionary process to run its course. The role and personality of the leader become more important as the movement's ideological appeals are diffuse or incoherent, as its organization is weak, and as the revolutionary process is extended in time. Under these circumstances, the leader must constantly reassure his followers that they are achieving their goals, that history is on their side, that defeat is only temporary setback, and that tomorrow and the next encounter will bring the movement to the threshold of victory.

The relative sociological mix of fascist movements also helps to explain the critical role of charismatic authority in holding the movement's diverse supporters together.[32] Workers, peasants, white-collar employees, and members of the middle and upper classes must be able to find their common identity in the personality of the leader. It is more his presence than his argument that expresses the causes of their discontent and gives them confidence in their revolutionary power. But charismatic leadership, whether on the left or on the right, is no substitute for a firmly implanted grass-roots organization, especially after power has been captured and the leadership faces the even more difficult tasks of consolidating power and realizing the more fundamental goals of the revolution. And it is notable that fascist movements, unlike communist movements, do not survive the death of their leaders.

Nor is it likely that Iran's clerical dictatorship will long survive the death of the Ayatollah Khomeini. What explains Khomeini's power in the first place? (1) The Shah's earlier centralization of power and his ruthless suppression of dissent and organized opposition. (2) The power vacuum that consequently was created by the relatively rapid disintegration of the Shah's regime in 1978-1979. (3) The presence of a clerical hierarchy that expressed the anti-Shah hostilities of a broad segment of Iran's population, that constituted Iran's only organized political force, and that had as its acknowledged leader (even in exile) the undoubtedly charismatic Khomeini. But it was unlikely that Iran's Islamic clergy would be able to compose its factional differences in Khomeini's absence. And the eventual and inevitable test of strength between the clergy and either Iran's military or the Iranian communists (or both) was almost certain to close the book on a curious experiment in anti-modernization. What's the point? That charismatic leadership, if only in the long run, is no substitute for strong organization.

It is in this context that many students of revolution have noted the necessary alteration of leadership roles and characteristics as the revolutionary process is extended in time. Brinton's typology identifies the changing roles of revolutionary leaders in terms of their varying skills, including the idealist, the formulator, the propagandist, the agitator, and the organizer. Rex D. Hopper identifies the prophet, the reformer, the statesman-leader, moderates, radicals and—in the final stage of the revolutionary process—the administrator. Eric Hoffer distinguishes between men of words, fanatics, and practical men of action. Harry Eckstein summarizes Harold Lasswell and Abraham Kaplan's typology as including ideologues, organizers, experts in violence, demagogues, and administrators.[33]

These categories are not mutually exclusive, and various leadership characteristics and roles may overlap in the same person and over time. David Schoenbaum observes that Max Weber's charismatic and bureaucratic types (which are mutually exclusive) in fact "were indissolubly merged" in the ruling elite of Nazi Germany.[34] And no one (except the Stalinists) disputes the critical role of Trotsky in the Russian Revolution, first as propagandist and agitator swinging the Petrograd military garrisons over to the side of the Bolsheviks, then as organizer of the Bolshevik coup of October 1917 and, subsequently, as organizer and strategist for the Red Army in the civil war against the Whites.[35]

Especially since the late nineteenth century, the role of the orator, spellbinding and eloquent, has frequently been of major importance in the early stages of mass mobilization, and much of the revolutionary impact of Mussolini, Hitler, Madero, Castro, as well as Lenin and Trotsky, has been attributed to their convincing and impassioned rhetoric from the public rostrum. And yet such great forensic talent does seem to give way eventually to the more mundane skills of the organizer. George K. Schueller, for example, characterizes the changing composition of the Russian Communist Politburo as follows: "the revolution was made, in the first instance, by the urban-born intellectuals and was later taken over by the rural-born organizers."[36] Stalin thus became the chief symbol and instrument of ideological rigidity and the consolidation of earlier revolutionary gains.

Different revolutionary techniques also require different leadership skills. The architects of successful guerrilla warfare or a military coup d'état are notable for their coalition-building and organizational skills from the outset of their revolutionary activity. The importance of organization increases as the movement encounters organized resistance, which inevitably prolongs the revolutionary process.[37] We can add that organization also is more determining of the final outcome as revolutionary leaders are prevented from haranguing crowds and are unable to take advantage of modern systems of mass communication. Especially in the context of a peasant society and a governmental system of informants and spies, the successful revolutionary leader must be more durable than brilliant, moving toward the revolutionary objective more by short steps than by giant strides. North and Pool summarize the characteristics of the effective organizer of peasant guerrillas in China: "He had to be tough; he had to command respect; he had to be able."[38]

REGIME ACCESS
AND SUCCESSFUL REVOLUTION

It is a self-evident (and tautological) proposition that revolutionary movements do not succeed without capable leadership. Where we observe a potentially strong movement enfeebled by factionalism, as in the case of the Dominican left after 1965, it is difficult to determine whether the factionalism exists because of the lack of leadership or the lack of leadership is the result of factionalism.[39]

We may reduce some of the ambiguity in assessing the role of revolutionary leadership by answering the following question: to what extent does the revolutionary leadership enjoy access to the decision-makers of the established regime, in terms either of overlapping personnel or covert sympathizers?

The answer to this question, and the answer to any other single question on revolutionary movements, will not explain the whole story of a particular movement's success or failure. But it is clear that despite the greater sociological similarity between leftist revolutionary leaders and established political elites (in comparison with rightist movements), leftist revolutionaries have much less access to existing political elites than do either bourgeois or rightist revolutionaries.

This finding helps to explain the greater organizational competence of leftist revolutionary movements that succeed. Leadership is not the critical variable; it is organization. But this is not true of either bourgeois or rightist revolutionary movements.

In fact the relative ease of revolutionary penetration in Stuart England, Bourbon France, Weimar Germany, and in Republican Italy was precisely because of the greater coincidence between political elites and revolutionary leaders, in terms of either overlapping personnel or revolutionary sympathizers within the existing regime. The consequently greater access to the centers of policy-making was reflected in the revolutionary leadership's contentment, once in power, with existing political institutions, and in the relative weakness of their revolutionary organizations. By contrast, communist revolution is distinguished by a powerful organization and the complete restructuring of political institutions after the capture of power. Under certain conditions, communists obviously can capture power without enjoying any personnel overlap or policy-making access in the existing regime.

In the case of noncommunist or even anticommunist movements, however, the extent of personnel overlap or policy-making access between political elites and revolutionary leaders is a useful index of the movement's chances of success. It is probably true, for example, that the Mexican Revolution should be judged a failure in terms of the social objectives of its early leaders. May this failure not be explained, in part, by the pronounced lower-class origins of its key leaders? To recite the characteristics of only the early principals, Emiliano Zapata and Pancho Villa, is to suggest the obstacles confronting the revolution's realization of its egalitarian ideals. Both were virtually illiterate; Zapata was a peasant, and Villa (born Doroteo Arango) had worked as a hacienda laborer, a muleteer, and was eventually forced to live as a bandit because of his involvement in a case of revenge murder. Neither of them was sensitive to the imperatives of political organization, and this may be attributed in part to their understandable inexperience in prerevolutionary government and their inability to draw on the experience of existing political elites.

The unsuccessful revolutions of 1848 that swept across Europe were almost everywhere led (insofar as they were led) by members of the intelligentsia—writers, students, teachers, all with liberal-republican ideals but lacking in organizational capability and without any support from established political elites and the property-owning middle classes. The relative quiescence of the English working class, even in the midst of the horrors of early industrialization, may also be explained in part by the lack of coincidence between elites of the established political system and those radical leaders that did emerge. In England in the early nineteenth century there were not even many intellectuals to publicize the plight of the disenfranchised lower classes. Most English intellectuals and political elites were in the ideological grip of Locke, Smith, Ricardo, and Malthus, and accepted as inevitable the mass suffering that was implicit in liberal economic dogma.

A study of slave revolts in North America by Stanley Elkins again confirms our findings of the unrepresentative status, in relation to their clienteles, of revolutionary leaders seeking to extend equality. In every instance of slave revolt, it was not the most miserable and exploited plantation slaves who took the initiative, but former slaves who were free artisans or, as in the case of Nat Turner, literate lay preachers.[40] In every instance the revolt also failed. And it is significant that the dynamics of the antislavery movement had to be supplied by activists from the northern political and social establishments.

Eric R. Wolf notes that the unsuccessful slave rebellions in Cuba of 1810, 1812, and 1844 were led by "a large group of free Negroes."[41] And in reference to the suppressed rebellion of the higher-status sepoys against British rule in India in 1857, Marx wrote: "The Indian Revolt does not commence with the *ryots,* tortured, dishonored and stripped naked by the British, but with the sepoys, clad, fed, petted and pampered by them."[42] Especially in the case of anticolonial movements, the measure of their almost certain defeat is not only the weakness of revolutionary organization but also the extreme institutional separation of revolutionaries from colonial elites.

In Czechoslovakia and East Germany in 1953, revolts against the Stalinist regimes in each country were easily suppressed. The rioters were unorganized, without recognized leaders, and the political elites were unified in the face of a serious challenge to their authority. But in Hungary and Poland in 1956 and in Czechoslovakia in early 1968, violence against the established regimes achieved much greater success. In each of these last three cases, factions of the dominant elites, both bureaucratic and intellectual, broke with the regime and lent their support to reformists and revolutionaries.[43] Only intervention by an external power, the Soviet Union, reversed the dominant trends in Czechoslovakia and Hungary, while the ideals of the "Polish October" were more slowly sabotaged by the old political elites who were returned to power in 1956 in the wake of popular mobilization.

But the point seems clear, and it may stand as a useful hypothesis in the study of the characteristics and roles of revolutionary leaders. However large or small the sociological gap between leaders and followers, and whatever the particular predispositions and skills of revolutionary leadership, the revolutionary movement improves its chances of success as it can gain access to the society's dominant institutions. This access, again, may be through defectors from the ruling class or through revolutionary sympathizers who continue to exercise some measure of legitimate political authority. Regime access is least characteristic of leftist revolutionary movements, and most characteristic of bourgeois revolutionary movements. This in turn helps to explain the greater emphasis on organization by leftist revolutionary leaders, and their haste to re-place existing political institutions with revolutionary forms of government as soon as the movement captures power. Lacking regime access and weak in organizational structure, no revolutionary movement should expect to succeed—regardless of the personal talents or ideological resolve of its leaders.

FOR FURTHER TESTING

Some Propositions:

1. Compared with their followers, leftist revolutionary leaders are likely to be better educated, more widely traveled, and drawn from higher social classes.
2. In terms of their social characteristics, bourgeois revolutionary leaders are representative of their followers and similar to ruling political elites.
3. Rightist revolutionary leaders are drawn primarily from the middle and lower-middle classes and are sociologically representative of their organizational base.
4. Regime access is highest for bourgeois revolutionary leaders and lowest for leftist revolutionary leaders.
5. Students and intellectuals in underdeveloped societies ruled by authoritarian elites are likely to have a leftist ideological orientation—especially if they are acquainted with the ideals of modernization and have experienced at first hand the repressive power of the state.
6. Revolutionary leaders are typically young, male, and without family responsibilities.

Some Hypotheses:

The personality and role of the revolutionary leader are more important to the survival and success of the movement,

1. as the movement's followers are socially diverse;
2. as the movement's ideology is less coherent and difficult to articulate;
3. as the movement's organization is weak;
4. as the movement's regime access is low;
5. as the revolutionary potential of the society is low;
6. as the coercive power of government is strong;
7. as the orientation of the movement is toward the ideological right.

NOTES

[1] Studies documenting the unrepresentative character of political elites in various countries, including the United States, are summarized in Davies, 1963, pp. 285-86.

[2] On the characteristics of Italian anarchist elites, see Hobsbawm, 1959, pp. 93-94.

[3] On the Sandinistas, see Bowdler, 1981. On the Malayan CP see Molnar, 1965, p. 76. On the NLF, see Rolph, 1971, p. 50.

[4] Calculated from data reported in Wolf, 1969, p. 185.

[5] Quoted in Wolf, 1969, p. 269.

[6] Lane, 1969, p. 32.

[7] North and Pool, 1965, Table 2, pp. 378-79. On the bourgeois origins of the founders and members of the early Chinese Communist party, see Lewis, 1970, Ch. 1.

[8] Moore, 1966, pp. 511-12.

[9] Brinton, 1965, p. 101.

[10] Melotti, 1965, pp. 211-14, summarizes the social class characteristics of many of the leaders of the Puritan, American, French, Russian, and Cuban revolutions.

[11] Support for this hypothesis may be found in Berelson and Steiner, 1964, p. 430.

[12] North and Pool, 1965, pp. 328 and 395.

[13] Rivero, 1962, p. 76.

[14] On the Vendée, see Tilly, 1964, and on Spain, Hobsbawm, 1959, p. 77.

[15] Lerner, Pool, and Schueller, 1965, pp. 207 and 212.

[16] Andreski, 1969, pp. 100-101.

[17] Lasswell and Sereno, 1965, pp. 181-82.

[18] Lerner, Pool, and Schueller, 1965, p. 203.

[19] Brinton, 1965, pp. 39-49. Brinton himself appears to recognize the theoretical difficulties in his argument in the 1956 preface to his book (originally published in 1938). See p. vi of the 1965 edition.

[20] Snow, 1971, p. 71.

[21] North and Pool, 1965, p. 376.

[22] Kautsky, 1969. On the Vietnamese and Algerian revolutionary leaders, see Wolf, 1969, pp. 181 and 234. On revolutionary leaders in Angola, see Marcum, 1978.

[23] Lipset, 1970, pp. 251-52, summarizes some of the relevant studies. Also see Huntington, 1968, pp. 198-208. By the 1970s and especially the 1980s, however, it was obvious that the cohering characteristics and modernizing capabilities of military elites in the Third World had been badly overestimated. See, for example, Degalo, 1976, and Nordlinger, 1977.

[24] On Kenyatta and Castro, see Beals, 1970, pp. 213-14 and 241.

[25] Trotsky, 1957, Vol. II, p. 308.

[26] Berelson and Steiner, 1964, p. 421.

[27] Leiden and Schmitt, 1968, p. 86, summarize some of the relevant studies on the age of revolutionary leaders.

[28] Flacks, 1970, and Baird, 1970.

[29] Ellul, 1970, pp. 501-2.

[30] Zinner, 1962, p. 262.

[31] Leiden and Schmitt, 1968, p. 203, argue that "without Castro there would have been no social revolution in Cuba." However, the "great man of history" thesis is disputed by a number of other authors, including Smelser, 1963, pp. 358–59; Davies, 1963, p. 278; Berelson and Steiner, 1964, p. 343; Hunter, 1940, p. 225; and Huntington, 1968, p. 303. These authors emphasize the more determining role of objective circumstances. But the problem is largely moot; in summarizing studies of small-group behavior, Cecil Gibb observes that "because there is such close interaction between the leader and the led it is often difficult to determine just who affects whom and to what extent" (Gibb, 1966, pp. 92–93).

[32] Max Weber defined charisma as "a certain quality of an individual personality by virtue of which he is set apart from ordinary men and treated as endowed with supernatural, superhuman, or at least specifically exceptional powers or qualities." Quoted in Smelser, 1963, p. 355.

[33] Brinton, 1965, pp. 107–19; Hopper, 1950; Hoffer, 1951, Chaps. 15–17; Eckstein, 1964, p. 26.

[34] Schoenbaum, 1967, p. 199.

[35] But to his own undoing, Trotsky "was clumsy and ill-suited to the small-scale work of Party organization" (Lunacharsky, 1968, p. 66). Lunacharsky's *Revolutionary Silhouettes* (first published in 1923) provides many fascinating insights into the characteristics and roles of the Bolshevik elite.

[36] Schueller, 1965, p. 109.

[37] Gurr, 1970, p. 291.

[38] North and Pool, 1965, p. 374.

[39] In his report from Santo Domingo, Francis B. Kent identifies the lack of leadership as the cause of the left's weakness in the Dominican Republic. *Los Angeles Times,* April 26, 1972, p. 6.

[40] Elkins, 1971.

[41] Wolf, 1969, p. 253.

[42] Quoted in Avineri, 1969, p. 63.

[43] Dallin and Breslauer, 1970, pp. 205-7, and Skilling, 1970, pp. 220-21.

CHAPTER
FIVE

FOLLOWERS

LEADERS AND FOLLOWERS

While it may be conceptually sound to distinguish revolutionary leaders from their followers, it is not easy to take a particular revolutionary movement and divide its hierarchy into two parts, saying that here stand the leaders and there stand the followers. Nor is it easy to determine where the followers of a revolutionary movement give way to less active supporters, and where these latter merge into a neutralized or apathetic mass that neither supports nor opposes revolutionary change. These conceptual categories become even more difficult to fit to reality when the revolutionary process is drawn out and each of the different categories of citizens plays several different roles over time.

The merging of leaders with followers at some point in the revolutionary hierarchy is also suggested by the applicability to followers of many of the generalizations about leaders offered in the preceding chapter. Revolutionary followers typically are young, male, and unmarried. They frequently are intellectuals and students. The society's ranks of unemployed and underemployed are very likely to be overrepresented among the rank-and-file of revolutionary movements. By definition, revolutionary followers also are drawn from the more activist and politically conscious sectors of their society. And their greater

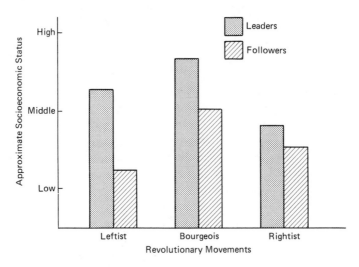

FIGURE 5-1 Sociological distance between leaders and followers, by type of revolutionary movement.

activism usually reflects greater sensitivity and exposure to the forces of social change, modernization, war, economic crisis, or governmental repression.

The generalizations in the preceding chapter about social class also may be briefly repeated here. The sociological base of leftist revolutionary movements is located in the lower social classes of the society, particularly among peasants and workers. Bourgeois revolutionary movements focus their appeal on the middle and upper-middle classes, including the urban professionals and the larger property-owning classes of the countryside. Revolutionary movements on the right receive their initial impetus from the lower-middle classes, in both rural and urban areas. The degree of sociological similarity between leaders and followers, discussed in Chapter 4, may be conveniently summarized here in graphic form (see Figure 5-1).

PEASANTS

These broad categories of social class may be divided into several subcategories, each playing various roles in the revolutionary process and each with varying levels of revolutionary potential. Peasants, for example, are *unlikely* to be mobilized as leftist revolutionary followers insofar as they are intensely religious, extremely poor, closely tied to landed elites (e.g., with sharecropping or feudal-type obligations), or where their property holdings are secure and provide them with economic self-sufficiency.

It was Castro's great good luck, for example, to have established his guerrilla base among the relatively independent, mobile, and squatter peasantry of Oriente Province and not among the less revolutionary and wage-earning laborers of Cuba's sugar plantations. And in Mexico, Russia, China, Algeria, and Vietnam, the sociological base for revolution was among the middle-strata peasants who owned a small amount of land and who were relatively independent of the controls exercised by government and landlord.[1]

On the other hand, there is no more potent force for conservatism and the status quo than a self-sufficient landowning peasantry, as urban revolutionaries in France since 1789 have discovered to their constant dismay. In Mexico after the 1930s, in India, Japan, and Korea after the Second World War, and in Bolivia after 1952, agrarian reform improved the property-owning status of peasants and consequently lowered their revolutionary potential.[2] In Bolivia in March 1971, armed peasants protesting the violence of leftist revolutionaries seized the municipal administration in Santa Cruz and turned it over to the military.

WORKERS

In the case of potential revolutionary followers in the urban environment, the very lowest social classes again are among the least likely to respond to appeals for revolutionary action. Extreme poverty breeds apathy and social withdrawal, not political activism.[3] The personal ties and extended family groupings of urban slum dwellers, for example, limit their mobility and independence, and they are the first to suffer from the disruption of municipal and welfare services that results from urban violence.[4]

Compared with unskilled and semiskilled workers, it is those workers who are skilled and who enjoy relatively higher income that appear to be the most susceptible to radical appeals. This is especially true of skilled workers who have experienced unemployment at some point in their vocational history. On the other hand, the antirevolutionary bias of contemporary communist parties and trade unions means that revolutionary sentiment may frequently predominate among the lesser-skilled categories of workers; at least this was the case in pre-Castro Cuba.[5] And reporting on the mobilization of workers in Petrograd before the February Revolution, Trotsky notes the important role played by women textile workers, "the most oppressed and downtrodden part of the proletariat."[6] The picture is obviously complex, and many variables intervene to complicate any assessment of the revolutionary potential of the working class. But as in the case of peasants and the bourgeoisie, it probably is correct to say that the revolutionary potential of workers declines as they are organized and integrated into the economic and political systems of their society.

What is perhaps most clear about the revolutionary role of workers is their relative *under*representation in revolutionary movements on the right. This is the finding of a study of Nazi party membership in 1933,[7] and it confirms our earlier finding of the lower-middle class orientation of rightist movements. The ranks of both the Italian Fascists and the German Nazis were swelled by shop-owners and merchants of provincial towns, small businessmen, and the urban unemployed. And while many in this last category came from a proletarian environment, they were unlikely to identify with traditional working-class aspirations or to be integrated into the growing trade union establishment. Seymour Martin Lipset's picture of the typical Nazi voter in 1932 includes the following characteristics: Protestant, self-employed, living on a farm or in a small community, and strongly opposed to big business and big trade unions.[8] With reference to the Nazis, David Schoenbaum observes that "real workers . . . were as rare as civil servants and those with higher education."[9] The same generalizations may be applied to other varieties of fascism, and in the 1950s to Poujadism in France and McCarthyism in the United States.[10] Thus the follower of rightist movements in industrial societies is likely to be a believer in free enterprise and the ideals of classical liberalism and, at the same time, fearful of the erosion of these ideals by the actions of big government, big business, and big labor. This picture hardly describes the typical worker, but it is true that workers in Rome and Berlin, or in Chicago and Oakland, may be readily mobilized by rightist groups to protest against the threat of job insecurity or social change, especially when the threat appears to come from a foreign enemy or from a racial minority within the society. But if workers are susceptible to *revolutionary* appeals for basic social change, the appeals are least likely to come from revolutionary leaders on the right.

MOTIVATION

And, in fact, the industrial working class has been most prominent in leftist and bourgeois revolutionary movements. The apparent irony of proletarian revolt in pursuit of bourgeois goals suggests the complexity of interests that motivate revolutionary leaders and followers. It is plainly wrong to assume that leaders and followers hold the same opinions, attitudes, and beliefs only because they are temporary allies in their assault on the bastions of power. The frequent rupture of the revolutionary alliance once power has been won makes clear the different motivations at work in the revolutionary process. And it also suggests the words that are given to an Algerian rebel organizer in Gillo Pontecorvo's film, *The Battle of Algiers:* "To begin a revolution is very difficult. To sustain it is even more difficult. To win it is almost impossible. But once you have won, then your troubles really begin." The unhappy sequence of events in Algeria following Algerian independence in 1961 confirms his point.

The difference in motivation between followers and leaders seems to be especially characteristic of rightist revolutionary movements. In the case of German National Socialism, the leadership began with an urban-industrial orientation, but the substantial support that the Nazis received from rural voters with different interests induced the leadership to revise its program, namely by promising a moratorium or cancellation of peasant indebtedness.[11] The pronouncements of radical right leaders in the United States in the 1950s and 1960s also had little to do with the nature of the radical right's fundamental appeal: less the anticommunism and Christian fundamentalism of the leaders than the distress of traditional Republican conservatives over their party's apparent support for the development of a welfare state.[12]

But the followers of revolutionary movements on the left also are less likely than their leaders to think in terms of sweeping principles related to morality, the social order, and political organization. A study of twenty-four guerrilla insurgencies between 1946 and the early 1960s finds that the reasons for joining the movement were "most frequently personal and situational in nature. Ideological or political reasons seem to have inspired only a small percentage, and propaganda promises appear to have had little effect." Once he is a part of the movement, the follower's revolutionary commitment may be reinforced by indoctrination and ideology, but his reasons for remaining are more often related to the small group loyalties generated by his guerrilla activities.[13]

While the revolutionary leader talks about freedom and justice for all, then, the revolutionary follower is more likely to think in terms of greater security and material well-being for himself.[14] Of course these ideals are not contradictory or mutually exclusive, and only reflect different levels of conceptual abstraction. Greater freedom and justice for the worker mean job security and a higher wage; for the peasant, enough land to feed his family and an end to the oppression of landlords and money lenders; for the shopowner, a fair return on his merchandise and services and protection from unionized labor and big business.

The critical question for any revolutionary movement, however, is the extent to which these and other interests can be brought together in a single revolutionary alliance against the apparent injustice and exploitation of the status quo.

CROSS-CUTTING ALLIANCES

Whatever the motivations, characteristics, or relationships of leaders and followers, there is one obvious common denominator that cuts across all successful revolutionary movements, whether of the left, center, or right. Revolutionary movements do not succeed where only the workers are mobilized, or only the peasants, or only the middle classes. They succeed only where a critical mass of most or all of the major classes in the society is mobilized in the revolutionary process. The dustbin of history is filled with revolutionary leaders and followers who thought only in terms of the parochial interests of their special clienteles.

Writing in 1850, Friedrich Engels argued that the German Peasant Revolt of 1525 failed because it was strictly a revolt of the German peasants. And the Protestant Reformation, perhaps the principal revolutionary movement of the premodern era, succeeded precisely in those areas of Europe where the peasantry *and* the upper social classes were united by their common hostility to the papacy.[15]

Many of the same issues and institutional conflicts that agitated French revolutionaries in 1789 were raised during the Fronde, a series of revolutionary outbreaks in France between 1648 and 1653 and the first largely secular revolutionary movement of the postmedieval age. The French nobility, bourgeoisie, and urban artisans were at first allied in their efforts to check monarchical authority. But the decisive base for revolutionary change, the French peasantry, was not mobilized in the revolutionary process, and instead was terrorized by marauding bands led and supported by the nobility. In the local parliaments, the bourgeoisie, apparently identifying its interests with a centralizing monarchy, eventually withdrew its support from the rebellious nobles. The nobility's enforced collection of provisions from town and country, and its attempts to enlist the support of France's enemies (notably Hapsburg Spain), further alienated the bourgeoisie and peasantry. The failures of the Fronde (and the German Peasant Revolt) suggested that neither the nobles nor the peasants, by themselves, constituted a critical mass for successful revolution.[16]

By contrast, the French Revolution of 1789 was notable for its de facto alliance among nobility, peasantry, the urban artisan classes, and a bourgeoisie grown larger and stronger since the Fronde of more than a century before. The French peasants were in revolt regardless of events in Paris. The antagonism between nobility and bourgeoisie did not surface until after the initial events of the revolution, and then as before the Parisian lower classes intervened at critical junctures to continue the revolutionary process. Even the village priests played a revolutionary role by identifying their interests with and lending their support to the Third Estate.[17] A study of the socioeconomic status of the reported dead and wounded during the revolutionary events in Paris in both 1789 and 1830 finds that they represented a cross-section of the total population: 19 percent were laborers and servants of the lowest social classes; 6 percent were from the professions; 4 percent were shopkeepers; and 65 percent were skilled artisans and craftsmen. It obviously was not a revolt of urban scum, the desperate, or the dispossessed.[18]

Trotsky explained the failures of Pugachev's Rebellion of 1774 and the Decembrist Revolt of 1825 in terms of their narrow social class base. The peasantry supporting Pugachev was without any urban support, in part because of the very weakness or nonexistence of a bourgeoisie and proletariat. The officers and progressive nobility in revolt against the tsar also lacked a bourgeoisie with whom to ally, and were decisively defeated by their fears of rousing the peasantry.[19]

The weakness of radical and revolutionary movements in England, Germany, and France during the nineteenth century can also be attributed to the absence of cross-cutting alliances among the major social classes. The English working class itself was divided and lacked support from the more liberal middle classes. Without middle-class support and regime access, the Chartist movement of the English working class was bound to be more an expression of noble ideals than an effective challenge to the established political system.[20] In Germany, during the revolution of 1848, the working class was led by revolutionaries who had only contempt for the bourgeoisie, while the bourgeoisie feared the socialist objectives of the working class. The Frankfurt Assembly was consequently an easy mark for Imperial power and the Prussian Army.[21] Without any support from the French peasantry, and with the French bourgeoisie and Church alienated by the working-class oriented programs of the Paris Commune (March–May 1871), the Commune was also a stationary target for the forces of counterrevolution.[22]

The record of nationalist movements against Ottoman rule in the Balkans from the seventeenth through the nineteenth centuries is one of unrelieved failure. The frequent revolts of the peasants seeking land reform and an end to feudal obligations were opposed by the upper social classes. And the nationalist leadership opposed to Ottoman control was in the hands of upper classes bent on retaining their feudal privileges. Especially after the Ottomans guaranteed property and legal rights to the peasants, the upper-class nationalists lost the basis for an appeal to the peasantry, and consequently were perennial losers in their struggle against Ottoman supremacy. Balkan independence had to wait until the disintegration of the Ottoman Empire after the First World War.[23]

The American Revolution is in large part the story of British policies which inadvertently created cross-cutting alliances between the various social classes of the colonies. The Stamp Act, Revenue Act, Townshend duties, and especially the Quebec Act (seen by the colonists as a barrier to westward expansion) heightened anti-British sentiment among merchants, frontiersmen, journalists, businessmen, lawyers, clergy, workingmen, wealthy land speculators, independent farmers, and people of the coastal towns and backwoods country.[24] The great majority of the debtor classes supported the revolution, but so did important parts of the wealthy landowning classes, especially in Virginia where the patronage influence of the British Crown was weak. J. Franklin Jameson identifies those categories of the more prominent Tory supporters, clearly a minority in colonial society; officeholders appointed by the Crown, merchants trading primarily with Great Britain, the wealthier landowners in New York and Pennsylvania, clergy of the Church of England, Episcopalians (especially in the north), the richest physicians and most prominent lawyers, recent immigrants from England and Scotland, and the larger part of the small but educated minority. While "the strength of the revolutionary party lay most largely in the plain people, as distinguished from the [colonial] aristocracy," the movement for separation from Great Britain was obviously based on a broad cross-section of the colonial social classes.[25]

This point is so important to the study of revolution that it deserves further documentation, and in the context of more contemporary revolutionary movements. The reader will not fail to note that we continue to test the hypothesis with reference to both revolutionary movements that fail and those that succeed. Only in this way can we minimize the uncertainty that is invariably associated with any hypothesis on revolution.

CROSS-CUTTING ALLIANCES IN REVOLUTIONARY MOVEMENTS OF THE TWENTIETH CENTURY

As in the case of the Fronde, the major issues that would be raised in 1917 in Russia were also present in an earlier and unsuccessful revolution, the Russian Revolution of 1905. In its initial stages, the 1905 revolution mobilized land-hungry peasants who were the de facto allies of a working class that wanted higher wages and shorter working hours, mutinous soldiers and sailors, and liberals and urban professionals who wanted constitutional reform. But the tsar's promises of civil liberties and an elected parliament (Duma) won the support of the bourgeoisie, already fearful of proletarian revolution. The broken ranks of the revolutionaries were then crushed by loyal army units returning from the Far East, following the tsar's hasty conclusion of peace with Japan.[26]

But the tsar's woeful mismanagement of Russia's role in the First World War, and the war's disintegrative effects on all sectors of Russian society, created a much more explosive situation. By 1916, the progressive nobility and liberal bourgeoisie were alienated by the regime's incompetence, while the tsar (who had been less than forthright in meeting his promises of 1905) continued to show his disdain for the nobles and bourgeoisie in the Duma. Their speeches were censored, and their antagonism for the German-born tsarina and her coterie of corrupt ministers only reinforced their tendencies to move with (if not support) the more extremist revolutionaries.

And as in the case of the French Revolution, the Russian peasants were burning manors and seizing land without any encouragement from the cities. The military, especially those soldiers who had deserted from the trenches, was no longer the pillar of support the tsar had leaned upon in 1905. Nor was the state bureaucracy. The workers were better organized than in 1905, and their strikes and demonstrations in the key industrial centers proved to be the linchpin in the wheel of the February Revolution. The problem was to determine just who opposed the revolution: "the most conservative of conservatives—a few army officers, a few members of the Court and old nobility."[27]

It was no coincidence that the First World War ignited revolutions in all the defeated countries. The Bolshevik victory in November 1917 added even more fuel to the fires kindled by peasants and workers in Austria, Hungary, and Germany in early 1918. But the military forces of the Central Powers remained intact, the workers were divided among themselves, and those industrial general strikes that did occur were not coordinated with the revolutionary activity of the peasants. They only reinforced the divisions of the working class and terrified the bourgeoisie. Of more importance was the conservative orientation of the greater part of the peasantry of Europe: only in Russia did the peasants prove to be an almost solid phalanx working for revolutionary change.[28]

Just as successful revolutionary movements of the working class have depended on support from the peasantry and the bourgeoisie, successful revolutionary movements on the right have depended on support from the working class. The support of one social class for another, however, may be more tacit than overt, or the revolution may succeed simply by *neutralizing* the large majority of the society's nonrevolutionary classes. And successful fascist movements have been able both to neutralize and mobilize important sectors of the population not classified as lower-middle class (the typical base of fascist strength). In fact the nationalist and racist appeals of right-wing movements are intended precisely to recruit followers from across the society's spectrum of classes.

Robert Hunter, for example, estimates that approximately 40 percent of the Italian Fascists were recruited from Italy's trade-union movement. Just prior to the Fascists' "March on Rome" in October 1922, Mussolini's oratory and the Fascist Manifesto were credited with neutralizing the army and civil service, appealing to their national pride and reinforcing their suspicions for "that class of imbecile and mentally deficient politicians, who, during four long years, have not known how to give a Government to the Nation."[29] Mussolini's overtures to "the productive bourgeoisie" also received a positive response from some of Italy's largest industrialists, including those in automobile and tire manufacturing, armaments and munitions, electrical, steel, and engineering combines, and from leaders of other business enterprises in Italy's industrial north. And his reassurances to "the working classes, the people of the fields and of the factories," found a resonant echo among landowners, peasants, and workers, all those who supported the Church, feared the left, rejected the peace settlement of Versailles, and detested Italy's feeble parliamentary institutions.

These generalizations also may be applied to German National Socialism, which similarly mobilized support from all the major sectors of German society, including landed aristocrats, peasants, businessmen, workers, government officials, and military elites. The fascist coalition typically comes apart with military defeat. But its end is also signaled by the defection of the bourgeoisie, the Church, and the military, which in 1955 proved fatal to Peronism in Argentina. In this sense the study of revolutionary movements may be treated as a subcategory of "group theory" and understood in terms of the political norms of coalition-building and maintenance.

It may seem that all that is at issue in the case of peasant-based revolutions is the extent of peasant mobilization and the movement's military power. But these in turn depend on the cross-cutting alliances effected among the various strata of the peasantry. The unsuccessful Malayan guerrilla movement after 1948, for example, never mobilized support from either the urban social classes or the several categories of Malayan peasants—with the exception of squatters in outlying jungle areas and the poorer peasants of Chinese ethnic extraction. The Malayan Communists consequently were relatively "easy prey for security forces" directed by an effective government staffed with British personnel.[30]

Following more orthodox Marxist doctrine and the Comintern's directives, Chinese Communism also failed to achieve its mobilization objectives before the 1930s. Its early focus on the Chinese urban proletariat, to the exclusion of either bourgeois or peasant support, only enhanced the party's vulnerability to the Nationalists and Chiang Kai-shek. Mao's capture of the party's leadership and its consequent reorientation toward the peasantry meant an important increment in the party's revolutionary potential. But the initial line was in terms of radical agrarian reform, including land expropriation and the organization of peasant collectives, which threatened both the upper and intermediate strata of the peasantry. Mao's subsequent emphasis on "winning over all possible allies" entailed an appeal to the "new middle peasants": some land from large estates was redistributed in those areas controlled by the Communists, usury rates were reduced, a progressive land tax was instituted, but even the land of most rich peasants was left intact. The resulting support from across the social spectrum of the Chinese peasantry enabled the Communists to consolidate their political position in the villages. And on the threshold of victory in 1949, the Chinese Communist party was fairly representative of the Chinese population: 80 percent of party members were of peasant origin, and of these approximately three-fourths were poor peasants and one-fourth were from the middle-stratum of the Chinese peasantry.[31]

Vietnamese resistance to Western colonialism developed from the very outset of French penetration of Indochina after 1850. Major uprisings occurred in the north of Vietnam between 1885 and 1896, and again in 1906. But these movements were primarily urban and upper-class based, and their suppression by the French was facilitated by the very low involvement of the Vietnamese peasantry. Organized in 1927, the Vietnamese Nationalist party was composed of members from the urban middle classes, especially Vietnamese in the colonial administration, and it too failed to make much headway against French control. The uprising of 1929 was marked by the emergence of the Vietnamese Communist party, which distinguished itself from other nationalist organizations by seeking the support of both peasants and workers. The Communists' success in developing a mass-based revolutionary movement was especially apparent following the defeat of the Japanese in the Second World War and France's attempt to reassert control over Indochina. The rank-and-file of the Vietminh army were workers and peasants, while the lower-echelon leaders or "linking cadres" were from the lower-middle classes and the colonial administration in both urban and rural areas. Most of the linking cadres had some Western-oriented education and experience, as did the majority of the Vietminh's upper cadres who were primarily intellectuals and sons of the bourgeoisie.[32] The victory of the Vietminh over the French in 1954 may be attributed to a number of factors, but they all turned ultimately on the Communists' ability to build a broad base of support among the various social classes of Vietnam, especially within the older and more structured society of the north.

Colombia in 1957 provides us with another example of students playing the role of "detonator" in an explosive situation. But the hostility of students for antiliberal politics must be shared by other sectors of the population, otherwise their threatened or actual violence only strengthens the support of the existing regime. In Colombia, however, the plainly rigged elections of dictator Rojas Pinilla triggered student riots that dramatized the regime's corruption and incompetence. The student riots in turn led to a general strike which was aimed at preventing the formal reelection of Rojas as president. The subsequent support for the students and strikers from both the Church and the military created the critical mass of opposition that toppled the regime from power.[33]

One of the more curious anomalies of the Cuban Revolution is the insistence of its theorists (including Régis Debray, Che Guevara, and others) on the determining role of peasants and the guerrilla *foco*. But the principal role of Castro and his army (which never numbered more than 2,000) appears to have been that of focal point for the anti-Batista hostility that cut across increasingly broader sectors of Cuban society.

Urban intellectuals, radical students, and rural campesinos found in Castro's movement a means of expressing their opposition to the regime. But the more decisive revolutionary alliance was created only as the guerrillas' continued survival demonstrated the weakness of Batista's supporting coalition. The more organized sectors of the working class supported Castro in the last stages of the revolution. It was really the urban middle classes, including business and the professions, that were the important source of money and supplies, responding to Castro's stated objective of resolving the economic difficulties associated with Batista. Pro-Castro support from the Catholic hierarchy and the urban middle classes, even tacit support from the Cuban upper classes, increased after Batista's resort to terror in 1958. The Lions and Rotary clubs, the medical, dental, and legal societies, and the middle-class sporting clubs, were all politicized and registered pro-Castro sentiments before the Batista government collapsed in January 1959. Thanks in part to the withdrawal of American support for Batista, the blunders and repression of his government, and the ambiguity of Castro's intentions, the core alliance of intellectuals, students, and a small part of the Cuban peasantry mobilized support from all the major sectors of Cuban society.[34]

By contrast, the anti-Castro movement of 1960 and 1961 was notable for the weakness of its social class base: almost exclusively the Cuban middle class, with the force of the movement deriving from the large landowners dispossessed by the Castro government. Castro reported that of the 1,000 counterrevolutionaries captured after the unsuccessful Bay of Pigs invasion approximately 800 came from wealthy families, and many of the others were former soldiers in Batista's army. In much the same way, the fate of the Somoza dictatorship in Nicaragua was sealed in 1979 when the Somoza family could count on the support of only the wealthiest of Nicaragua's families and the highest ranking army officers. The anti-Somoza alliance eventually came to include Marxists and businessmen, shopkeepers and workers, bankers and peasants, housewives and professionals, Indians and clergy, with the most active representatives of these groups joining in the demonstrations, election boycott, and general strike that helped to rid Nicaragua of the family that had ruled the country since 1933.[35]

CRITICAL MASS

The above should help to make clear why most revolutionary movements fail, and why the great majority of revolutionary leaders and followers drown in a sea of hostility and apathy even when they claim to be riding the waves of revolution. A rampage of Weathermen through the streets of Chicago (as in 1969) may suggest a feeble beginning in the revolutionary process, but until such efforts enlist the support of substantial numbers of citizens from all the major sectors of society they signify more the self-gratification of a few than the revolutionary mobilization of the many.

But what do we mean by "substantial numbers," "important percentage," a "large part"? How do we determine what constitutes the "critical mass" in the fusion and fission processes of revolution? I have used these vague descriptive labels in the preceding sections with self-conscious awareness of the ambiguity they represent. It is true that the success or failure of revolutionary movements cited above seems to lean heavily on the extent to which the movement effected cross-cutting alliances among most or all of the dominant classes of the society. But even revolutionary movements that succeed are based on a small percentage of the total population. A revolution involves minorities fighting minorities. And if the revolutionaries have any advantage over the loyalists, it probably begins with the revolutionaries' greater *intensity* of commitment to their cause.[36] We can add that this is especially true of colonial societies, where the established government is likely to be regarded by most citizens as very low in legitimacy.

But whether the great mass of the society is apathetic, neutralized, or supportive of the revolution, the movement and its followers are a tiny minority whose intense commitment to revolution is their most valuable resource. The Algerian rebellion was initiated in 1954 by no more than 500 men, 300 of them in the Aurès Mountains with fewer than fifty shotguns. By 1956, French authorities estimated rebel strength at 8,500 fighters and 21,000 auxiliaries. But the French were unable to control the activities of the rebel guerrillas until the French Algerian Army mobilized 450,000 troops. This forced the rebellion into the urban areas of Algeria, mainly the Muslim quarter of Algiers where a population of 80,000 supplied 4,000 recruits to the rebel Army of National Liberation.[37] By the end of 1957 this rebel force also was crushed, and subsequently it was events in France rather than Algeria that determined the end of French colonialism in North Africa.

The success of the Cuban revolution also seems to have been largely beyond the immediate control of either Castro or his followers. Some authorities put the maximum size of Castro's army at even less than the 2,000 cited above. And while his urban supporters also could be numbered in the thousands, they were never organized and there was nothing approximating mass participation in the revolution until its successful end was a foregone conclusion.[38]

It has been estimated that throughout most of the American Revolution one-third of the 2.5 million population were neutral, another third were pro-British, and only the remaining third supported the Patriot cause.[39] Of the approximately 700,000 men of fighting age (18 to 60), the maximum strength of the Continental Army was around 90,000. But for the greater part of the military conflict that extended over seven years, the Continental Army managed to enlist only about one man for every sixteen of fighting age.[40]

With 100,000 members in 1920, the Italian Fascists had only 2.5 members per 1,000 population. This ratio increased to 11.9 in 1922 when the Fascists came to power. Comparable ratios for German Nazis were 1.6 in 1928, 5.8 in 1930, 12.2 in 1931, and, prior to the capture of power in 1933, 1.4 million party members or 21.4 per 1,000 population.[41]

Only about 12,000 persons were active in the Russian Social Democratic party between 1898 and 1905.[42] On the eve of the February Revolution in 1917, the Bolsheviks numbered no more than 30,000 members in all of Russia.[43] The population of Petrograd was 2 million, with 600,000 employed as workers. Events in the February Revolution began with strikes and demonstrations by 90,000 workers, most of whom did not intend a revolution. On the third day of strike activity, government figures estimated the total number of demonstrators at 240,000 or 12 percent of the total population of Petrograd. Trotsky refers to this as "the entire active mass of the people," and the turning point in the revolutionary process of February 1917.[44] The October Revolution in Petrograd was carried out by no more than 25,000 to 30,000 armed insurrectionists, while the number of troops in and around Petrograd (most of whom were either neutralized or Bolshevik supporters) numbered 200,000.[45]

A study of the percentage of participants in seven insurgencies between 1940 and 1962 again shows the very small number of the total population involved in revolution. Including both insurgents and government forces, the average is 7 percent, with a range from 0.7 percent in the Philippines to 11.2 percent in Greece.[46] There is no apparent relationship between the success or failure of these movements and any of the variables that can be derived from the data.

It is obvious, then, that when we talk about the mobilization for revolution of workers, peasants, or the middle classes, we are talking about a small minority of activists within each of these categories. Even among the more revolutionary-prone category of students we must be cautious of misleading generalization. Of the 160,000 students in Paris during the events of May–June 1968, no more than 40,000 participated in the demonstrations. Of the 600,000 students in all of France, only about 10 percent played an active role in a movement (initiated by the students) that seriously threatened the Gaullist state.[47] Opinion surveys in the United States and in many European countries in the late 1960s also make it clear that the extreme student left consists of less than 10 percent of the total student population in each country.[48]

What is at issue for any revolutionary movement, then, is the extent to which the active minority of one social class is able to ally with the active minorities of other social classes. The percentage of any particular social class and the scope of cross-cutting alliances involved in successful revolution will depend in turn on the strength of the regime under attack, the appeal of the revolutionary ideology, the qualities of organization, the techniques employed, and many of the other characteristics of revolutionary movements discussed in the following chapters. But it should be clear at this point in our study that just as government in a stable society is the affair of a minority, so is revolution.

FOR FURTHER TESTING

Some Propositions:

1. The very rich and the very poor are the least likely to revolt.
2. Support for leftist revolutionary movements is likely to come primarily from the society's lower classes (including peasants and workers).
3. Bourgeois revolutionary movements are likely to be supported primarily by the society's middle classes.
4. The lower middle classes are the primary base of support for rightist revolutionary movements.

Some Hypotheses:

The chances of capturing power increase as the revolutionary movement,

1. mobilizes a critical mass of followers from most or all of the society's classes (cross-cutting alliances);
2. finds ways to focus the diverse interests and varying motivations of leaders and followers on revolutionary objectives (see the next chapter).

NOTES

[1] See Wolf, 1969, pp. 202-3, where his findings and those from other research on revolutionary peasants are summarized. Hobsbawm, 1959, pp. 67 and 76, notes the importance of small landholders—not the absolutely landless—in peasant millenarian and anarchist movements in Tuscany and southern Spain.

[2] Huntington, 1968, pp. 375-76.

[3] Davies, 1963, pp. 11-15, summarizes the findings of social psychology supporting this generalization.

[4] Lewis, 1965.

[5] Zeitlin, 1967, pp. 97-98. Also see Hamilton, 1967, p. 121, on the characteristics of French working-class voters. And on the characteristics of communist voters, including those of higher working-class status, see Greene, 1971.

[6] Trotsky, 1957, Vol. 1, p. 102.

[7] Woolf, 1969, p. 112.

[8] Lipset, 1970, p. 235.

[9] Schoenbaum, 1967, p. 21.

[10] Lipset, 1963, Chap. 4. On the characteristics of the followers of Spanish fascism, see Linz, 1968, p. 16.

[11] Converse, 1964, pp. 252-54, summarizes the findings of Herberle and others.

[12] Wolfinger et al., 1964.

[13] Molnar, 1965, p. 5 and Chap. 3.

[14] Gurr, 1970, p. 148.

[15] Engels, 1971.

[16] On the Fronde, see Palmer, 1956, pp. 156-59.

[17] Palmer, 1956, p. 349; Brinton, 1965, pp. 56-57; Moore, 1966, pp. 75 and 480.

[18] Pinckney, 1964. The percentages apply to the Parisian crowds of the 1830 Revolution, but Pinckney observes that "the composition of the crowd in 1830 was strikingly similar to that of the crowds in the Revolution of 1789."

[19] Trotsky, 1957, Vol. 1, p. 8.

[20] Birnie, 1962, p. 127.

[21] Palmer, 1956, pp. 486-89.

[22] Hunter, 1940, pp. 73-74.

[23] Fischer-Galati, 1963.

[24] Palmer, 1956, pp. 324-26; Brinton, 1965, p. 99.

[25] Jameson, 1956, pp. 13-18.

[26] Palmer, 1956, pp. 714-17; Trotsky, 1957, Vol. 1, pp. 12-13.

[27] Brinton, 1965, p. 100. Also see Trotsky, 1957, Vol. 1, p. 27; Wolf, 1969, p. 300; Palmer, 1956, pp. 721-22.

[28] Borkenau, 1962, pp. 91-95.

[29] Quoted in Hunter, 1940, pp. 241-44.

[30] Molnar, 1965, p. 102.

[31] Mao Tse-tung, 1970, p. 417; Huntington, 1968, p. 295; Wolf, 1969, pp. 148-51.

[32] Wolf, 1969, pp. 180-85, summarizes the relevant bibliography and data.

[33] Huntington, 1968, p. 213.

[34] Beals, 1970, p. 246; Leiden and Schmitt, 1968, pp. 188-90; Mills, 1960, pp. 43-46. Llerena, 1978, emphasizes the crucial role played by Cuba's middle class in support of Castro's revolution.

[35] See Kenner and Petras, 1969, p. 83, on the sociological composition of the anti-Castro movement and Bowdler, 1981, on cross-cutting alliances in Nicaragua in 1978-1979.

[36] Gurr, 1970, p. 276.

[37] Wolf, 1969, pp. 236-39.

[38] Leiden and Schmitt, 1968, p. 190.

[39] Deutsch, 1964, p. 105.

[40] Jameson, 1956, p. 48.

[41] Linz, 1968, table following p. 109.

[42] Lane, 1969. See Part I for the methodology and data supporting Lane's estimates.

[43] Neumann, 1949, and Lane, 1971, p. 515.

[44] Trotsky, 1957, Vol. 1, pp. 102–110.

[45] Trotsky, 1957, Vol. 3, pp. 190, 227, 246, and 294. Total Bolshevik membership claimed by the Sixth Party Congress in August 1917 was 200,000 (or 0.12 percent of Russia's total population).

[46] Molnar, 1965, Table 1, p. 74.

[47] Ellul, 1970, p. 496. The force of events in France in 1968 was much greater than in the United States precisely because the French students were able to effect a cross-cutting alliance with the French workers.

[48] Lipset, 1970, p. 261. A Harris opinion survey of American citizens in March 1970, commissioned by *Time* Magazine, found that 9 percent of the total United States population call themselves "revolutionaries." Students and blacks were the social categories most overrepresented in these findings, confirming the narrow social class base of revolutionary sentiment in the United States.

CHAPTER
SIX

IDEOLOGY

FUNCTIONS

The alert reader will already have understood the principal function of revolutionary ideology: to facilitate the development of cross-cutting alliances between the active minorities of the society's major classes. The more heterogeneous its actual or potential clientele, the greater the movement's challenge to fashion an ideology that offers something for everyone—or almost everyone.

Communist ideology is probably the most coherent and articulate belief system in the history of revolution. But the broad-range theory that supports communist doctrine functions largely as a system of cues and symbols for intra-elite communication, reinforcing the revolutionary commitment of the movement's upper hierarchy or expressing its factional conflicts in terms other than those of personality and power.

But for the majority of followers and the great mass of the society, the broad-range principles of historical inevitability and class conflict have been de-emphasized or completely ignored by communist ideologists and propagandists. Instead they have focused on general problems relevant to the whole society, such as national independence, and on the specific grievances of clearly identified clienteles.

Lenin's slogan of "land, peace, and bread" was a succinct invitation for revolutionary support from oppressed peasants, war-weary soldiers, and hungry workers and their families. "All power to the soviets" directed attention to the weakness and indecision of the Provisional Government, and at the same time avoided reference to the Bolsheviks as the dominant force in the soviets (or "councils") organized by revolutionary peasants, soldiers, and workers.

Benefiting from the experience of the Chinese Communists, the Vietnamese Communists also avoided the theme of class conflict in favor of nationalist appeals against a common enemy—the Japanese military occupation and, subsequently, French colonialism. During the Indochinese war of 1946 to 1954 and in the areas they controlled, the Vietminh shunned issues and politics that threatened to divide Vietnamese society into classes and waited until after their capture of power before attempting radical agrarian reform.

In fact an ideology that appeals to national identity is the most powerful symbolic means of mobilizing revolutionary support. Nationalism alone has the greatest potential for cutting across all the society's classes. It can unite young and old, male and female, peasant and landowner, industrialist and worker, businessman and intellectual, the religious faithful and the nonbelievers, rich and poor, and people in the villages and in the cities.

The Algerian National Liberation Front, for example, was constantly threatened by factional strife whenever issues were raised on the more general problems of the future social and political organization of Algeria. Only the dynamic provided by anticolonialism papered over the conflicts and lent the movement whatever cohesion it enjoyed. The Chinese revolutionaries of 1911 were divided on all the issues of socioeconomic and political reform. What united them was their "angry complaint . . . that China's position in the world was humiliating . . ."[1] And in the case of Castro's revolution in Cuba, the long-standing hostility of Cubans for the economic and political penetration of the United States—dating from the end of the Spanish-American War—gave Castro's doctrinal statements a focus that was otherwise lacking in his more liberal and moralistic exhortations.

Where nationalism has not been an issue in revolutionary mobilization, as in the case of extreme left movements in England, France, and in the United States, the movements have been doomed to a narrow class-based appeal and, consequently, political insignificance. Marx himself would appreciate the irony of apparently class-based movements depending on nationalist passions for their revolutionary power. (Although he would probably insist on the peculiarity of nationalism to specific stages of socioeconomic development.)

What small-group loyalties and charismatic authority are to the cohesion of the revolutionary organization, ideology is to the intellectual and symbolic cohesion of the minds of revolutionary leaders and followers. Each man and woman in the movement must be able to identify in the ideology those themes and symbols that correspond to his or her personal needs and ambitions. And it is true that the impact of revolutionary ideologies is in terms more of "a congeries of phrases, vague ideas, and symbols" than a coherent belief system penetrating the collective consciousness of the revolution.[2]

But it also is true that where there are competing ideologies, there is no cohesion to the revolutionary movement. In France in 1968, workers were divided over the extent to which economic gains should be joined with structural reform of the production process, while radical students and anti-Gaullist politicians competed with each other under the headings of communism, socialism, anarchism, Maoism, Trotskyism, neo-Sartrianism, situationalism, and even subcategories of these various systems of belief and action.[3] In this sense, too much ideology undermines the cohesion of the movement. And revolutionary organization is likely to be better structured by a loosely knit system of issue-oriented programs overlaid with an appeal to national self-interest.

The mix of various cues and symbols along with nationalism is especially characteristic of fascism. Mussolini talked in terms of economic growth, personal discipline, an end to political instability and social disorder (much of it the result of Fascist violence!), and especially the attainment of national glory. But Mussolini himself seemed to exult in the "extraordinary intellectual poverty" of his movement:[4] "Action! Deeds! These alone matter. Leave theory to the scribblers!"[5] The ideology may be largely incoherent, then, but nationalism and charismatic authority can give it the appearance of logical unity, which in turn can reinforce the cohesion of the movement.

The even greater cohesion and militancy of German National Socialism may be explained in part by these same ideological characteristics, overlaid with the insidious veneer of anti-Semitism. With only 600,000 Jews in Germany, Hitler's emphasis on the responsibility of the Jew for every foreign and domestic evil did not at all threaten the mass base of his movement. On the contrary, it strengthened it and gave it apparent ideological unity, especially as the Nazis sought to recruit followers from those social classes ranked above the lower-class status of their original clientele. In his 1934 study of motivations for joining the Nazis, Theodor Abel found that only 25 percent of working-class members identified anti-Semitism as a principal reason for their Nazi support. The higher the social status of the party member, the more likely his reference to anti-Semitism: "60 percent of the professional classes mentioned it as a major reason for joining the party." But "everyone was moved by nationalism."[6]

Nationalism, however, has also imparted cohesion to cross-cutting class alliances mobilized by revolutionary movements on the center and left. In their revolts against the oligarchical elites of Turkey and Egypt, Kemal and Nasser first emphasized national unity and power. Only after consolidating power did they turn to the far-reaching social reforms that, if advocated at an earlier time, would have seriously weakened their power base.[7] Especially when the organization of the revolutionary movement is weak and its followers are less subject to direct command, a nationalist ideology can provide the persuasive force that renders the movement self-sustaining. T. E. Lawrence makes this point in his narrative of the Arab revolt against Turkish rule between 1916 and 1918. As is made clear by the rapid disintegration of the Arab alliance after the Turkish defeat, however, a compelling ideology is no substitute for organizational strength, and the Arabs in 1918 only exchanged one colonial overlord for another.[8]

If a strong ideology is functional to revolutionary mobilization, even where organization is weak, it also is true that a weak ideology is an almost insuperable obstacle to revolutionary success. In Mexico after 1915, the Zapatista guerrilla movement withered away as the men in Zapata's army secured the parcels of land that had inspired their revolutionary activity. The army failed to extend its area of operations beyond the vicinity of Morelos, and Zapata himself seems to have had no understanding of how to capitalize on anti-American sentiment in order to fuse the efforts of his guerrillas with the activities of those in the north and with workers and intellectuals in the cities.[9]

But there is no doubt that the Communists in South Vietnam well understood how to transfer the nationalist sentiments of the Vietnamese from hostility for the French to hostility for the Americans. And wherever revolutionary movements have been able to monopolize the tissues of anticolonialism and agrarian reform, they have proved to be an almost unbeatable force. The success of Chinese Communism in areas under the Japanese occupation confirms the point. On the other hand, the relative weakness of Communism in India reflects the Communists' failure to capitalize on the issues of anticolonialism and agrarian reform, issues earlier captured by Gandhi and Nehru.

At the same time, we should recall our findings of the different motivations mobilizing revolutionary followers and leaders, and the different cues and interpretations that revolutionaries read into the same ideological appeals. Of those participants interviewed after the 1830 revolution in Paris, almost half cited personal grievances against the state, including dismissal from the army or navy or premature retirement from the civil service, as the primary reason for their insurrectionary activity.[10] A study in 1965 of more than 1,300 defectors from the Viet Cong in South Vietnam reports that almost none explained their defection in ideological terms, while the majority of defectors referred to shortages of food and medical supplies.[11] A survey of students participating in the 1968 French revolt found that most students were agitated less by the repressive character of the Gaullist state and the university than by their apprehensions over unemployment following graduation.[12] Even where there is an obvious basis for nationalist appeal, a commitment to armed insurrection may be triggered by only the most immediate personal circumstances: the principals in the French Resistance during the Second World War—peasants, workers, and students— were initially mobilized by the Germans' introduction of compulsory labor service for Frenchmen in German factories and not by the earlier appeals of a few intellectuals and military leaders for national liberation from a foreign oppressor.[13]

As in the case of the roles of revolutionary leaders, then, the functions of ideology are more to reinforce than to create the conditions conducive to cross-cutting alliances and revolutionary mobilization.

LEGITIMACY

The function of revolutionary ideology is also to legitimate the movement, to sanction its means and ends in terms of basic values accepted by its followers and, perhaps, all mankind. The ideology is likely to be better developed and more articulated, then, as the intended break from the established regime and the society's conventional norms is more extreme. Ideological justification for revolution is especially important when sustained violence is a principal technique employed by the movement.

Thus there are frequent references in the ideologies of revolutionary movements to metaphysical sanctions for revolutionary activity. The Puritans in England and the leaders of the Protestant Reformation thought in terms of divine election to authority and social prominence. Revolutionary liberals in the American and French revolutions justified their acts in terms of natural law and the inalienable rights inherent in human existence. Socialists and communists have relied on earlier liberal notions of social contract and the right of labor to the full value of the product produced, and they have sought justification for revolution in the historical dialectic of proletarian progress.

But as in the case of religious conflicts, ideological divisions in the society are closed only with great effort and over an extended period of time.[14] Differences over the distribution of political power, patronage, and welfare are more susceptible to bargaining and compromise. The formulation of specific grievances into general principles, however, makes the resolution of differences between social groups more difficult. When basic values are at stake, the intensity of the conflict is higher and its duration is longer. The monarchy's censorship required liberals in prerevolutionary France to talk in terms of universal norms and absolute rights, and these generalized claims laid the basis for ideological and political divisions that persist in France to this day.[15]

At the same time, the presumption of absolute right typical of revolutionary ideologies helps to lend certainty to the activities of the revolutionaries. Revolutions are not for those who are filled with self-doubt and moral skepticism. Revolutionaries see the world in shadeless black and white, and their allies are thought to be motivated by high idealism while their opponents are the picture of self-interest and opportunism.[16] The certainty of revolutionaries in the legitimacy of their acts helps to inspire them with optimism for the future and self-sacrifice for the present. The first test for the revolutionary is his willingness to die for his cause, a willingness that turns on the presumed rectitude of his faith.[17]

This helps to explain the weakness of most counterrevolutionary movements, which are motivated less by abstract ideals than by the urge to recapture the privileges of an earlier day. And this generalization appears to apply with equal force to counterrevolutionary movements in France after 1789, in Russia after 1917, in Cuba after 1959, and to the Nationalist Chinese hopelessly anchored on China's offshore islands and Taiwan.

But revolutionary ideologies not only function as legitimating sanctions for revolutionary action. They also are intended to weaken or eliminate the legitimacy claimed by the existing regime. The regime itself claims legitimacy in terms of what Gaetano Mosca called "the political formula" of the ruling class. The political formula justifies the existence and actions of the government with reference to basic values—authority derived from God (Divine Right), natural law and the apparently unequal distribution of virtue and talent (and so property and wealth), or the notions of consent, representation, and majority rule. Revolutionary ideology attacks the political formula as plainly wrong, or as right but inconsistent with the actual performance of the regime. The evils and injustices of present society are linked to the political elite, the constitutional order, and to the structure of society itself. And the ideology of the revolutionary movement typically assumes that wrongs can be righted by the transfer of power from one elite to another. Especially where the political formula advances the presumption of citizen efficacy in the functioning of government, revolutionary ideology attempts to demonstrate that efficacy is more myth than reality and that elections and parliamentary representation are only more subtle devices of repression and exploitation.[18]

CONTINUITY

Revolutionary ideology enhances its own legitimacy and threatens the legitimacy of the existing regime insofar as it can claim continuity with the fundamental values and goals of the society. Even leftist revolutionary ideologies frequently cite traditions of the past and argue that revolution is only the necessary means of realizing the society's basic cultural identity and historical purpose. Invariably the choice of traditions is selective, but it enables the revolutionary movement to link its actions to a part of the past and lessens the threat to its clientele of a radical break in the future.

Chinese Communism could legitimately claim continuity with earlier popular upheavals in China, including the Taiping Rebellion of 1850 to 1865 and the revolution led by Sun Yat-sen in 1911. And each of these movements in turn could claim continuity with the long-standing aspirations of important segments of Chinese society. Both Sun and Mao advocated a more equitable distribution of wealth and land, an end to poverty and economic exploitation, emphasis on the nation instead of the family and clan, and a definition of freedom in terms of collective responsibility. Both the Chinese Communists and the Taiping rebels mobilized popular support from among the same social strata and in the same regions of south China, and they both sought an end to inherited privilege, the elimination of status differences between gentry, military, and the peasantry, equality between the sexes, prohibitions on foot-binding, prostitution, the marriage of sons and daughters as arranged by parents seeking financial and social advantage, and the abolition of private ownership in land.

In fact the collectivist ethic of communism is typically based on long-standing collectivist traditions in the society itself, at least where the indigenous communist movement has been strong and has not been imposed on the society by external military force. In Russia and in parts of Yugoslavia the peasantry was long-accustomed to collective village organization, and in Russia collectivist traditions prevailed even among the landed aristocracy. The Vietnamese Communists insisted on using the Vietnamese word *xa* for "socialism," and thereby "put the future of Vietnam under the constraint of its past and of a tradition anterior to that of the French."[19] *Xa* evoked the norms of communal responsibility and collective discipline traditional to Confucianism and enabled the Communists to organize support in the Vietnamese villages in terms of past traditions as well as future hopes. Part of the explanation for Castro's success, his support from the Cuban bourgeoisie and the hesitant neutrality of the United States before 1960, was his representation of the traditions of José Martí and Castro's promise to restore the liberal constitution and to guarantee free elections.

As subsequent counterrevolution in both Cuba and North Vietnam suggest, then, the successful revolutionary movement is threatened insofar as its actual policies prove inconsistent with earlier ideals and promised programs. The very utopianism of the revolutionary ideology threatens the legitimacy of the new regime as it seeks new directions or confronts the harsh realities of implementing socioeconomic change. As is suggested by the fate of many successful anticolonial movements in the underdeveloped world, the ideology of the movement can lay the basis for its own revolutionary defeat. The extent of political stability after the capture of power, as well as the efficacy of the revolutionary movement itself, is of course closely related to the characteristics of revolutionary organization—our subject in the following chapter.

But as in the case of Mexico and Russia, continued lip service to the original ideals of the revolution can inspire commitment and sacrifice, even under the same circumstances that earlier inspired revolutionary activity. Among the animal species, man alone will die for an idea. It is the source of both his nobility and his folly. How much is nobility and how much is folly is for subsequent ideologies to judge.

FOR FURTHER TESTING

Some Propositions:

1. Nationalism and anticolonialism are the ideologies that are the most effective in creating cross-cutting alliances.
2. The weakness of counterrevolutionary movements is explained in part by their failure to develop an ideology that goes beyond the promise to return to prerevolutionary conditions.

Some Hypotheses:

1. The chances of success increase as the revolutionary movement develops an ideology that appeals to diverse strata of the population.
2. The importance of ideology varies directly with,
   a. the extent of the revolutionary movement's reliance on violence,
   b. the length of time required for the movement to capture power,
   c. the political legitimacy of the regime under attack,
   d. the extent of change (in the existing society) that is intended by the movement once it captures power.

NOTES

[1] Gasster, 1969, pp. xxiv–xxv.

[2] Gurr, 1970, p. 195. For a study of populism in Colombia and the "disparate and basically unachievable promises aimed at attracting the support of as many groups as possible," see Sanders, 1970.

[3] R. Johnson, 1972, Chap. 4.

[4] Halperin, 1964, p. 4.

[5] Quoted in Berger and Neuhaus, 1970, p. 207.

[6] Woolf, 1969, p. 112. On the function of ideology as a "scapegoating" mechanism and as a means of personalizing hostility and distress, see Smelser, 1963, Chap. 8.

[7] Leiden and Schmitt, 1968, Chaps. 8 and 9.

[8] Lawrence, 1962, Chap. 33. Confirming our finding in the preceding chapter on the small minority mobilized for revolution—even where the great mass of the population is sympathetic to the movement—Lawrence notes (p. 199) that only about 2 percent of the Arab population participated directly in the revolt against Turkish rule.

[9] Wolf, 1969, p. 32.

[10] Pinkney, 1964, p. 13.

[11] Molnar, 1965, p. 85.

[12] Boudon, 1971, pp. 140–42.

[13] Pickles, 1947, pp. 64–66, summarizes the data supporting this generalization.

[14] Berelson and Steiner, 1964, p. 621.

[15] de Tocqueville's interpretation of the effects of censorship on French revolutionary thought is summarized in Richter, 1966, p. 98.

[16] Davies, 1963, p. 349; Parsons, 1964, p. 66.

[17] The bone-chilling "Catechism of a Revolutionist," written by the Russian anarchists Bakunin and Nechaev in the nineteenth century, concluded that the "revolutionist is a doomed man" because of the moral code necessarily attached to his revolutionary commitment. On the "Catechism," see Berger and Neuhaus, 1970, p. 204.

[18] In their findings from survey research in Mexico, Italy, West Germany, Great Britain, and the United States, Almond and Verba suggest a close relationship between stable democratic government and the citizens' belief in their ability to influence its policies. See Almond and Verba, 1965, Chap. 6 and pp. 344–54.

[19] Paul Mus, as quoted in Wolf, 1969, p. 189.

*CHAPTER
SEVEN*

ORGANIZATION

SPONTANEITY

The spontaneous eruption of masses of people determined to alter the immediate circumstances of their life is a frequent event in the first stages of revolutionary movements. But despite its frequency, we understand very little about the elemental forces that suddenly galvanize thousands or even millions into collective action—action that, in an instant of history, lays bare the superficiality of constraints that structure behavior in the stable social order and in more tranquil times. What is clear is that, by itself, spontaneity is incapable of effecting revolutionary change. The study of spontaneity, then, helps to demonstrate the essential role of organization in the realization of revolutionary goals.

By definition, it is the unorganized who revolt spontaneously. But it is not tautological to say that those who revolt spontaneously are most likely to be drawn from those social groups that are the least organized and that have few if any institutional channels for expressing their claims on the system: blacks in the urban ghettos of the United States, nonunionized and disenfranchised workers, urban artisans, students, and especially peasants.

The basis for revolution in France in the eighteenth century and in China and Russia in the twentieth century was the largely spontaneous revolt of peasants. Their assault on the privileged structures of agrarian society triggered revolts in the cities and laid the foundations for more enduring revolutionary organization. In Russia after July 1917, the incidence of peasants attacking the manors of landlords and seizing their property increased as Bolshevized soldiers defected from the war zones and returned to their villages. The collapse of the Bulgarian front in 1918 was immediately followed by a spontaneous revolt of Bulgarian peasants. The Hungarian Communist government's announcement in 1953 of the ending of collectivization roused the Hungarian peasants to a spontaneous dismantling of the collective farms and the staking out of farmland for their own personal use. But precedent for these and other peasant uprisings may be found in the nineteenth century in the spontaneous mobilization of peasants in Italy and Spain, during the Taiping Rebellion in China, and even earlier during the Protestant Reformation in Central Europe.

A measure of the unpredictability of spontaneous revolt is the failure of the apostles of spontaneity (Blanqui, Bakunin, Sorel, Luxemburg and, more recently in France, Daniel Cohn-Bendit) to actually provoke the spontaneous upheavals that they considered essential to revolution. Blanqui's repeated calls for the rebellion of the Parisian artisans and workers fell on deaf ears. And yet, unaided by revolutionary leaders or ideology, these same classes spontaneously rose to overthrow the Bourbon monarchy in 1830, the Orléanist monarchy in 1848, and Louis-Napoleon in 1870. The same social classes with equivalent spontaneity attacked monarchical authority from Copenhagen to Palermo and from Paris to Budapest in the revolutions of 1848.[1]

The first industrial general strike appeared spontaneously in Russia in 1898, and spontaneous general strikes of the Russian working class occurred again in 1905 and in the February Revolution of 1917. Despite his misgivings about unorganized revolutionary activity—typical of Marx, Lenin, and all those who call themselves Marxists-Leninists—Trotsky grudgingly admitted that the February Revolution was a largely spontaneous event.[2] Spontaneous industrial strikes also took place in 1918 in Austria, Hungary, and in whole regions of the Ruhr, Upper Silesia, and in central Germany. General strikes occurred in Shanghai and Hong Kong in 1925 and in Vienna in 1927. Following the Popular Front election victory of the French left in 1936, the French working class ignited a general strike that swept from Paris to the provinces and back again to Paris, mobilizing workers, peasants, and the urban artisan classes in its wake. Spontaneous sit-down strikes and the occupation of factories by workers first appeared on a massive scale during the Popular Front movement in France. These same tactics were used again in 1968 when French workers at the Sud-Aviation plant in Nantes struck first to express economic grievances; but as the strike movement spread to other factories throughout France and was joined by other social classes, it became politicized and was aimed at toppling the Gaullist government. In Czechoslovakia and East Germany in 1953, in Hungary in 1956, and in Poland in 1956, 1970, and 1980, workers spontaneously struck to protest low wages and price increases and to express their hostility for the established regime.

As workers have become better organized and have felt represented by working-class parties in government, their potential for spontaneous collective action has declined. When they are mobilized, it frequently follows the spontaneous action of students. In Paris in 1968, police violence radicalized students whose continued resistance to authority brought the workers into the struggle, despite the protestations of the French Communist party and trade union. In Hungary in 1956, it also was the initial heroics of the Budapest students that mobilized worker, and then peasant, revolutionary activity. In Shanghai and Hong Kong in 1925, the workers acted before the students, but the students extended the movement by resorting to street demonstrations and initiating a boycott of British goods and services. Especially where the society's revolutionary potential is low and where students are without any institutional mechanism for expressing their interests, as in the United States, collective action by students is likely to be spontaneous: the United States' invasion of Cambodia in May 1970 triggered student strikes on at least fifty university campuses without any national coordination and without local student leaders knowing the full extent of the movement.

As these examples and our earlier findings on revolutionary motivation suggest, spontaneous action by peasants, workers, or students can be stimulated by a wide variety of incidents and circumstances: unemployment, inflation, military defeat, the spontaneous outburst of another social class, political crisis, or a change in government. Thus the spontaneous actions of the mass are not necessarily aimed at revolutionary change, but may be concerned only with the redress of immediate grievances.[3] It remains for revolutionary leaders, ideology, and subsequent events to give the movement a more general purpose and revolutionary direction.

Typically, however, spontaneous outbursts begin when popular attention is focused by a central event, associated with or immediately followed by some kind of confrontation with authority. A study of seventy-six race riots in the United States found that in fifty-two of them the riots followed a report of interracial strife.[4] Rumor diffusion is especially rapid in the densely populated urban environment, and the arrival of police in the black ghetto only heightens the tension that can explode spontaneously into collective violence. In Budapest in October 1956, a peaceful student demonstration with government sanction attracted large crowds of onlookers; the growing excitement of the crowd led to a clash with police; a greater mass of citizens and workers from nearby factories was drawn into a movement increasingly revolutionary in orientation.[5]

The weather, transportation routes, the availability of recreational facilities, the role of public media, and the opportunities for face-to-face communication can all affect the mobilization of the crowd for collective action.[6] But once the crowd is mobilized, the basis is laid for social behavior that would be atypical for most of the participants in a different social context. What Herbert Blumer calls "the milling process" facilitates the creation of "a common mood, feeling, or emotional impulse" that intensifies sentiment and reduces or eliminates the more normal inhibitions on individual behavior.[7] As the crowd moves from one confrontation with authority or its symbols to another, a sense of solidarity is established and the participant ceases to think of himself as a specific individual in an atomized social structure. He more willingly imitates the actions of others and is carried along by the "suggestive power" of mass participation.[8] One writer on the Hungarian Revolution of 1956 describes the more youthful partisans as inspired by a kind of "psychic compulsion" and fighting in a "somnambulistic trance . . . . It did not matter whether they lived or died. Only one thing counted: getting weapons and using them as much and as long as possible."[9]

The crowd attacks the most visible symbols of authority: the lord's manor, the tax collector's office, or the headquarters of military recruiters. The immediate object of the crowd's hostility may have functional relevance to the crowd's continued activity: a police station or military depot where the regime's authority is clearly symbolized and where arms and ammunition are stored (the Paris Bastille). A measure of the collective discipline and political intent of the crowd is its refusal to engage in random violence and general looting (unlike ghetto riots in the United States). In Budapest, the crowd attacked the central radio station in order to broadcast its demands; it invaded the offices of the Communist party newspaper and built bonfires of party literature; it tore the red star from the Hungarian flag and toppled a statue of Stalin; it attacked police stations and executed known members of the hated secret police. But the crowd's targets were selective and there was "no looting, no storming of shops, no general breakdown of discipline. The crowds did not even start an indiscriminate persecution of Communists. Even in small towns, where Party members were highly conspicuous, 'decent' Communists were left unharmed."[10]

As these examples suggest, the crowd in spontaneous revolt is not a totally amorphous mass without guidance or direction. An important part of the history of mass-based revolutionary movements is the unwritten and untold story of individuals who see what must be done and take the initiative in doing it. Who were the workers in the 1905 Russian Revolution who first determined the necessity of organization and initiated the election of delegates to a workers' soviet? Or the men and women in the February Revolution of 1917 who fraternized with soldiers and converted them to the side of the people? In the Hungarian Revolution of 1956, the street fighters organized themselves into groups and assigned each group to a specific military task. Drawing on the workers' councils in Yugoslavia and the Bolsheviks' experience with soviets, workers in Hungary and Poland in 1956 created their own workers' councils and, in Hungary, even developed a national coordinating council. But who took the initiative in these organizational efforts? And in Paris on at least a half-dozen occasions of spontaneous revolutionary activity between 1789 and 1968, who organized the construction of street barricades, the occupation of a factory, the transportation of food, blankets, and medical supplies, the intelligence network that kept the crowd informed of the movements of police and army? Small-group theory admits that there is no way of predicting when or explaining why these "central persons" undertake such "initiatory acts."[11] But the impulse toward some incipient form of organization, even in the case of "spontaneous" revolt, makes clear the impossibility of destroying one governing structure without putting another in its place.

The revolutions in Hungary in 1956 and in France in 1968, however, are perhaps the best confirmation of Rosa Luxemburg's insistence on the creative force of spontaneous revolution.[12] Revolutionary leaders and organizations, she argued, inevitably lag behind events and lack the revolutionary ingenuity inherent in the masses mobilized under their own power. She was right. But both the revolutions in Hungary in 1956 and in France in 1968 failed, as have other revolutions that lacked the means of coordinating the revolutionary movement beyond the first tremor of its spontaneous eruption. By themselves and even in de facto alliance, peasants seizing land, workers occupying factories, and students in the streets cannot accomplish revolutionary change. Spontaneity may demonstrate the potential power of revolutionary sentiment, but only organization can give it lasting effect.

STRUCTURE

The importance of organization in revolutionary movements increases as the movement's leadership lacks charismatic appeal, as its regime access is low, as the ruling political elite and its coercive apparatus remain unified, and as the revolutionary struggle is protracted through time. The comparatively short period of time involved in the capture of power by successful fascist and military-based movements, the fragility of the governments they have replaced, their relatively high regime access prior to capturing power, and the charismatic appeal of their leaders help to explain the relative weakness of rightist revolutionary organization—especially as compared with revolutionary organization on the left.

The example of communist movements also suggests that revolutionary organization is likely to be strong where the movement's ideology is a coherent and highly articulated system of values linked to prescriptions for revolutionary action. A "strong" revolutionary organization has a minimum of factional conflict and a clearly established chain of command running from the top of the organization's hierarchy to the bottom. A "strong" revolutionary organization is capable of surviving tactical military defeat and the loss of one or more of its top leaders. The organizational strength of revolutionary movements also is measured by the extent to which the movement institutionalizes the recruitment and training of its cadres, provides formal mechanisms for their socialization and continuing indoctrination in the norms of the movement, maintains channels of communication that facilitate feedback from the rank-and-file to the leadership, and creates functionally specific suborganizations charged with clearly defined tasks.

History, consequently, is filled with examples of defeated revolutionary movements that failed to meet most or all of these criteria for revolutionary organization. The Taiping Rebellion in China in the mid-nineteenth century was based on a supernatural ideology that the leaders were unable to communicate to the movement's rank-and-file; there was no system for recruiting, training, or indoctrinating its cadres; the movement's decision-making process was as unstructured as its hierarchy; and it rapidly lost vitality after the assassination of its principal leader. The efforts of Irish rebels against England since at least the late seventeenth century, and more recently the attempt of the Irish Republicans to unite Northern Ireland with the Catholic South, have been constantly plagued by intense factionalism and weak leadership. The youthful rebels in the jungles of Ceylon in 1971 were without any discernible leadership and had almost no organizational structure; armed mostly with ideals, they were an easy mark for government forces enjoying the logistical support of the Soviet Union. Unlike their revolutionary counterparts in Vietnam, the Malayan Communists were unable to secure a geographic base for their operations; they thus had no opportunity to build organizational strength on the foundations of peasant village society; and they lacked leaders with the revolutionary experience and organizational ingenuity of Ho Chi Minh and Vo Nguyen Giap.

The "stages" that revolutions traverse are determined less by the force of ideas ("extremist" or "moderate") than by the distribution of organizational strength among the competing revolutionary groups. In their struggle with the bourgeoisie, the unorganized lower classes are almost certain to fail: the bourgeoisie has "property, education, the press, a network of strategic positions, a hierarchy of institutions."[13] The revolutionary upheavals in Europe in 1848, and in France in 1789, 1830, 1848, 1870, 1936, 1944, and 1968 were based largely on the revolutionary activity of the nonpropertied classes, but it was the bourgeoisie that captured or retained power in every instance. In France in May–June 1968, attempts to organize a federation of student strike committees were regularly defeated. It was no coincidence that the organizational efforts came mostly from Trotskyites, and that their defeat reflected the militantly antiorganizational bias of the students' principal leader, Daniel Cohn-Bendit. Nor was it coincidental that the French Communist party played the major role in preventing the students from establishing organizational links with the workers' strike committees. If in 1968 there had been a French Communist party sympathetic to revolutionary change, it would have been something very different from the French Communist party.

In Mexico, too, the radicals led by Villa and Zapata were unable to coordinate their activities and, even when the two leaders met in Mexico City in 1914, they failed to develop a political organization for governing. Power first fell to the generals, and then into the hands of the oligarchs of new wealth. Only with the presidency of Lázaro Cárdenas between 1934 and 1940 were industrial and agrarian reforms implemented that approximated the ideals of the earlier revolutionaries.

Anarchist movements also have invariably failed because of the anarchists' disdain for political organization. Suited to the uncoordinated activities of workers in small workshops distributed throughout the provincial areas of industrial Europe, or to the independent status of pueblo societies in southern Spain, anarchism purposefully neglected organization and leadership. The grand assumption was that knowing the truth of human nature and understanding the appropriate form of social organization would guarantee the movement's success, and on a worldwide scale. Andalusian peasants in Spain committed to anarchism might be asked, "How would the great change come about? Nobody knew. At bottom the peasants felt that it must somehow come about if only all men declared themselves for it at the same time." [14] Anarchism has thus been characterized by a high degree of spontaneity but no organization, and so perpetual defeat.

Movements based on the sentiments generated by cultural separatism also have invariably failed without organization. Ted Gurr notes that, in northern Spain, "Basque separatists have been violently opposing foreign rulers quite literally from the beginning of recorded history, though ordinarily in the context of persisting communal rather than associational organization." [15] Basing their movement on shared values instead of on institutionalized membership and participation has meant for the Basques constant subordination to the superior organization of a centralized government.

On the other hand, the success in 1973 of the Anyanya rebels of the southern Sudan may be explained largely by their effective maintenance of an army and supporting organization for more than ten years of political and military struggle. This too was a war of cultural conflict, with the black and mostly pagan Sudanese rebels in the south seeking regional autonomy from the dominant Arab and Islamic population of the north. The rebel army consisted of between 5,000 and 8,000 soldiers (against a northern army of 15,000 to 20,000), organized into large regular combat units and smaller units of guerrillas, functioning with typewritten orders and radio communication, wearing uniforms (a useful measure of the extent of rebel organization in underdeveloped societies), supported by medical teams, and receiving part of their supplies from the air drops of Israeli aircraft. [16]

But certainly the prototype of guerrilla organization is that developed by the Vietnamese in their struggles against the Japanese, the French, and the client government of the United States in Saigon. Not one but two systems of organization linked sympathizers to followers and leaders: a territorial system of personnel drawn from villages grouped into districts, with each district subordinated to a provincial committee, the provincial committees organized into zones, and each zone reporting to the Central Committee of the Communist party; and a cross-cutting system of special-interest organizations focused on peasants, workers, women, youth, and urban cultural associations directed especially at students and intellectuals. Each member of a clientele organization was responsible for maintaining a close relationship with three nonmembers, thereby extending even further the movement's reach into the grass roots of Vietnamese society. Following Mao's insistence on *political* control over military operations, the party's authority was initially ensured through overlapping personnel who occupied the higher echelons of both the political and military hierarchies. The escalation of the war in South Vietnam after 1964, however, required increasing adaptability to changing circumstances: the military and political hierarchies became more functionally distinct, while the National Liberation Front (NLF) exercised "a tightly centralized control of policy with considerable decentralization of execution . . . ."[17]

There is the danger, however, that as the revolutionary movement is extended through time, its supporting organization will become bureaucratized and deflected from its original goals. This is especially true of political parties based on the working class, and their tendencies toward deradicalization over time have been observed by political sociologists since at least the first decades of the twentieth century (including Roberto Michels and Max Weber). Preoccupied with survival, operating in nonrevolutionary circumstances, and anxious to extend their trade-union influence and enlarge their parliamentary representation, socialist and subsequently communist parties have put political tactics in the place of revolutionary strategy. It was these trends that induced Lenin to insist on the organization of a revolutionary vanguard composed exclusively of intellectuals devoted to revolution and that convinced Rosa Luxemburg of the necessity of relying on the revolutionary spontaneity of the masses.

But there is an additional danger, perhaps even more of an obstacle to the realization of revolutionary goals. The movement's actual capture of power in no way implies that its original ideals will be implemented. Capturing power is not the same as consolidating it, and even consolidating power does not mean that the movement will achieve the socioeconomic transformations that inspired its revolutionary activity. To exercise power requires a structural change in the organization of the movement, and this is especially difficult where the struggle for power has involved the mobilization of large numbers of citizens from many social classes. The importance to successful revolution of cross-cutting alliances, emphasized in Chapter 5, may become a source of fatal weakness to the movement after its capture of power. New forms of organization are essential, and where they have not been developed (as in Republican Spain and in many of the former colonies of Black Africa), the frustration and failure of the movement is usually a matter only of time.

The Bolsheviks, however, replaced the soviets of workers', peasants', and soldiers' deputies with the Communist party. The party's consolidation of power in turn depended on the organization of the Cheka (secret police) and the Red Army. The effectiveness of Red Army units was ensured by Trotsky who reinstated the death penalty for mutiny but, more importantly, organized each military unit around a nucleus of proletarian faithful: the hard-core revolutionaries in each military unit won the loyalty of the less committed workers, and these two groups in turn were able to marshal the support of the less dependable soldier-peasants. Ultimately, as Rosa Luxemburg and even Trotsky predicted, the entire political and military apparatus was subordinated to the dictatorship of the Political Bureau of the party's Central Committee. The emergence of Stalin as dictator of the Politburo, and so dictator of the party and state apparatus, spelled the end to hopes for revolutionary social democracy, but no one could doubt the effectiveness of the organization.

And in China after 1911 and Cuba after 1959, the consolidation of revolutionary power depended on the creation of new organizational structures. The Nationalist Chinese government lacked an army and a unified party organization, and depended on "the whimsical good will of local war lords for its security."[18] Only after 1923, and with the assistance of the Soviet government and its representative Michael Borodin, were the Nationalists provided with a solid institutional base: the Kuomintang was organized along the lines of the Bolshevik party, and the Whampoa Military Academy in Canton (directed by Chiang Kai-shek) ensured a cadre of trained and trusted military officers for the Nationalist Army.

In Cuba, Castro's revolution against Batista had been relatively brief and easy, and thus there was no organization suitable to the needs of revolutionary government once power was won. The military hierarchy of the rebel army could not function as a political administration. But after 1959 there was at hand a disciplined cadre of personnel, the Cuban Communist party, characterized by a high degree of organizational and ideological cohesion. With its members infiltrated into the army, government administration, and the trade unions, and with its competitors eliminated or controlled, the Communist party provided Castro with the organizational support essential both to consolidating power and to implementing new programs. What was at issue was the replacement of Castro's 26th of July Movement with the Cuban Communist party, and Castro's own assertion of control over the latter: the purges and maneuvers of 1959 through 1962 ensured the accomplishment of both. In this sense, the imperatives of political organization can determine the ideological and programmatic orientation of the movement.

FUNCTIONS

"Structure" implies "function," and some of the principal functions of revolutionary organization should already be clear from the above. Generally, the organization of successful revolutionary movements must maintain effective command and communications links between leaders and followers. It must recruit and coordinate the efforts of activist minorities drawn from the society's various social strata. It must sustain the movement's members and their ideological commitment, and ensure logistical support for their revolutionary activities. It must adapt to new conditions as the revolutionary process is extended through time, and it must prove especially flexible and innovative after the capture of power. There are at least two specific functions of revolutionary organization, however, that deserve special emphasis.

The first relates to the cohering functions of revolutionary organization. The organization exists in part to reinforce the commitment of its members, to isolate them from nonmembers and competing sources of information and values, and to generate group loyalty and a homogeneity of opinion essential to the tasks of revolution.[19]

It may be only in the context of the revolutionary organization that an intellectual, worker, or peasant is able to develop the interpersonal relationships that give his or her life meaning and direction. And only as a member of a revolutionary organization may the individual have the sense of equality and status that he or she is denied in the larger society. There also is some evidence from social psychology that the individual's propensity for risk-taking is increased when he or she is involved in group participation and decision-making.[20]

It is typical of the history of revolutionary movements that mechanisms designed to meet these functional goals should be furthest developed in communist organizations. A local guerrilla unit of the Viet Cong is assigned a military objective, but after the plan for attack has been presented by its officers the guerrillas are asked for their comments and suggestions. There at least is the illusion of participation in decision-making. Communist regulars, semiregulars, guerrillas, and their network of supporters are periodically exposed to small-group meetings for retraining and reindoctrination. The frequent sessions of criticism and self-criticism serve to reinforce group norms, maintain ideological unity, and are an important means of communication from the lower cadres to the movement's upper hierarchy. Given authority over a local village or guerrilla unit, assigned to organize the collection and transportation of food or military supplies or to monitor and report on the movement of government troops, an individual is very likely to enjoy more status among his or her peers than he or she does in the factory, field, or office. Performing well is also likely to be rewarded by promotion and greater responsibility, thus providing the individual with an opportunity for status mobility that is unavailable outside the context of his or her revolutionary activity. And the greater his or her responsibility and status in the organization, the more the individual is compromised by his or her revolutionary role, and so the less likely he or she is to defect to the side of the government or counterrevolution.

At the same time the revolutionary organization must walk a thin line drawn between the group isolation of its members and their association with the general population. The former helps to ensure the organization's cohesion, but the latter is essential to the movement's growth and popular support. Just as Bolshevik agitators had to mingle with soldiers, workers, and peasants in order to prepare the masses for the Bolsheviks' seizure of power, Vietnamese and Chinese Communist rank-and-file were urged to practice the "three withs": eating with, working with, and living with the people. The revolutionary organization that walks this line without losing its balance is very likely to be closer to the masses than the government that claims their allegiance. It also is another measure of the structural integrity of the revolutionary organization and the effectiveness of its functioning.

The second function of revolutionary organization that deserves special attention may be described in terms of "countergovernment," "dual sovereignty," or (Trotsky's term) "dual power." The effectiveness of revolutionary organization and the likelihood of success increase as the movement is able to develop institutions that actually function as agencies of government.

The greater regime access of bourgeois and rightist revolutionary movements enables them to focus on the capture of existing institutions for the prosecution of their revolutionary objectives. The critical step for Hitler and Mussolini was their constitutional appointment as executive head of government. Subsequently, they both were able to engineer a grant of authority from parliament that, at least on the surface, appeared to legitimate their assumption of dictatorial power. Burgeois revolutionaries in France in 1789 and the Puritan revolutionaries in England in 1640 were able to seize on existing legislative institutions as the means of challenging the authority of monarchs. The Russian Duma was also the institutional basis for the liquidation of the Romanov Dynasty in the February Revolution of 1917. The task of all these revolutionaries was obviously easier because the power of the state was centralized and because existing institutions served as a basis of legitimacy for revolution. It also is obvious that the organizational structures of these revolutionary movements did not have to be as developed or as functionally specific as in the case of revolutionary movements on the left.

The case of the American Revolution helps to illustrate the relationship between revolutionary organization and the degree of centralization characterizing the existing regime. The anticolonial effort of the Americans was complicated by the diffuse structure of British authority in the colonies. The development of American revolutionary organization was consequently slow and equally diffuse. The example of leftist revolutionary movements also supports the hypothesis that the structure of revolutionary organization tends to reflect the structural characteristics of the regime under attack.

The organization of the American Revolution thus began with alliances among merchants boycotting English goods. The revolution's institutional base also was reinforced by the long experience of the colonial legislatures with virtual self-government. During the periods of declining revolutionary sentiment, the Sons of Liberty and the Committees of Correspondence helped to keep alive the revolutionary commitment of a small but ultimately influential minority of the total population. After 1774 and the convocation of the Continental Congress, the Committees of Correspondence functioned as an intelligence network observing and reporting the movements of British troops. And they eventually became the effective countergovernment to British authority in the colonies: "they punished offenders, confiscated Loyalist properties, fixed prices, collected army supplies, fitted out privateers, recruited men." [21]

It was appropriate that in 1966 Tom Hayden, perhaps the best informed and most thoughtful of young American radicals, urged "building institutions outside the established order which seek to become the genuine institutions of the total society." Hayden referred explicitly to the model of the Continental Congress during the American Revolution and suggested "a kind of second government, receiving taxes from its supporters, establishing contact with other nations, holding debates on American foreign and domestic policy, dramatizing the plight of all groups that suffer from the American system." [22]

It was precisely this kind of organizational network that the Communists in China and Vietnam were able to develop during their struggle for national power. In the areas under Communist control, and frequently in areas under the nominal control of the government, a parallel system of governing institutions collected taxes, ran the village government, organized and administered schools and courts, and implemented the economic and military policies established by the Communist party. The functional sophistication of the party's organization was indicated by the Central Committee's appointment of ministers charged with administering party policy in each of these specific areas of government. When a revolutionary organization has reached the point where it functions as a parallel government with its own shadow cabinet and fiscal resources, it is as much of an institutionalized opposition to the established regime as it is a revolutionary movement.

But the important role of dual power in revolutionary movements is perhaps best illustrated by the functions of the Russian soviets during the February and October revolutions of 1917. The Petrograd Soviet could claim political legitimacy from the very outset of the February Revolution: the Duma's appointment of Prince Lvov to head the Provisional Government was made in consultation and with the approval of the Petrograd Soviet. Even before the Bolsheviks captured a majority in the Soviet, it operated as a countergovernment, "fulfilling a whole series of governmental functions . . . ."[23] Between February and October it often was the case that the Provisional Government continued to exist only on the sufferance of the workers', soldiers', and peasants' representatives organized by the Soviet. Time and their own organizational competence worked to the advantage of the Bolsheviks.

Following the February Revolution, a system of soviets developed nationally, appearing first in March in all the industrial centers and towns and reaching the rural villages in April and May. Thus the institutional basis was finally laid in Russia for coordinating the revolutionary activity of peasants, workers, soldiers, and conspiratorial groups of intellectuals. And after July, the Bolsheviks augmented their influence in soviets throughout the country as the soviets increased their governmental functions. In many cities they were the only authority capable of organizing industrial production and supplying the local population with water, food, light, and fuel.

Coordinating the activities of the soviets was the formal task of the National Congress of Soviets, and the First Congress was convened in Petrograd in March. But the local soviets naturally tended to follow the lead of the capital, and between April 1917 and January 1918 the Petrograd Soviet sent more than 2,500 agitators into the villages and towns of sixty-five Russian provinces. Well before the October Revolution, Bolshevik organizers had engineered the support of a majority of soviet deputies.

It was through the soviets, then, that the Bolsheviks captured political power and claimed government legitimacy. Trotsky's organization of the Military Revolutionary Committee was authorized by the Petrograd Soviet, and it was this group of trained insurrectionists that carried out the actual coup d'état of October. The Congress of Soviets, with a Bolshevik majority, subsequently authorized the creation of the Council of People's Commissars, headed by Lenin. The Bolshevik government was in place, and could begin (in Lenin's words) "to construct the socialist order."

The indispensable role of the soviets in preparing the way for the Bolsheviks' seizure of power was admitted by Trotsky: "Attempts to lead the insurrection directly through the party nowhere produced results."[24] Power was not won by the Bolshevik party, but by the Bolshevik party working through the dual power structure represented by the soviets. It was an important lesson in the organization of revolutionary movements. Later revolutionaries who ignored it, including communists, courted almost certain disaster.

FOR FURTHER TESTING

Some Propositions:

1. Those who are the least integrated into society are the most likely to revolt spontaneously.

2. Revolutionary success depends in part on the organization of followers whose revolutionary sentiments may be expressed initially by spontaneous action. By itself, spontaneous revolt is not enough.
3. The characteristics of the organization must change as the revolutionary movement becomes a governing power intent on implementing its program.

Some Hypotheses:

1. The more developed and highly articulated the ideology, the stronger the organization.
2. The more that the organization is able to structure the lives of its members, the stronger the organization.
3. The chances of revolutionary success vary directly with the movement's capacity for organizing parallel structures of government within the society under attack.

NOTES

[1] Palmer, 1956, Chap. 12.

[2] Trotsky, 1957, Vol. III, pp. 172 and 280.

[3] Hobsbawm, 1959, p. 7.

[4] Gurr, 1970, p. 197.

[5] Kecskemeti, 1961, Chap. 5.

[6] Smelser, 1963, pp. 240–41.

[7] Blumer, 1939, p. 234.

[8] Le Bon, 1971, p. 164.

[9] Kecskemeti, 1961, p. 113.

[10] Kecskemeti, 1961, p. 112.

[11] Redl, 1966, pp. 82-83.

[12] See the writings assembled in Luxemburg, 1967.

[13] Trotsky, 1957, Vol. III, p. 169.

[14] Hobsbawm, 1959, p. 88.

[15] Gurr, 1970, p. 316.

[16] See the article by Stanley Meisler in the *Los Angeles Times,* Oct. 18, 1971, Part I-A.

[17] Rolph, 1971, p. 11. On the characteristics of communist guerrilla organization, also see Pike, 1966; Wolf, 1969, pp. 188–89 and 203-7; and Molnar, 1965, especially Chap. 2.

[18] North and Pool, 1965, p. 325.

[19] Gusfield, 1968, p. 448; Lipset, 1963, pp. 74–75.

[20] On the "risky shift" and the "enhancement role" of group discussion, see Myers and Bishop, 1970, and Cartwright, 1971.

[21] Beals, 1970, pp. 38–39.

[22] Hayden, 1966.

[23] Trotsky, 1957, Vol. II, p. 321. Also see Janos, 1964, pp. 136–37.

[24] Trotsky, 1957, Vol. III, p. 283.

TECHNIQUES

VIOLENCE

"Violence" refers to those actions by individuals or groups that endanger the physical security of people or property. The threat of violence, its actual employment, and its ideological justification for political ends are among the clearest indicators of a social movement's revolutionary intent.

Violence may precede or follow the movement's capture of power, or it may prove indispensable to the movement throughout most or all of the stages of the revolutionary process. But the range and intensity of violence are likely to vary from one revolutionary movement to another according to several variables, including the following: the extent of the movement's popular support and regime access, the strength of its organization, the unity and violence of its opposition, the degree of political and socioeconomic change intended, and the role of foreign states in support of or in opposition to the movement.

These several variables may interact and thereby complicate the explanation of the range and intensity of violence characterizing the movement. By themselves, high regime access and strong popular support are likely to coincide with a low level of violence. But weak organization and an entrenched opposition, in government or on the political left or right, may require heavy reliance on violence in order to win power and to consolidate it.

With reference to the role of foreign states, however, it seems clear that the level of violence is raised when foreign intervention supports the revolutionaries or, after their capture of power, their counterrevolutionary opponents. In Turkey, Egypt, and Cuba, for example, the level of revolutionary violence was relatively low, especially in comparison to the violence of the French and Russian revolutions. This may be explained largely by the weakness or absence of "an émigré group plotting with foreign invaders to overturn the revolution and reinstall the *ancien régime.*"[1] In Cuba, where foreign intervention did occur (in 1961 at the Bay of Pigs), the lack of popular support for the counterrevolutionaries and their own logistical weakness enabled the Castro government to beat back the invasion with a minimum of effort. The consolidation of power after the Mexican and American revolutions also was a relatively nonviolent undertaking: compared to more violent revolutions, the degree of socioeconomic change projected by the new elites was slight, and the consolidation of the revolution's political authority was largely unchallenged by domestic interests and foreign states.

Whatever its range or intensity, however, violence is a common thread running through all revolutionary movements, whether on the left, center, or right. Despite the gloss of legality that attended Hitler's and Mussolini's accession to constitutional power, the force of their movements depended in large part on the blatant use of violence against the opponents of fascism and the threat of violence against the state itself. With its ideology glorifying the ethic of violence and claiming that authority was inherent in physical superiority, fascism organized gangs of thugs and its own paramilitary units to beat up and intimidate socialists, communists, trade unionists, uncooperative public officials, Jews, and all those who subscribed to norms more suitable to a civilized society. Once in power, fascism immensely strengthened the police apparatus of the state in order to eliminate its opposition and centralized political authority in order to consolidate its hold over the whole population. It is in this sense that fascism deserves to be classified among the several types of revolutionary movements discussed in this book.

The pervasive role of violence in revolution, and the broad implications of violence as a conceptual category, suggest the utility of distinguishing violence according to at least three specific techniques: terror, guerrilla warfare, and coup d'état. The first two techniques characterize revolutionary movements with low regime access; successful guerrilla warfare demands especially competent revolutionary organization and substantial popular support; but the technique of coup d'état is appropriate to a variety of revolutionary (and nonrevolutionary) circumstances. Coups d'état, in fact, are so adaptable to varying political circumstances that only hindsight can tell us whether or not a particular coup deserves to be classified as a part of the revolutionary process in any given political system. But there is no doubt about the revolutionary intent of organized guerrillas and terrorists.

TERROR

Terror includes assassination, kidnapping, and bombing, and is intended to disorient the psychology of the individual in the social mass in the same way that sabotage is designed to disrupt the production, transportation, and communications systems of the state. Terror ultimately attacks men's minds while sabotage directly attacks the tangible instruments of government and authority.

The principal function of terror, then, is to convince people that the revolutionary movement is powerful and that the power of the state is weak. Terror is designed to increase the individual's feeling of isolation and helplessness, thereby enhancing his susceptibility to the appeals of the revolutionary movement.[2]

It is absolutely essential to understand that terror is an effective instrument of social mobilization only in the initial stages of revolutionary activity and only where the general population is sympathetic to the goals of the revolutionaries. This of course is most likely to be the case in underdeveloped societies dominated by a foreign state, and where the large majority of the population is unorganized and unrepresented in the policy-making apparatus of government.[3]

An exclusive reliance on terror as a revolutionary technique, however, is a certain sign of the movement's weakness. In Malaya, the Communists resorted to mass terror when it became apparent that they could not win a guerrilla war, but their terror campaign only further alienated potential supporters and strengthened the resolve of the government to liquidate the insurgency.[4] As its use and effects become familiar, terror ceases to be efficacious in creating social and psychological disorder and in mobilizing support for the movement. Marx, Lenin, and Régis Debray are among those proponents of revolution who have admitted that terror alone can never bring about revolutionary change, that having to rely primarily on terror reflects the impossibility of achieving revolutionary goals under prevailing circumstances, and that revolutionary movements on the left invariably deviate from socialist ideals insofar as terror is their principal weapon for capturing and maintaining power.[5]

The initiation of a campaign of terror, then, should coincide with other revolutionary strategies—including sustained efforts at grass-roots organization and the widespread dissemination of antigovernment propaganda. The terror campaign itself should begin with a crash, broad in range and high in intensity. The objects of attack should appear to be randomly chosen, thereby heightening the population's sense of physical and thus psychological insecurity.

But, in fact, the terrorists must choose their targets with care in order not to alienate the very sectors of the population essential to the further development of the movement. History is filled with examples of terrorists who generated counterproductive results by indiscriminate slaughter, and children, women, and political leaders with whom the public identifies are targets that must be scrupulously avoided. The fate of anarchist terrorism confirms the point. And the results of terrorist bombings and shootings in the southern United States by white supremacists, in Quebec by French-speaking separatists, in England and Northern Ireland by Protestant and Catholic extremists, in Italy by the Red Brigades, and in West Germany by the Baader-Meinhof gang, are only more contemporary indications of the counterproductive effects of terrorism where there is neither political organization nor popular support to lend it revolutionary impact. Terrorists must be sensitive to that ill-defined threshold beyond which continued terror lays the basis for their own betrayal and defeat.

The function of terror is also to provoke massive and indiscriminate violence against the population by the state's police and military apparatus. Not knowing where the terrorists will strike next can immobilize thousands of government troops, constrained to take up a defensive posture by guarding officials, residences, offices, and utilities and communications installations. Soldiers and police, frustrated by their inability to provoke a direct confrontation, and thinking themselves the next target of terrorist violence, can be made to behave irrationally and with brutality. House-to-house searches by government troops in the Moslem quarter of Algiers, transportation check points, curfews, citizen harassment, and the imprisonment and torture of suspected rebels, all helped to confirm the Algerian rebels' claims that French colonialism was repressive and thereby reinforced nationalist sentiment among the Arab population. Insofar as the government itself is provoked into committing random acts of terror and violence, its claims of being the guardian of law and order and the source of legitimate authority are seriously weakened.[6]

Terror on a sufficient scale can also disrupt the functioning of government. In South Vietnam between 1959 and 1964, the Viet Cong assassinated more than 6,000 minor government officials, including province chiefs, police, medical personnel, and schoolteachers, many of whom played additional roles as government informers and intelligence operatives. These targets of Viet Cong violence were frequently viewed by local peasants as outside authority figures imposed on them by the centralizing government in Saigon.

But the terror campaign of the Viet Cong also was coordinated with the organization of a guerrilla army and the implantation of Communist political organization in Vietnamese villages. Terror was not the principal technique of the Communist insurgency in South Vietnam. As the Vietnamese war escalated and the United States intervened on a massive scale, however, terror continued to play an important role: declining Viet Cong and NLF recruitment was positively correlated in the same areas with an increasing incidence of kidnapping. And after the defeat of the Communists' Tet New Year's offensive in 1968, terror in South Vietnam seemed to be primarily for the purposes of maintaining the cohesion of the rebel cadres, advertising their continued if weakened presence, and enhancing the Communists' bargaining position in international negotiation.[7]

GUERRILLA WARFARE

Unlike the Communist insurgency in South Vietnam, however, Communist revolutionary movements in North Vietnam and China were largely devoid of terror. This reflected the early establishment of secure areas of rebel control serving as a base for guerrilla operations and political organization, and confirms our finding of the utility of terror (if at all) only in the initial stages of revolutionary organization. Where a solid basis for revolutionary organization already exists, terror is unnecessary, even counterproductive, and Ho Chi Minh and Mao Tse-tung consequently have little to say about the role of terror in revolution. Their emphasis instead is on the techniques of guerrilla warfare.

But guerrilla warfare is peculiar to neither Communist revolution in Asia nor mass-based insurrection in the twentieth century. Some form of guerrilla organization and activity characterizes most of the violent efforts by native peoples to resist collectively the invasion and oppression of foreigners, especially where the foreigners are superior in military organization and armament. The ancient Hebrews and the early Romans were acquainted with the rudimentary techniques of guerrilla warfare. Caesar's legions encountered guerrilla resistance in Gaul. French and British soldiers and, subsequently, white frontiersmen and settlers from the eastern United States fought the guerrilla tactics of American Indians in order to deprive them of the land that was essential to the Indians' economic and cultural well-being. British troops in the American Revolution were harassed by irregular American forces that frequently took advantage of the British military's commitment to conventional warfare. South African Bushmen organized guerrilla resistance against the territorial invasion of Dutch-descended Boers and were defeated only after a prolonged struggle in 1795. Counterrevolution in France after 1789 often took the form of guerrilla warfare, in the Vendée as well as in other parts of western France.

The word "guerrilla" derives from the Spanish word for "war" (*guerra*) and was first applied to the popular Spanish resistance to Napoleon's armies that invaded Spain in 1808. The unity of the Spanish peasantry, clergy, and nobility in their guerrilla resistance to Napoleon was enhanced by their common devotion to "Religion, King, and Country," and the French armies never completely pacified the Spanish population. But Spain itself was later troubled by guerrilla warfare in the Spanish American colonies, especially in Cuba where prolonged conflict finally erupted into full-scale war in 1896.

In the twentieth century, T. E. Lawrence was the first theorist of guerrilla warfare and, at the same time, a leader of guerrilla partisans. Lawrence drew an explicit parallel between the mobility of naval vessels at sea and the tactical advantages of his Arab followers in the desert. Between 1916 and 1918, the Arab guerrillas under Lawrence's leadership weakened the Turkish Army by attacking its lines of communication and supply, while avoiding a direct military confrontation.

> Our cards were speed and time, not hitting power. The invention of bully beef had profited us more than the invention of gunpowder, but gave us strategical rather than tactical strength, since in Arabia range was more than force, space greater than the power of armies.[8]

During and after the Second World War, guerrilla warfare marked the struggles of insurrectionary movements in Palestine, Greece, Yugoslavia, Malaya, Ceylon, the Philippines, Algeria, behind the military lines in Korea, in China, Vietnam, Laos, and Burma, in the southern regions of Oman and the Sudan, in the Portuguese colonies of Africa, and—after 1959—in almost all of the countries of Latin America. Nor is this a complete listing, but it gives us a better understanding of the important role in revolutionary movements of guerrilla warfare and provides us with a respectable sample for generalizing about its prominent characteristics.

As in the case of terror, guerrilla warfare cannot succeed without the support and sympathy of a broad sector of the population. The guerrilla leans heavily on the willingness of the rural or urban dweller to provide him with food, shelter, information, additional recruits, and to remain silent about guerrilla identities and activities when questioned, even tortured, by government police and military. Thus the critical importance in peasant guerrilla warfare of winning the support of the peasantry: in Andalusia in the 1950s and in Ceylon in 1971, hard-pressed guerrillas attacked local villages and isolated peasants in order to steal food and money, thereby alienating the population on which they depended and signaling the imminent defeat of the guerrillas by government forces. The weakness of guerrilla movements in South America since the high point of their activities between 1963 and 1965, especially in Bolivia, Colombia, and Venezuela, may be explained in part by the apparent apathy, even hostility, of the peasantry to guerrilla organizers and insurrectionary adventure. The first mistake of the guerrilla revolutionary is also his biggest mistake: to assume, as did Che Guevara in Bolivia, that all that is needed for peasant-based revolution is the presence of armed men preaching liberation from oppression.

In China, Vietnam, and Cuba, however, great care was taken to cultivate the sympathy and support of the peasantry, a task made all the easier in China and Vietnam by the visible presence of foreign troops and colonial authority. Vietminh and Viet Cong guerrillas were constantly urged by their leaders to treat prisoners humanely and to respect the property of peasant villagers. Mao frequently won converts to Chinese Communism by showing captured government soldiers (usually of peasant origin) the salutary effects of Communist agrarian reform and then releasing them with enough money to make their way back to their homes and villages. Régis Debray has emphasized the importance of raising the political consciousness of peasants by ensuring their daily contact with the guerrillas, who must share the peasants' living conditions, work by their side, and help them with concrete tasks that improve the material circumstances of peasant life. A major advantage of capturing peasant support is the kinship network that is consequently made available to the movement: each peasant guerrilla operating in his own village or province can take advantage of acquaintances as well as relatives for the purposes of refuge, recruitment, and information.[9]

Only with local support, then, can the guerrillas establish the geographic base necessary for extending their military and political operations. Ideally, the guerrilla base is in rugged terrain that impedes the movement of government troops. It should be near the border of a country friendly to the guerrilla movement, where sanctuary is available for the guerrillas and where the intelligence operations and jurisdiction of the government are less well established. It should provide the guerrillas with economic self-sufficiency. But it must not be so isolated that the guerrillas are removed from the native population that, again, is the ultimate source of their strength.[10] Debray's emphasis on the importance of constant mobility, and the necessity of a daily relocation of the guerrilla base, reflects the weakness of guerrilla movements in Latin America in the 1960s. Without a base of operations, without a "liberated zone" that enables the movement to implant its political organization and to demonstrate its program for social and economic reform, the guerrillas are forever on the run and are more concerned with tactical survival than with the conquest of political power.

Mobility, however, does characterize the early and intermediate stages of the guerrillas' military operations. Ambush is the principal military tactic (and in South Vietnam a variant of ambush, the booby trap): surprise and maneuver must be made to work to the advantage of the guerrillas, and for every successful ambush they gain weapons and supplies, lower the enemy's morale, and, politically, demonstrate the vulnerability of the government and thereby enhance their appeal to a population normally subdued by the myth of the government's invincibility. Mao's canons on the appropriate tactics for the Red Army may be summarized as follows.

1. Guerrilla warfare is a protracted struggle, and the enemy is defeated more by attrition and demoralization than by decisive military confrontation.
2. Military engagement, then, must be undertaken only when it will produce a quick and favorable result for the guerrilla forces.
3. The guerrillas must maintain their mobility and avoid positional warfare and the establishment of fixed lines of battle.
4. Military operations must be designed to destroy the fighting capability of the government units under attack and not merely to force their retreat.

5. Guerrilla forces, then, should be concentrated rather than dispersed, and the enemy should be attacked at one point rather than at several points at the same time.
6. The guerrilla units must be largely self-sufficient, and logistical and supply organizations must be kept to the barest minimum.
7. The party must control the military.
8. The command structure of the military hierarchy must be centralized, but the lower levels of the hierarchy must be allowed tactical independence for guerrilla organization and operations.
9. The guerrillas must never plunder the peasantry and, instead, must "oppose bandit ways, and uphold strict political discipline." [11]

Guerrilla warfare obviously is not for innocent youths motivated primarily by romantic idealism. It is for seasoned veterans whose living conditions are constantly in flux, but are always hard and verging on the intolerable. "Guerrilla warfare," Debray writes, "is above all an endurance test of forced marches in difficult terrain rather than a series of military engagements, which in fact should be avoided rather than sought. In this perspective, romanticism is swiftly dissolved." [12]

This explains the importance of careful recruitment in the building of the guerrilla cadre and its hard core of guerrilla fighters. New recruits may be added only on the personal recommendation of trusted veterans, and they in turn will be held accountable in the event of the recruit's defection or betrayal. But as the guerrillas are transformed by their success into a large army, and as the protracted struggle moves toward its final stage of decisive engagement along the lines of conventional warfare, a less discriminating recruitment program is initiated appealing to the mass base of the society. Attrition and demoralization of the government's fighting personnel have taken their toll, and the mounting military success of the movement encourages both rural and urban citizens to join its ranks. The organizational network is developed that will enable the revolutionaries to consolidate power and administer the society after the enemy's defeat. And the enemy's defeat is close at hand when the life of the cities is choked off by guerrilla control of the countryside (as in China in 1949) or when the enemy is dealt a major military blow (as befell the French at Dienbienphu in 1954).

But this happy scenario of events, from the guerrillas' perspective, is likely to be troubled by frequent reverses and many unanticipated difficulties. By the late 1960s the development of sophisticated counterinsurgency techniques suggested the declining utility of guerrilla warfare for revolutionary change in all but the most underdeveloped and strife-torn societies. The following section, then, may be read from a negative point of view: what guerrilla movements in the 1980s and beyond must take advantage of or avoid if they are to maximize their chances of success.

COUNTERINSURGENCY
TECHNIQUES

Counterinsurgency obviously failed in North Vietnam and, in retrospect (typical of the problems of hypothesizing about revolution), it seems that everything the French did only contributed to their defeat. Betraying an "administrative mentality" that insists on pacifying even the most remote areas under colonial jurisdiction, the French refused to concentrate their forces in the more easily controlled urban centers of Indochina. They instead sought to hold outlying positions in mountainous terrain where the Vietminh enjoyed a marked advantage. The French fought conventionally, from fixed positions, and frequently overextended their forces, which were heavily dependent on logistical supply from urban areas. The defeat of guerrilla insurgency requires a personnel ratio of *at least* five to one in favor of government forces. But the French were never able to field more than 450,000 men against a Vietminh force of 350,000. In Greece, the insurgent guerrillas were defeated by government troops enjoying an eight to one advantage. And in Algeria, the French eventually mobilized sixteen counterinsurgents for every one Algerian rebel.[13]

In Algeria between 1954 and 1956, however, the French were unable to suppress the guerrilla activities of the rebel Army of National Liberation (ALN). The ALN operated in the desert and mountainous areas of Algeria and enjoyed the active support or sympathy of most of the Arab and Berber populations. But in 1956 a substantial increase in the size of the French Algerian Army and a major revision in French military strategy reversed the earlier success of the guerrillas. Contrary to their counterinsurgency efforts in Indochina, the French in Algeria concentrated their military forces in the towns and centers of transportation and communication. They also used mobile units of seasoned fighters (including paratroopers and Foreign Legionnaires) to probe the Algerian hinterland, harassing guerrillas and breaking down their systems of intelligence and supply. The success of these tactics and the subsequent defeat of the ALN's urban terrorist campaign forced the guerrillas into border areas adjoining Tunisia and Morocco. The French then cordoned off each of the ALN's military districts, isolating each from the other thereby preventing the coordination of guerrilla activities, and proceeded to attack each district in turn. A major part of the French counterinsurgency effort involved the massive relocation of almost two million Algerian peasants and tribal people to areas more easily controlled by the government. The ALN was consequently isolated and unable to carry out effective guerrilla operations. But the repression characterizing the French counterinsurgency campaign, and especially the effects of the relocation program, intensified Algerian nationalism in inverse relation to the military success of the French. And the extreme costliness of the war, plus the factionalism and war-weariness of the French government in Paris, laid the basis for eventual Algerian independence.[14]

Counterinsurgency warfare, then, is primarily a struggle by the government for the minds and sympathies of the native population. The guerrillas, even if defeated, can thus force the government to atone for years of neglect and exploitation, and the record of history—unfortunately for the millions who have suffered—shows that violence can indeed induce governments to implement needed social, economic, and political change.[15]

The fall of South Vietnam to the Communists in 1975, however, confirmed the prior suspicions of many students of southeast Asian politics: that the agrarian reform program of the South Vietnamese government, finally implemented in 1970, was a classic example of much too little far too late. Counterinsurgency in South Vietnam also was impeded by the coercion that underlay the antiguerrilla programs of Saigon and the United States. Jungle defoliation, chemical warfare, the destruction of crops and animals, indiscriminate bombing, and the beating and torturing of Viet Cong captives and suspects only confirmed the arguments of Communist propaganda. The strategic hamlet program, designed to isolate the peasantry from the guerrillas (as in Algeria and Malaya), was initiated by the forced removal of peasants from their homes and villages, which frequently were destroyed by government troops in the process of evacuating the population.

It is true that massive repression can succeed, at least temporarily, in curtailing guerrilla activities. But the lasting success of counterinsurgency warfare depends on inducement, not coercion. The minds and sympathies of people are won by convincing them that their life is likely to be better under the existing government, and not by destroying their crops and homes and killing their friends and relatives. When guerrilla insurgency has reached the point where it can be defeated only by the widespread destruction of natural resources and the indiscriminate killing of citizens, reasonable men are likely to doubt that the costs to humanity are justified by the guerrillas' defeat.

The successful counterinsurgency campaign of the Philippine government against the Huk guerrillas, concluded by 1954, thus involved major efforts aimed at agrarian reform and controlling the indiscriminate violence of government troops. A "military complaint office" was established to carry out a rapid investigation of all charges of military brutality, and severe sanctions were administered against government personnel in substantiated cases.

The success of the British in Malaya and Kenya also confirms the importance to counterinsurgency warfare of minimizing citizen contact with the government's military forces. In Malaya a specially created federal police proved more effective than government troops in working with the native population, especially where the police resided in those areas under their supervision and were known by the local population. In striking contrast to counterinsurgency in Algeria and South Vietnam, the government's strategic hamlet program in Malaya was based more on inducement than on coercion: the Briggs Plan included the resettling of 400,000 Malayans in 410 "New Villages," more easily policed but also offering citizens improved living conditions and better health and school facilities. The relocated Chinese squatter peasants were given leases for the farming of their own land. Defections from the guerrillas' ranks were encouraged more by the persuasion of the guerrillas' friends and relatives (especially in Kenya) than by the propaganda of the government media. Through these personal contacts defectors were promised not punishment but monetary rewards and job training to develop employment skills. The British also accelerated their program for Malayan self-government and established political parties and a government coalition composed of representatives from Malaya's major ethnic groups, including the indigenous Chinese who had been the recruitment base for the Communist guerrillas.

The inducement part of the counterinsurgency campaign in Malaya was supplemented by the use of small mobile units of seasoned jungle fighters and the centralization of all intelligence operations in the office of the British High Commissioner. Malaya's border with Thailand was sealed off from the guerrillas thereby denying them sanctuary and external supply, and they were unable to establish a fixed base of operations. Antiguerrilla activities consequently came to be better coordinated than the activities of the guerrillas themselves, and the elimination of their military advantage was reinforced by the government's institution of photo-identity cards for all citizens and careful monitoring of the distribution of food: in areas of guerrilla concentration, canned goods were punctured to prevent the guerrillas from accumulating large food supplies. In the implementation of their counterinsurgency program, the British were aided by a well-trained and professional civil service, whose administrative competence far surpassed that of the corrupt civil service systems of the Kuomintang in China and the Saigon government in South Vietnam. The best counterinsurgency program on paper is likely to remain a dead letter if those responsible for administering it and servicing the civilian population are dedicated more to personal gain than to social welfare.[16]

The administrative incompetence and political corruption of the Batista regime in Cuba also worked against its antiguerrilla efforts, which were largely uninformed on the counterinsurgency techniques developed by the French and British in Asia and Africa. The success of the Castro guerrillas in Cuba in 1959 meant, however, that similar revolutionary techniques were likely to fail elsewhere in Latin America. Alerted to the importance of developing sophisticated counterinsurgency warfare, Latin American governments by the mid-1960s had effectively eliminated the threat of large-scale guerrilla activity. The beneficiaries of substantial military supply and training programs provided by the United States, they have been able to coordinate amnesty and inducement programs with the coercive skills of mobile ranger units armed with the most modern weapons. Even the Batista government, with all its vulnerabilities, would very likely have succeeded in altering the fate of the Castro guerrillas in the Sierra Maestra with the surface and aerial mobility provided by a handful of helicopter gunships. The appearance of urban guerrillas in Latin America in the mid-1960s, especially the Tupamaros in Uruguay, suggested in fact the effectiveness of counterinsurgency techniques and the low potential for guerrilla organization in the Latin American countryside.

But urban-based revolutionaries deserve more the label of "terrorist" than "guerrilla." Their mobility is extremely limited, it is almost impossible for them to concentrate and move groups of armed men, and they obviously have no opportunity to establish a fixed base and liberated zone for revolutionary operations and government. The assassination of an agent of government repression, an occasional attack on police, or the kidnapping of public officials or wealthy citizens to secure the release of imprisoned partisans, to force the government's extension of civil liberties, or to collect ransom money (even when it is distributed to the urban poor and unemployed), represent more of a harassment to the regime than a revolutionary threat. The weakness of both urban terrorists and rural guerrillas, now and in the foreseeable future in most of the countries of the world, suggests the necessity of developing new techniques if revolutionary movements are to enhance their chances of success. But an old technique is almost always close at hand, and it is likely to remain a principal means of effecting political change—the coup d'état.

COUP D'ÉTAT

The French word *coup* has the same meaning as its Latin and Greek origins, "blow," and *coup d'état* literally means "blow" or "stroke of state." Thus the term originally implied a sudden and unconstitutional seizure of power by individuals or groups already in a position of political authority.

This meaning is accurately represented by the coup d'état that Louis-Napoleon engineered after his election as president of the Second French Republic in 1848. On December 2, 1851, he dissolved the legislature and government troops occupied its meeting place. An uprising of Paris workers was suppressed. The assumption of dictatorial power was quickly ratified (in January 1852) by a national plebiscite marked by voter intimidation and electoral manipulation. Louis-Napoleon nonetheless enjoyed substantial popularity, and his repression of republicans and working-class radicals received the support of French conservatives, including the large majority of the peasantry, the army, and those in the hierarchy of the Church.

This in turn suggests that, however sudden and efficient the technique of coup d'état, the durability of the new regime depends on the range and representativeness of citizen interests mobilized in its behalf. And, as in the case of terror and guerrilla warfare, a successful coup d'état involves much more than the ingenuity or ambitions of those who are responsible for the firing of bullets or the stuffing of ballot boxes. Its chances for lasting success increase as the coup conspirators are more unified among themselves, as their regime access is higher prior to the coup, as they can generate popular support before and after the coup, and insofar as they can avoid alternative techniques of political violence that depend on the mobilization of larger numbers of citizens. Mass insurgency or a general strike, for example, are more difficult to control; they give the coercive apparatus of the state an opportunity to deploy and use its power; and they can lay the basis for revolutionary activity that might threaten the very objectives of the coup conspirators.

The political objectives represented by a coup d'état, however, can range widely: from reaction (Louis-Napoleon's coup in 1851 or, in 1923, General Primo de Rivera's coup against the Spanish parliament) through conservatism to radical socioeconomic change. Most military coups in Latin America since the mid-1930s have been conservative in inspiration, designed "to thwart the election majority" and to prevent reformist politicians from threatening the status of an entrenched oligarchy.[17] Trotsky and the Bolsheviks, however, made it clear that a coup d'état can also serve the interests of left-wing revolution. The adaptability of the coup to varying political objectives reflects the variety of circumstances in which coups d'état can be mounted against the state. But we are likely to be forewarned of attempted revolutionary change the more that the coup conspirators include nongovernmental personnel within their ranks and the more that the actual seizure of power is accompanied by collective violence.

The revolutionary intent of the architects of a coup d'état is especially obvious when, after seizing power, they attempt to build new structures of political organization outside the framework of the existing government and party system. Such was the case in both Egypt and Bolivia after 1952 when military coups overturned existing regimes as a prelude to efforts toward far-reaching socioeconomic change. But unlike revolutionary movements based on guerrilla warfare or other techniques of mass mobilization, ideology is likely to play a minimal role in the revolutionary movement initiated by a coup. Nasser's reform programs after 1952, for example, were characterized more by improvisation than doctrinal direction, and a relatively coherent ideology of Egyptian socialism emerged only in 1961.[18]

"Coup d'état," then, has come to mean any alteration in policy-making personnel according to unconstitutional procedures, whether or not the coup conspirators enjoy prior political authority. But they are likely to have some institutional base of power within the existing political system (typically in the military hierarchy),[19] a largely nonideological orientation, and low organizational support (especially as compared with the organizers of guerrilla warfare); and the incidence of violence and the number of citizens involved in the seizure of power are likely to be relatively small. As in the case of "revolution" or "revolutionary process," the problem of defining a "coup d'état" is one of more-or-less, not either-or.

The adaptability of the coup d'état to varying political and social objectives is conveniently illustrated by the similarities between the Bolsheviks' seizure of power in 1917 and the techniques employed by the Italian Fascists in 1922.[20] In fact, Mussolini and the leaders of his Black Shirt *squadri* appear to have studied closely the coup techniques implemented by Trotsky, who rejected the strategy of general strike and mass insurrection advocated by Stalin and Lenin's argument for "dealing the chief blow against the government from outside Petrograd," mainly by relying on "military forces from Finland."[21] Trotsky clearly understood that the organizational strength of the Bolsheviks, the pro-Bolshevik orientation or neutrality of the military garrisons, and the weakness of the Provisional Government were conducive to revolutionary techniques of a much lower profile, and that the "art of insurrection" is in part the application of the least amount of force necessary to seize the strategic centers of power.

Both the Bolsheviks and the Italian Fascists, then, were able to neutralize or capture the support of the military and police. Both relied on the coercive effectiveness of paramilitary units of trained insurrectionists and technicians, the latter skilled in the operation of telephone and telegraph exchanges, electrical power facilities, and railway and traffic control systems. Both the Bolsheviks and the Fascists capitalized on the unwillingness or the inability of the existing governments to act swiftly and with resolution and decisiveness against the revolutionary threat. And at the appointed hour, both quickly occupied the principal centers of communication and transportation. The Bolsheviks could rely on their control of the mass organizations and the soviets organized by workers, soldiers, and peasants. The Fascists, prior to their "March on Rome" in October 1922, already had seized power in Tuscany. Mussolini's appointment by the king as premier and the Bolsheviks' dissolution of the Constituent Assembly (where they were in a minority) only ratified a *fait accompli.*

But by far the greatest number of coups d'état have occurred in the underdeveloped countries of Asia, Africa, the Middle East, and Latin America. In these countries a successful coup typically has involved fewer personnel and lower levels of violence and organization than in the case of the Bolsheviks' and Fascists' seizures of power. Most of these coups have been initiated by junior or middle-rank officers in the military. But politicians, civil servants, and business leaders have frequently played an important supporting role.[22]

It is the military, however, that is especially sensitive to the need for modernization in order to augment the military power of the state. The military also is likely to be especially intolerant of the factionalism of civilian politicians and the high incidence of corruption typical of government bureaucracies in most underdeveloped societies. The military's seizure of power is facilitated by the extreme centralization of political authority in the hands of a few political leaders who are concentrated in the capital, where the public media play a minimal role in political communication, where the urban population is small, and where most citizens are unorganized and without an established political orientation. These preconditions for a successful coup d'état are, obviously, most likely to be found in an underdeveloped society, small in population and geographic size, where the legitimacy of the state is more a function of political personality than institutionalized authority.

The potential for a coup d'état is especially high after the civilian politicians, frequently handicapped by an economy dependent on a single export commodity, have been unable to fulfill the popular expectations generated by the winning of independence from a colonial power. But once the military seizes the reins of government and finds itself confronted by the same intractable problems that overwhelmed its predecessors, the stage is set for factional conflict within the military, and a succession of apparently unending coups d'état. The coup becomes an established convention of political life, and its frequency even lends it a kind of quasi-constitutional legitimacy.

This explains the high incidence of military-based coups d'état in the underdeveloped world since the Second World War. There were fourteen successful coups in the thirty-five independent and nonwhite African countries between 1946 and 1967, and in these same countries there was a much larger number of unsuccessful coups, insurrections, and army mutinies.[23] Of the fifty-six states that achieved independence after the Second World War, one-third had their governments overthrown by the military by 1968.[24] Even in the older states of Latin America, there were thirty-one successful coups between 1945 and 1955, and one student of Latin American politics (E. Fossum) has counted ninety-five successful coups in the twenty Latin American countries between 1907 and 1966.[25] The 1970s, however, proved to be a banner decade for successful coups, with military elites seizing power at various times in Ecuador, Honduras, Uruguay, Argentina, El Salvador, and also in Pakistan, Thailand, Portugal, Ethiopia, Ghana, Niger, and Uganda.[26] Nor is this a complete listing. But no listing could even approximate completeness without the addition of Bolivia, which underwent successful coups in 1970, 1971, 1978, 1979, and in 1980.

That violence begets violence is suggested by the close relationship between the high frequency of coups d'état and earlier anticolonial struggles characterized by prolonged and intensive conflict: two-thirds of the countries included in this category experienced a successful coup after winning their independence.[27] That coup begets coup is suggested by the concentration of coups in a handful of countries, especially in Latin America: for example, during their approximately 160 years of independence, Bolivia has recorded 189 assorted coups and uprisings, while the comparable figure for Honduras is 137.

A critical factor helping to explain the frequency of coups d'état is the extent to which the winning of political independence was accompanied by the development of a mass-based organization oriented toward socioeconomic change. Here again is the obvious advantage accruing to revolutionaries of an ideology based on nationalism, an ideology that is given its most powerful political expression through the technique of guerrilla warfare as directed by a strong revolutionary party. Especially in Latin America, however, the relative weakness of revolutionary movements and the high incidence of coups d'état reflect the early attainment of independence from Spain and Portugal (in the early nineteenth century), well before the advent of social and economic modernization. The independence movement in these countries was largely an affair of the indigenous elites, and nationalism only entrenched the feudal-type oligarchies of Latin America, uniting landowners, Church, and military in the preservation of their social status, wealth, and political power.[28] More contemporary radicals and revolutionaries in most Latin American countries (Cuba and Chile are exceptions) have been unable to give their efforts the authority imparted by a strong nationalist appeal against a clear case of colonial exploitation. The frequency of coups d'état in Latin America is a sobering comment on the low (rather than high) revolutionary potential of these particular societies.

It is through the military coup d'état, then, that upwardly mobile citizens (especially in the junior officer ranks) may most readily express their claims on the society's existing institutions. For them, the issue is related more to personal status, political power, and patronage distribution than to fundamental social change. Many students of the coup d'état in general and Latin American politics in particular agree that the functions of a coup d'état are analogous to those of elections and popular referenda in more stable societies. In this sense, the coup d'état represents an institutionalized means of political competition.[29] This is especially true of political systems where parties are weak and, consequently, where there are few if any channels for the expression of political opposition. The military becomes the principal, in some cases the only, vehicle for political opposition and status mobility.[30]

But the use of a coup d'état for narrow political or personal advantage is obviously inconsistent with the pursuit of revolutionary goals. It is worth repeating here that we can judge only after the fact whether or not a coup d'état merits classification as part of the revolutionary process for a particular society. And this is likely to be the case only where the new elite organizes political support on a mass base and outside the existing structures of government. Otherwise, the leaders of a successful coup lay the basis for their own defeat (and another coup) as they advance programs that threaten the prevailing distribution of status, wealth, and power.

Samuel Huntington has argued that the objectives of the military and the functions of a coup d'état vary according to the type of political system and the society's level of modernization.[31] Where the level of modernization is low and the political system is based on a narrow oligarchy, the military is more likely to play a revolutionary role. Egypt in 1952 illustrates the point, and Israel's defeat of the Arab army in 1948-1949 helped to heighten the Egyptian military's sense of a need for radical domestic change.

But as the society undergoes modernization, as the middle classes grow in size and economic strength, and as the political system extends the opportunities for citizen participation, the role of the military and the objectives of a coup d'état are increasingly conservative. In South Korea and Turkey in 1960, in Greece in 1967, and again in Turkey in 1972 and in 1980, the military intervened to check an apparent drift to the left and to strengthen the hand of governments threatened by mass violence (especially marked by student unrest). It is clear that in the most modern societies and well-established political systems the military is either subordinate to civilian control or can be counted on to play only a reactionary role, especially in the case of threatened political violence on the left.

Given the apparent trends toward modernization on a worldwide scale, then, we are likely to be more right than wrong in concluding that the coup d'état, like the techniques of terror and guerrilla warfare, is of declining utility in the initiation of revolutionary change. This is not to say that the coup d'état, implemented with or without occasional manifestations of popular unrest, will cease to be an effective instrument of change in the political personnel of the ruling elite. But in fact it may be true that revolution, peculiar to the early stages of modernization and to the intense nationalism of anticolonial movements, is more a relic of the past than a promise for the future. Contemporary revolutionaries must consequently place all the more emphasis on a frequent characteristic of the revolutionary process: the external support that foreign states can provide for revolutionary movements abroad.

FOR FURTHER TESTING

Some Propositions:

1. As compared with coup d'état and terrorism, the technique of guerrilla warfare is most closely associated with peasant societies, leftist ideologies, low regime access, strong revolutionary organization, protracted struggle, and foreign intervention.
2. Coups d'état are most likely to occur in countries that,
   a. are economically underdeveloped,
   b. are newly independent,
   c. have gained their independence primarily through violent instead of peaceful means,
   d. have a prior record of coups d'état.

Some Hypotheses:

1. The lower the revolutionary potential of the society, the greater the revolutionaries' commitment to violence and terror.
2. The more that the revolutionaries rely on terror, the less likely they are to succeed.
3. The chances of successful *counter*insurgency increases as the guerrillas,
   a. are forced to plunder and terrorize the population,

b. are denied a secure geographic base of operations,
c. are physically isolated from the population,
d. are outnumbered in fighting personnel by a ratio of at least five to one,
e. induce the government (indirectly) to implement parts of the guerrillas' program.

NOTES

[1] Leiden and Schmitt, 1968, p. 210.

[2] Thornton, 1964, pp. 71-99, discusses many of the findings on the role of terror summarized here.

[3] Kecskemeti, 1961, pp. 153-54.

[4] Molnar, 1965, p. 171.

[5] On Marx's view of the role of terror, see Avineri, 1969, pp. 188 and 193; on Lenin and Debray, see Debray, 1970, p. 461.

[6] Gurr, 1970, p. 354.

[7] On the characteristics of Communist terror in South Vietnam, see Fall, 1965; Mallin, 1966; Molnar, 1965, Chap. 11; and Rolph, 1971, pp. 46-50.

[8] Lawrence, 1962, p. 199.

[9] Molnar, 1965, p. 74, reports that between 70 and 80 percent of the guerrillas in the Malayan, Philippine, and Korean insurgencies operated in their native provinces, while this was true of only 30 percent of the government's counterinsurgency forces.

[10] McColl, 1967.

[11] Mao Tse-tung, 1970, p. 416. Also see Giap, 1964, and B. Schwartz, 1958, esp. pp. 189-90.

[12] Debray, 1970, p. 457.

[13] Kelly, 1970, p. 427. Also see Kelly's summary of the counterinsurgency principles advanced by Jacques Hogard, pp. 432-35.

[14] Wolf, 1969, pp. 238-41. Also see Murray and Wengraf, 1963.

[15] Moore, 1966, p. 505; Gurr, 1970, p. 358; and for some specific examples in the case of the United States, see Iglitzin, 1972, p. 150.

[16] On counterinsurgency in Malaya and South Vietnam, see Thompson, 1966, and Molnar, 1965, esp. Part VI. On counterinsurgency in an urban context, see Burton, 1976.

[17] Needler, 1966.

[18] Beling, 1970, p. 191.

[19] Huntington, 1968, p. 218.

[20] Hunter, 1940, pp. 213-49.

[21] Trotsky, 1957, Vol. III, p. 135.

[22] See especially Stepan, 1971, where the political intervention of the military in Brazil in 1944, 1954, 1955, 1961, and 1964 is shown to be a positive response to the interests and demands of the Brazilian middle classes as expressed in the editorials of the bourgeois press.

[23] Luttwak, 1969, pp. 17-24. The studies by Luttwak, Goodspeed (1962), and Stepan (1971) are the contemporary classics on the characteristics and circumstances of a coup d'état. An earlier classic that concentrates on Europe after the First World War is Malaparte, 1932.

[24] von der Mehden, 1969, p. 92.

[25] Kling, 1956. Fossum's findings are reported in Gurr, 1970, p. 219.

[26] See Miller, 1971, for a detailed study of a typical coup scenario in an underdeveloped country (Uganda) where ethnic cleavages fragment both the society and the military.

[27] von der Mehden, 1969, p. 92.

[28] Beals, 1970, pp. 9-10.

[29] Degalo, 1976, emphasizes the play of personal ambition that marks so many of the military coups in Africa. Also see Bwy, 1968; Rapoport, 1966; Huntington, 1962; Blanksten, 1958; Kling, 1956.

[30] Huntington, 1968, pp. 408 and 422. Taylor, 1970, finds a multiple correlation coefficient of .62 (explaining 38 percent of the variance) between "coup proneness" and, (1) economic underdevelopment, (2) general instability ("turmoil"), and (3) no organized political opposition. The study is based on approximately 300 instability events in 103 countries between 1948 and 1967, controlling for the number of years of each country's political independence. Putnam, 1967, p. 98, reports a strong inverse relation ($r = -.63$) between his index of military intervention in Latin America between 1956 and 1965 and a variable (drawn from Banks and Textor, 1963) measuring interest aggregation by parties.

[31] Huntington, 1968, p. 221.

*CHAPTER
NINE*

EXTERNAL
SUPPORT

SANCTUARY AND SUPPLY

Only in the very last stages of guerrilla warfare is sanctuary a secondary factor in the success of the revolutionary movement. Throughout the formative and intermediate stages of organization and military operations, the guerrillas depend heavily on the geographic security provided either by remote areas in their native country or by neighboring states sympathetic to the guerrillas' revolutionary goals. And where the guerrillas lack sanctuary, they also usually lack the supply and matériel available from foreign sympathizers and essential to the guerrillas' military success.

Between 1910 and 1916, the armies of Pancho Villa operating in the north of Mexico enjoyed the support of the border population of the United States, which provided the Villistas with both sanctuary and military supplies in exchange for cattle and cotton expropriated from the haciendas of northern Mexico. The Vietminh in North Vietnam were able to accelerate their guerrilla activities against the French after the victory of the Communists in China in 1949, when the Vietminh gained access to the Chinese border areas and to the matériel and cadre training programs provided the Vietminh by the Chinese. The establishment of Bangladesh in East Pakistan in 1971 would have been impossible without the support of India. India gave sanctuary to the Bangladesh rebels after their decisive defeat by the West Pakistani Army, and only the subsequent invasion of West and East Pakistan by the Indian Army enabled the Free Bengal movement to secure its political objectives.

Elsewhere in the early 1970s, guerrilla revolutionaries proved very dependent on external support for their continued survival. Guerrillas in the southern Sudan found sanctuary in Uganda. Rebels against the Sultan of Oman received sanctuary and support from the revolutionary government of South Yemen. Fighting against Portuguese colonialism, the Mozambique Liberation Front depended heavily on the sanctuary available in the border areas of Tanzania, Malawi, and Zambia. The effectiveness of these rebel movements also seemed to correlate highly with the extent of matériel and guerrilla training provided by foreign states, including China in the case of the Mozambique Liberation Front and both China and the Soviet Union in the case of the rebel movement in southern Oman. And without the substantial external support received by the Pathet Lao and the Thai Communists, these movements also would have been much more vulnerable to the inducement and coercive programs of counterinsurgency warfare in Laos and Thailand.

By contrast, the fate of the Communist guerrillas in Greece was sealed in 1948 when, following the split between Stalin and Tito, the Yugoslav government closed its borders to the Greek rebels. The defeat of the Huk guerrillas in the Philippines and the Communist insurgents in Malaya may be explained in part by their lack of sanctuary and external supply, which was largely the result of geographic isolation. The isolation of the Mau Mau in Kenya in the early 1950s and of the Ceylonese rebels in 1971 reinforced the counterinsurgency effectiveness of the British and the Ceylonese governments. Increasing cooperation between governments in Dublin and London in the 1970s helped to reduce the incidence of the IRA's terrorist activities in Northern Ireland, activities that had depended on the sanctuary and supply routes available from the south.

The fate of a particular revolutionary movement, then, is not only a function (in part) of the extent of its own external support, but also depends on the external support available to the government and the forces of counterrevolution. In Latin America, the United States has played a major role in defeating movements that stood for radical change, most obviously in Guatemala, Brazil, and Bolivia. In China in the 1920s and 1930s, the success of the Kuomintang in its struggles against feudal warlords and the Chinese Communists was largely a result of the substantial economic and military aid, along with political and military advisers, provided by the Soviet Union.

But where the existing government has been unable to marshal external support in the face of a strong revolutionary movement, the government's defeat is usually a question only of time. The United States' withdrawal of diplomatic support for the Batista regime in 1958 and (under congressional pressure) the Eisenhower Administration's embargo on arms shipments to Cuba facilitated Castro's capture of power. That, in fact, United States neutrality (or ambivalence) may be a precondition for the success of revolutionaries in Latin America was again suggested by events in Nicaragua in 1978–1979: the Carter Administration imposed a moratorium on U.S. arms sales to Nicaragua, prevented the Somoza government from receiving a $20 million loan from the International Monetary Fund, and helped to persuade the Organization of American States to condemn the Somoza dictatorship. Coupled with the sanctuary and supply provided the anti-Somoza guerrillas through Costa Rica (to the south) and Honduras (to the north), this combination of direct and indirect external support helped to make the success of the guerrillas a question of *when,* not *if.* And in England, during the Puritan Revolution, King Charles was defeated when he failed to win military allies from either the royalists in Ireland or on the continent, while the success of the Parliamentarians was assured by the military intervention in 1644 of the Presbyterian Scots on the side of the Puritan armies.

The example of the Puritan Revolution helps to make the point that external support frequently has been a critical variable in the success or failure of revolutionary movements well before the twentieth century and the advent of Communist guerrilla warfare. This is especially obvious in the case of independence movements against colonial control, where sanctuary is less important than the coalition of forces mobilized for or against the movement. It is very probably true, for example, that without the intervention of France, and particularly the French Navy, the British would have succeeded in their war of attrition against the American colonists. French, Russian, and British military support was even more instrumental in the victory of the Greek nationalists over Ottoman control in 1829. The Paris Revolution of July 1830 triggered independence movements in Poland and Belgium (and elsewhere), but in Poland the revolutionaries lacked external support and were easily crushed by tsarist troops from Russia, while the Belgian movement against Dutch control succeeded because of Britain's support for a neutral and independent Belgium.

The success of Latin American independence movements against Spain and Portugal in the early nineteenth century must also be explained with reference to the role of external support. Coincidentally, it was Napoleon's Peninsular Campaign and occupation of Spain that opened the way for Latin American independence, while the British Navy subsequently prevented Spain from reasserting colonial control in Latin America (and thereby added military force to the paper declarations of the Monroe Administration in the United States). The defeat of the Southern Confederacy in its war with the North, which was superior in military and industrial strength to the South, was a foregone conclusion without external support; although the major European states were sympathetic to the rebel cause, they refused to provide either diplomatic or military assistance to the South. And Spain's loss of Cuba was assured by the intervention of the United States in the Spanish-American War of 1898.

External support also may be essential to the creation of cross-cutting alliances that are the basis for a strong revolutionary movement. In their struggles against Ottoman control between 1593 and 1606, the Balkan peasantry and nobility were united only when and where they received the "promise of Habsburg support . . . ."[1] The always shaky alliance of Arab tribes organized by T. E. Lawrence against the Turks from 1916 to 1918 depended heavily on British money and arms and, of course, the leadership that made the Arab alliance an effective guerrilla force also had to be imported. But even when revolutionaries enjoy the widespread support of cross-cutting alliances, they are vulnerable to counterrevolutionaries with an overwhelming advantage in external support: without the military equipment and personnel provided by Nazi Germany and Fascist Italy, the Spanish Fascists under General Franco would very probably have been defeated by the Spanish Republicans.[2]

Where all the conditions appear to exist for revolutionary mobilization, but where revolutionary movements are weak or nonexistent, the determining variable is likely to be the absence of external support. Otherwise it is difficult to explain, for example, the consistent failure of Irish nationalists to raise a major rebellion against the economic exploitation and cultural repression imposed on Ireland by England from at least the sixteenth century. The clan warfare and intense factionalism of the Irish themselves suggested that revolutionary organization and leadership would have to depend on the intervention of external authority before cohesion and force could be imparted to the Irish independence movement. This apparently was what the French hoped to accomplish during the Napoleonic Wars (1803–15), but the plan to send a French fleet to Ireland was never implemented. The most notable uprising of the Irish against English rule, the Easter Rebellion of 1916, was in fact precipitated by the Germans during the First World War when a German submarine landed Roger Casement and German agents in Ireland precisely for the purpose of raising a rebellion.

Contemporary South Africa is another case in point: all the preconditions for a revolutionary movement against the privileged white minority appear to exist, but South African blacks are unlikely to be mobilized for revolutionary action except through the intervention of external force.[3] The example of South Africa suggests that, to be successful, external support must vary in degree according to the levels of violence and repression characterizing the regime under attack. There are other variables that must also be considered, however, and the above examples provide us with a respectable sample of cases for more systematic generalization.

EXTERNAL SUPPORT
AND REVOLUTIONARY
MOVEMENTS

First of all it is obvious from the above that external support frequently has been a determining factor in the success or failure of revolutionary movements, whether on the left or right, whether in the twentieth century or in earlier periods of anticolonialism and modernization. Even for the brief time span of 1961 to 1965, Ted Gurr's study of 114 countries identified fifty-four "internal wars," and in thirty of them the rebels took advantage of the external support provided by foreign states.[4] It consequently is difficult to see the logic behind the argument that revolutionary movements are best described as "internal wars." A recent study sponsored by the United States Government of more than "fifty cases of contemporary local violence concludes that the boundary between international and internal war is frail."[5]

This boundary becomes even less discernible as the revolutionary movement mobilizes greater numbers of participants and is extended through time. A coup d'état, even when carried out with revolutionary intent, is less likely to provoke external intervention than a prolonged guerrilla war. This is partly because of the relative brevity of a coup d'état and the low level of ideology, which helps to conceal the revolutionary ambitions of the coup conspirators. In Egypt in 1952, for example, King Farouk counted in vain on the intervention of the British against the military plot organized by Nasser and Naguib. The success of their coup along with their nationalist aspirations meant Farouk's loss of his throne and a major reduction of British influence in the Middle East and, eventually, the elimination of British control over the Suez Canal. If the Egyptian nationalist movement had been of longer duration and if it had employed different techniques for seizing power, external support would very probably have played a more prominent role, both for and against the revolutionaries.

External support for the revolutionaries also is very likely to stimulate external support for the government under attack. This is especially true of guerrilla warfare, where the level of ideological conflict is high and where the rebels plainly state their revolutionary ambitions. As revolutionary followers are exhorted to make greater sacrifices over a longer period of time, ideology plays a greater role in justifying their efforts and in cohering the movement. The political, social, economic, and foreign policy changes promised by the revolutionaries or implicit in their ideology provoke greater international concern, and foreign states are more likely to register their support for either the revolutionaries or the government in power. Thus the level of violence is likely to increase, and with international involvement the contesting parties are less able to compromise their differences. The intensifying struggle between the United States and the Communist insurgents in South Vietnam between 1965 and the early 1970s illustrates the point. So, too, does the intensification of big power, and client power, competition in Africa—beginning in the Congo in the 1960s and carrying beyond the struggles for Angola's and Namibia's independence in the 1970s. It is in this way that the impoverished and the innocent can suddenly find that their countries have become an arena of conflict for the competing interests of the Soviet Union, China, and the United States.[6]

Where the government is heavily dependent on external support for its continued survival, however, the revolutionaries may enhance their popular appeal by emphasizing their national identity along with the government's foreign dependency. The Chinese Communists succeeded in spite of (or, perhaps, because of) their low level of external support even while the United States supplied the Chinese Nationalists with two billion dollars in military and economic assistance between 1945 and 1949. But where the revolutionaries themselves are heavily dependent on external support, they compromise their popular appeal in terms of nationalist sentiment. They become vulnerable to the government's counterrevolutionary propaganda, which can claim that the struggle is not against domestic forces but against foreign invaders. This clearly was one of the obstacles encountered by Castroite guerrillas in Latin America during the 1960s, especially in Venezuela and Bolivia.

These risks are necessary, however, when the revolutionaries are low in regime access, charismatic leadership, organizational competence, popular support, and logistical supply. Insofar as the necessary external support is channeled through a single leader or group within the revolutionary coalition, the authority of the movement's leadership and the cohesion of the revolutionary organization may be enhanced. The leadership's task, then, is to maximize in fact the advantages accruing from external support while minimizing in word the movement's dependency on it, or else the revolutionaries may find that they themselves have been captured by foreign interests that were essential to revolutionary success. Nevertheless, as governments develop greater skills in counterinsurgency warfare and increase their coercive capabilities, the very survival of revolutionary movements is likely to depend on ever-heightened levels of external support.

FOR FURTHER TESTING

Some Propositions:

1. A significant increase in the external support received by a government under attack is likely to lower the government's political legitimacy. (From the government's point of view, then, this political disadvantage must be compensated for by the material advantages deriving from additional external support.)

2. A significant reduction in the external support received by a government under attack is likely to improve the revolutionaries' chances of success.

3. Heavy reliance by the revolutionaries on external support reduces the effectiveness of their ideological appeal.

Some Hypotheses:

1. The chances of revolutionary success are,
   a. directly related to the extent of external support received by the movement, and
   b. inversely related to the extent of external support received by the government under attack.

2. The incidence of external support for both the revolutionaries and the government under attack increases as the revolutionary struggle is extended,
   a. in time, and
   b. in geographic area.

3. The stronger the coercive capabilities of the government, the more dependent is the revolutionary movement on external support (if the movement is to succeed).

NOTES

[1] Fischer-Galati, 1963, p. 13.

[2] This opinion, and documentation on the massive support provided Franco by Germany, Italy, and to a lesser extent by the United States, may be found in Beals, 1970, pp. 182-85.

[3] This is the conclusion of Colin and Margaret Legum, 1964, who also describe in detail the conditions of the black population in South Africa.

[4] Gurr, 1970, pp. 270-71.

[5] Summarized and cited in Kelly and Miller, 1970, pp. 230-31.

[6] Rosenau, 1964. Marcum, 1978. Gurr, 1970, pp. 270-71, reports a correlation coefficient of .83 between external support for the insurgents and external support for the regime in his study of fifty-four internal wars between 1961 and 1965.

THE
SETTING
Accelerators

The titles of the chapters in Part Two of this book represent my understanding of the principal characteristics of revolutionary movements. Each of these chapters has presented hypotheses and propositions drawn from a variety of revolutionary movements, and each of these has been integrated into conceptual categories indicated by the chapter titles and section headings. Most of these hypotheses and propositions have been designed to help answer a single question: what factors appear to contribute to the success or failure of a particular revolutionary movement, whether on the ideological left, center, or right? Even in this relatively uncomplicated part of our study of revolutionary movements, then, we have been unable to avoid questions related to cause and effect.

Part Three trespasses even more boldly in the territory of causal inference. Here we ask questions not about the success or failure of revolutionary movements but about the conditions and circumstances that appear to be most frequently associated with their development. We are concerned less with why revolutionary movements succeed or fail than with why they arise at all. It is appropriate to warn the reader that we thus walk on much shakier ground. According to the formalities of scientific method, we can never really *prove* causality. At best, we *demonstrate* varying degrees of probability in the relationships of specific phenomena. And the persuasiveness of our causal inferences is more a matter of logical self-evidence than empirical certainty. In short, causality is an invention of the mind.

These observations on the necessary limits of our knowledge are especially relevant to the study of revolution as our analytical categories are extended in space and time. Our assumptions about the "preconditions" of revolutions are likely to be even more tentative than our conclusions about their "accelerators." We are well advised, then, to begin our study of the causes of revolutionary movements with reference to those events that are apparently the most closely associated with the outbreak of revolution. These "accelerators" are the "final, or immediate, causes of revolution . . . ."[1] They are discrete events and they occur at specific points in time. Their principal function is to cohere individuals with shared values into a group with revolutionary potential. Among the many accelerators of revolution that may be cited, the most obvious is the following.

MILITARY DEFEAT

The Puritan Revolution was immediately preceded by King Charles's unsuccessful military campaign against Scotland in 1639-40. In 1788, Louis XVI again went to war with Great Britain; the war exaggerated those weaknesses of the French monarchy—especially in terms of its financial administration—that contributed to the outbreak of the French Revolution in 1789. Austria's imperial domination of northern Italy was broken in 1859 by Louis-Napoleon, and the Austrian defeat was immediately followed by revolutionary agitation throughout the Italian peninsula. The failure of Louis-Napoleon's armies in the Franco-Prussian war of 1870-71 laid the basis for another revolution in Paris and the establishment of the Paris Commune. The magnitude of revolutionary events in Russia was directly related to the scope of military disaster suffered by the tsar's armies in 1905 and 1917.

Following the defeat of the Central Powers in the First World War, revolutions broke out in Germany, Austria, Hungary, and Turkey. Japan's military success in China and in the French and Dutch colonies of Southeast Asia laid the basis for communist and anticolonial revolutions in China, Vietnam, and Indonesia after Japan's defeat in the Second World War. Major anti-Fascist activity in Italy did not develop until 1944 and the Allies' defeat of Mussolini's armies in the Italian South.

Concentrating on Europe, Robert Hunter has counted nineteen revolutions between 1204 and 1919 "which have followed immediately after defeat in war."[2] And Pitirim A. Sorokin, in his study of political violence in Europe from the time of Ancient Greece and Rome to 1933, found a relationship between periods of international conflict and the frequency of domestic conflict that was especially obvious in the case of those countries defeated in war.[3]

What explains this apparently close association of international military involvement, particularly when it ends in defeat, and the outbreak of revolution? One of the most useful concepts in the development of a theory of revolution is that of governmental or political *legitimacy.* The potential ambiguity of this concept is a partial measure of its utility in explaining many of the more particular phenomena of the revolutionary process. But political scientists agree that "legitimacy" refers to the attitudes of citizens as they reflect on the personnel, policies, laws, and institutions of government. Where legitimacy is high, most citizens believe that the government has the right to do what it does. Where legitimacy is low, most citizens believe that the goverment is wrong in doing what it does. The institutions of government may be regarded as highly legitimate, but the personnel, policies, or specific laws of the government may be rejected because of their apparent illegitimacy. Deductive logic informs us, not surprisingly, that as any or all aspects of government decline in legitimacy, revolutionary potential increases.[4]

Ideally, we would be able to test the relationship between legitimacy and revolutionary potential with time-series survey data that carefully operationalize both variables. Lacking these obvious research advantages, we must infer variations in legitimacy for a given society from aggregate data and specific events in its political history. By definition, then, revolution indicates low legitimacy, and the close association of military defeat with revolution implies that failure in war drastically lowers the legitimacy of government.

We may assume that colonial governments already are relatively low in legitimacy. Their military defeat undermines their legitimacy even further and makes their continued claims to authority over the native population a meaningless exercise in the manipulation of symbols. Nationalist sentiment is likely to intensify. But even in noncolonial societies, the government's military defeat suggests that the myths employed by the government to inspire citizen loyalty and sacrifice are out of touch with reality and lacking in credibility. From the citizen's point of view, a government that is defeated militarily either bungled its conduct of the war or should not have gone to war in the first place. In either case, the government is plainly incompetent. This perspective is especially characteristic of military elites, whose readiness to identify the civilian government as the scapegoat for military defeat increases the military's susceptibility to revolutionary appeals—either from factions of the military or from revolutionary movements of the fascist variety.

Military defeat that does not entail occupation by a foreign invader also creates a power vacuum that can work to the advantage of revolutionaries who are better organized than the enfeebled government (for example, the Bolsheviks). But military defeat that is accompanied by foreign occupation opens the way for revolutionary movements that enjoy widespread support and are based on strong political organization implanted in the grass roots of the society (for example, Chinese Communism).

In economically underdeveloped societies with narrowly based political institutions, the very initiation of large-scale war increases the society's potential for radical change. War is one of the most rapid and effective agents of social mobilization. A newly emergent middle class may demand political representation as the condition for its continued economic support of the government. Especially in peasant societies, massive military conscription mobilizes the peasantry and raises its level of political consciousness. The peasant who is a soldier is also a peasant who is armed. And hundreds of thousands or millions of armed peasants dilute the elitist quality of the professional army and render less dependable the government's coercive apparatus. Military defeat increases the potential for armed mutiny, both at the front and at home where the refusal of troops to fire on crowds of demonstrators is itself an accelerator of the revolutionary process.

But for all citizens, war raises the level of violence of their social environment and accustoms them to the resolution of conflict through physical force. Old norms and established conventions may quickly disintegrate. The government that seeks to enhance its legitimacy and to raise the level of social cohesion by going to war instead raises the society's revolutionary potential as the war is long, bloody, and moves ineluctably toward defeat. Along with anticolonialism, military defeat is also one of the most certain means of effecting cross-cutting alliances that unite the society's major classes in common hostility to the existing government.

In the early stages of war, governments augment their role in the national economy and strengthen the administrative centralization of the state. Industrial production approaches capacity, unemployment declines, government spending increases, and wages rise. Government controls may be imposed to hold down prices, and the hard-core unemployed can be absorbed into the military. Even a successful conclusion to the war, then, is likely to bring temporary economic crisis and a period of relative instability as the government eases its economic controls and reduces its spending, and as the economy retools for peacetime production and demobilized soldiers search for jobs. But military defeat means not economic crisis but economic catastrophe: a rapid downturn in industrial production, economic scarcity, massive unemployment, galloping inflation as the government turns out paper money to meet its obligations, and the liquidation of savings for millions of citizens as the value of the currency is depreciated. The more severe the military defeat, the more staggering the economic problems that a weakened government, already low in legitimacy, must confront.

In this sense, military defeat magnifies the impact of the other accelerators of revolutionary movements, including those discussed below. These accelerators are not necessarily associated with the circumstances of war, but there is no doubt that when they are reinforced by military defeat the society's revolutionary potential is markedly increased.

ECONOMIC CRISIS

In Ghana on 13 January 1972, a military coup d'état overturned one of the few parliamentary governments remaining in postcolonial Africa. The civilian elite had been faced with lagging agricultural production, falling market prices for Ghana's major export commodity (cocoa), a large trade imbalance and a massive foreign debt, and rising rates of inflation and unemployment. To help solve its economic problems, the government instituted a program of economic austerity and devalued the national currency by 44 percent. It also attempted to cut expenditures for the civil service, the police, and—a fateful step— the army.

In Ghana, however, and in many other Third World countries, the cosmetic changes introduced by military dictatorship have had little or no impact on basic economic vulnerabilities. The consequence has been continued political instability. Following the military coup of 1972, for example, Ghana's economy continued to deteriorate and then, in the mid-1970s, it was devastated by the direct and indirect impact of skyrocketing oil prices. The annual rate of Ghana's inflation reached 100 percent. Shortages of food became more frequent and more severe. A new military elite seized power in 1978. There followed another military coup in 1979. And another in 1982. Before the 1982 coup, Ghana's cost-of-living was nine times what it had been in 1977, the cost of a loaf of bread was one-and-a-half times the minimum daily wage, 40 percent of the government's budget went to pay the salaries of public officials, the black market had become an accepted way of life, smuggling across Ghana's borders was thriving, and corruption in both private and public sectors was the rule instead of the exception. This last point also applies to the unconstitutional transfer of power from one ruling elite to another. In Latin America, too, the frequency of coups d'état rises in years of economic deterioration, while it declines in years marked by increases in real per capita income.[5]

There was a poor harvest in France in 1788. During the first months of 1789, prices rose, wages fell, and unemployment increased in the cities and rural areas. The mobilization of the Paris mob throughout the period of the French Revolution has been correlated with the price of bread, and in July 1789 its price was higher than at any time since the death of Louis XIV in 1715. For the two years preceding the Paris Revolution of 1848 there was depression and mounting unemployment. After 1848, in France and elsewhere in Western Europe, employment and wages rose and revolutionary agitation declined.[6]

In Italy before September 1920, there were 100,000 unemployed and the Fascists were a strident but small extremist party. By early 1922, there were 600,000 unemployed and Fascist membership was growing rapidly. In Germany, Nazi membership declined after economic stabilization in 1923. But with the onset of the depression in 1929 unemployment in Germany rose from 2 million to 6 million over the ensuing three years, and Nazi party membership increased from 100,000 in 1928 to 1.4 million in 1932. The depression in Germany also substantially increased voter participation, to the advantage of all the extremist parties, but Nazi electoral support exploded: from 810,000 votes in 1928 to 6.4 million votes in 1930 to 13.7 million votes in July 1932.[7]

In the Communist states of East Germany and Czechoslovakia in 1953, and in Poland in 1970 and in 1980, economic crisis and the regimes' attempts to restrict consumption while increasing production quotas for workers immediately preceded sudden outbreaks of collective violence. In Poland, spontaneous strikes and subsequent organization by the workers forced a change in the top leadership of party and state in both 1970 and 1980. Neither political elites with an ideology based on the welfare of the working classes nor authoritarian states with a sophisticated coercive apparatus are immune to the political effects of economic crisis. Neil Smelser makes clear just how old and wide-ranging is the relationship between economic crisis and collective violence:

> Economic factors, such as abrupt food shortages, unemployment, rising prices, and falling wages are closely associated with outbursts of violence in contexts so diverse as the French Revolution, lower-class riots in 17th Century Mexico and in 17th Century England, food riots in 18th Century England, Luddite violence in 19th Century England, American labor disturbances in the 19th and 20th centuries, American nativism, and peasant uprisings in Japan toward the end of the Tokugawa period.[8]

Men are likely to be roused to direct action more by their immediate economic circumstances than by ideological appeals on behalf of social justice. But once mobilized to protest food shortages, unemployment, or rising prices, they become more susceptible to revolutionary ideology and organization. Especially where the forces of order and repression prove sympathetic to demonstrators and strikers (as in Russia during the February Revolution), original economic grievances may be broadened to include demands for fundamental political and social change. In Ethiopia in 1974, for example, soaring inflation fueled by the rising world price of oil prompted students to take to the streets; demonstrations turned into riots; strikes spread among workers and paralyzed the country's transportation system; and then the military seized Ethiopia's second largest city and demanded pay increases—but soon found itself at the head of a revolution that deposed Emperor Haile Selassie and overturned a tradition of absolute monarchy that reached back over three thousand years.

This suggests that economic crisis, by itself, is unlikely to provoke collective violence with revolutionary intent. The immediate crisis must reflect more basic social and economic problems, which the crisis helps to dramatize and focus in the minds of potential revolutionaries. It is in this sense that economic crisis can serve as an accelerator of revolution, helping to lower the government's legitimacy as the political consciousness of citizens is heightened.

But of course the history of every society is filled with examples of economic fluctuation, the rise and fall of production and consumption, the expansion and contraction of the labor market, and changing wage rates and price levels. The frequency of downturns in the business cycle suggests that if we scratch the surface of almost any revolutionary period we shall find economic sores festering in the social organism. And while many instances of political violence and revolution can be linked to economic crisis, most economic crises do not lead to either violence or revolution. Other variables must intervene.

Most obviously, the economy must be relatively underdeveloped and most citizens must live on the margins of subsistence. Under these conditions, any increase in food prices or taxes, or drought or the threat of famine and unemployment, can raise the society's revolutionary potential.[9] In underdeveloped societies temporary economic setback can seriously affect the government's performance of all its functions, especially its provision of welfare and services to the underprivileged majority of the population. For these citizens, the government's legitimacy is closely tied to their immediate economic circumstances, and the legitimacy of the state's young institutions is unlikely to compensate for the administrative incompetence or economic bad luck of the political elite.

But economic crisis together with weak political institutions can raise the revolutionary potential of both agrarian and industrial societies. In the case of agrarian economies in a colonial setting, the result is likely to be in terms of leftist revolutionary movements. Depression and nationalist appeals in more developed economies with weak political institutions are likely to lead to fascist-type movements, as in Italy, Germany, and Spain after the First World War.

The social structure of an underdeveloped society is also especially sensitive to economic change, and in fact either rapid economic growth or depression can upset established norms and weaken social solidarity.[10] Economic depression intensifies job competition, while economic growth inevitably has an uneven impact on different strata of the population. In either case, ideological, ethnic, and racial cleavages are likely to be widened, raising the potential for communal conflict.[11]

Along with the legitimacy of the society's political institutions and its stage of economic development, another intervening variable affecting the relationship between revolution and economic crisis is the nature of economic change prior to the crisis period. James C. Davies has described this relationship in terms of a "*J*-curve": revolution is most likely to occur after a relatively long period of economic growth, followed by a sudden downturn in the economy.[12] Raymond Tanter and Manus Midlarsky have elaborated this hypothesis in terms of the *rates* of prior economic development and subsequent decline: the higher the rate of growth in per capita GNP prior to a given revolution, and "the sharper the reversal *immediately* prior to the revolution, the greater the duration and violence of the revolution." This hypothesis is tested statistically for fourteen countries, including six in Asia and four in the Middle East, where the respective correlation coefficients of the variables (rates of economic growth and decline and the level of violence) are a very high .94 and .96.[13]

It is appropriate that these findings are derived from societies with relatively underdeveloped economies. But it also is more than a little troubling that the research supporting the *J*-curve hypothesis has concentrated almost exclusively on societies that have undergone revolution. Having selected a revolutionary event, it is very likely that we can identify a period of economic growth preceding economic crisis and the revolutionary event that initially determined our research interest. *J*-curve trends, for example, can be discerned prior to notable increases in political violence in France in 1968, in Italy and Ceylon in 1970-71, prior to the French revolutions of 1789, 1830 and 1848, and in fact in probably all of the instances of revolution cited in this book.

This still says nothing about the many instances of a *J*-curve in the economic cycle that is unaccompanied by either violence or revolutionary activity. We obviously must look more closely at the underlying conditions of societies experiencing revolution, including their stages of economic development and the legitimacy of their political institutions, and at other accelerators of revolution that may reinforce the effects of economic crisis—including the following.

GOVERNMENT VIOLENCE

Not only revolutionaries use violence for political ends. Nor is the use of violence by governments restricted to international conflict. Government violence in domestic affairs, however, is invariably justified in terms of the maintenance of law and order. But all citizens in every society have in their minds some notion of a boundary that distinguishes legitimate from illegitimate government violence. The position of this boundary varies from one citizen to another according to ideological orientation, socioeconomic status, education, political experience, and the frequency of violence in the individual's social environment.

Even citizens in the United States, where political stability and legitimacy are relatively high, impose limits on the government's use of violence. In October 1969 a representative sample of United States citizens found that 9 percent would approve violent resistance to the government if the government "arrested and imprisoned many of the Negroes" in their communities, "even though there has been no trouble." The number of respondents approving citizen violence against the government increased as the hypothetical violence of the government increased: 48 percent approved acts of violence by citizens in the event "the government starts arresting and shooting large numbers of innocent people including members of your family."[14] That less than half of the population approved citizen violence even under these extreme circumstances is a dramatic comment on the high legitimacy attributed to United States political institutions by most Americans.

Government violence that appears to be arbitrary and indiscriminate, then, tend to lower the government's legitimacy and raises the society's revolutionary potential. Those already committed to reform may be radicalized by government violence, especially when police brutality or military repression is experienced at first hand. And those citizens who are normally passive or politically apathetic may be politicized by government violence, which thus enlarges the number of activists and helps to alter their goals from reform to revolution.

Demonstrators in Paris in February 1848 assembled before the premier's residence and were fired upon by police. Twenty persons were killed. Their martyrdom was immediately celebrated by a torchlight procession, followed by widespread rioting which in turn precipitated the fall of the monarchy of Louis Philippe. In St. Petersburg in January 1905, tsarist troops killed hundreds of peaceful demonstrators and thereby helped to trigger a wave of industrial strikes, the organization of workers' soviets, peasant rebellion, and the rapid growth of revolutionary groups in Russia.

Communist armies in Russia during the Civil War, in China, in South Vietnam, and Castro's guerrillas in Cuba, all benefited from the actions of government or counterrevolutionary troops who indiscriminately robbed, tortured, or killed peasants and destroyed their villages. By contrast, the Chinese Communist party "made it a cardinal rule not to let its troops enter a village to collect grain and recruits." [15]

In Paris in May 1968, police invaded the Sorbonne to break up a student rally. Student resistance acted as an accelerator for an industrial strike movement and further student violence that threatened the foundations of the Gaullist state. Almost all the urban riots of black citizens in the United States in the 1960s were touched off by initial incidents of alleged police harassment or brutality: "Moreover, increased police response to the initial incidents usually transformed them into major disorders." [16]

The wave of hostility and moral revulsion that swept away Iran's regime of the Shah in 1979 was raised in part by the widespread terror and repression associated with SAVAK, the Shah's army of secret police and spies. And the critical event that accelerated the revolutionary process in Nicaragua after 1978 was the assassination of Dr. Pedro Chamorro. Chamorro was leader of the conservative forces opposed to the Somoza dictatorship and he owned and edited the country's leading newspaper. His funeral was the occasion for a virtual antigovernment gathering of thousands of Nicaraguans, and his martyrdom helped to radicalize the anti-Somoza opposition and to broaden the cross-cutting alliance that eventually brought down the Somoza regime.

A factor analysis of eighty-four countries between 1948 and 1962 finds a close association between various types of government and citizen violence. Mass arrests load highly on a "turmoil" and "riot" factor, while the variable of government executions loads highly on a factor identified as "civil war."[17] A time dimension must be introduced, however, to clarify the causal relationship of the variables. And if we interpolate these cross-sectional data into time-series data for Latin America, we find that in nineteen of twenty-six cases martial law (our index of government violence) was in fact declared *before* the initiation of revolt.

As in counterinsurgency warfare, however, government violence on a sufficiently massive scale can suppress overt revolutionary activity. In Hungary in 1956 the initial violent confrontation between police and demonstrators "drove the crowd to frenzy, and the possession of arms, obtained from sympathizers among the military, gave it a feeling of unlimited power."[18] But the coercive advantage provided the government by Russian tanks, the subsequent dissolution of the workers' councils, and the arrest and imprisonment of the leaders of the workers' councils and strike committees, crushed the revolution and restored government power.

The relationship between government violence and most types of political violence, then, appears to be curvilinear: political violence increases along with government violence, until a threshold is reached where increased government violence coincides with a rapid decline in the collective violence of citizens.[19] (See Figure 10-1.) This threshold obviously varies from one revolutionary event

FIGURE 10-1 Political Violence and Government Violence: A Curvilinear Relationship

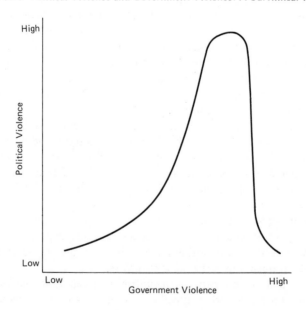

to another, and according to the intensity of the citizens' hostility for the regime. Their revolutionary potential, as well as the regime's capacity for counterrevolutionary violence, may in turn depend largely on the cohesion of the political elite.

ELITE FRAGMENTATION

Plato, Alexis de Tocqueville, and many contemporary writers on revolution have observed that revolution frequently begins with "divisions among members of the ruling class."[20] Elite fragmentation itself is closely associated with military defeat and economic crisis, and even the elite's resort to higher levels of government violence can threaten its cohesion. Whatever the immediate difficulties, factions within the elite are likely to disagree on how to resolve them, and rival personalities may take advantage of the crisis by advancing their claims for higher status within the government. The consequent fragmentation of the elite is an especially visible symbol of declining government competence and is likely to lower the regime's legitimacy in the minds of citizens.

This is especially the case when an autocratic ruler dies leaving in his wake a crisis of succession. The death of Tsar Alexander I in 1825 opened the way for elite dissension on the role of the Russian monarchy and the status of serfs, which contributed to the outbreak of the Decembrist Revolt. Stalin's death in 1953 was followed by violent clashes between police and demonstrators in Hungary, Czechoslovakia, and East Germany, and by a power struggle in the Soviet Union that was dramatized in 1956 by Khrushchev's attack on the memory of Stalin—a major symbol of legitimacy for all communist parties and states. The resulting conflict within communist elites led to popular revolt precisely where state and party personnel were most severely divided (in Poland and Hungary), and divided not only on the issue of Stalinism but on the means of solving prevailing economic problems and on the role of Russian authority in Eastern Europe.[21]

An important accelerator of Castro's revolution in Cuba was the increasing fragmentation of Batista's ruling coalition after 1956, including the high command of the Cuban military.[22] Taking the number of cabinet ministers dismissed from office as an index of elite fragmentation, a study of sixteen Latin American countries between 1948 and 1962 finds a close association between the frequency of dismissals and the outbreak of revolt.[23] A more statistically sophisticated study of Latin American instability also finds that "elite fragmentation and disorganization consistently takes place *prior* to the occurrence of Internal War."[24]

REFORM
AND POLITICAL CHANGE

Elite fragmentation may be accelerated by the attempts of a part of the elite to initiate reform. Especially where socioeconomic development has not been accompanied by changes in political institutions and representation, the regime's decision to implement reform represents an abrupt departure from the practices and policies of the past. Efforts at reform are usually half-hearted, in part a function of the elite's fragmentation, but they inevitably imply a repudiation of past inequities and can consequently lower the regime's legitimacy.

Writing in the 1850s with regard to the French Revolution, de Tocqueville proposed a generalization that applies equally well to the Manchu dynasty before the Nationalist Revolution in China, to Russia under Catherine II and Nicholas II, and to the Communist governments of Eastern Europe between 1953 and 1956:

> Revolution does not always come when things are going from bad to worse. It occurs most often when a nation that has accepted, and indeed, has given no sign of even having noticed the most crushing laws, rejects them at the very moment when their weight is being lightened. The regime that is destroyed by a revolution is almost always better than the one preceding it, and experience teaches us that usually the most dangerous time for a bad government is when it attempts to reform itself.[25]

The reforms attempted before 1789 by various ministers in the French government, however, not only fragmented the monarchy's traditional supporting elite. They also made even more intolerable the nobility's efforts to reassert some of its feudal prerogatives. In England, too, James I and Charles I attempted to revive feudal dues prior to the Puritan Revolution. The Paris Revolution of 1830 followed efforts by Charles X to restore the *ancien régime* and absolute monarchy. Attempts by governments to go either forward or backward in resolving their current difficulties, then, can precipitate revolution.

The political elite's decision to centralize the state's administrative authority can also accelerate the revolutionary process, especially where regional and cultural autonomy are threatened by centralization. The uprisings of Russian peasants and Cossacks in the seventeenth and eighteenth centuries paralleled the increasing centralization of the Russian state under Muscovy and the tsars, whose extension of power over the provincial nobility also meant the peasants' subordination to the nobility as serfs. Counterrevolution in southern and provincial France after 1789 coincided with the National Assembly's attempts to eliminate the relative independence of the regional parliaments. Part of the foundation for communist insurgency in South Vietnam was laid by the

Diem government's elimination of village autonomy after 1954. The outbreak of tribal conflict in Nigeria and the Nigerian civil war were immediately preceded in January 1966 by the central government's decision to create a unitary state and to recruit civil-service personnel without regard for ethnic representation.

The intensity of cultural or communal conflict also is likely to be heightened by abrupt changes in the political status of indigenous elites. The winning of independence from a colonial power, for example, can precipitate these types of conflict, as in the case of the Congo in 1960 and Zanzibar in 1964. The revolt of African blacks in Zanzibar immediately followed the departure of the British colonial administration, which left the Arab minority in nominal control—but the Arab elite itself had been fragmented in 1963 by the formation of an opposition Arab party.[26]

The political status of indigenous elites in both underdeveloped and developed societies also can be suddenly altered by critical elections, which in turn may serve as accelerators of violence and revolution. Elections in Nigeria, Pakistan, and Trinidad in the 1960s and early 1970s and in France, Spain, and Germany in the 1930s raised the level of political consciousness of citizens and polarized their conflicts along ideological and ethnic lines of cleavage. In Italy, Germany, and Spain after the First World War it was in part the electoral success of the left that enabled fascist movements to mobilize supporters from among the frightened middle classes, the Church, and the military and landed oligarchies. Especially in underdeveloped societies characterized by communal cleavage, national independence and the organization of competitive elections can mean major conflict insofar as the newly created political parties reinforce cultural divisions. Thus "democracy," in the context of weak political institutions and cultural conflict, can lay the basis for civil war, a military coup d'état as the threat of violence increases, or both.

But critical elections, the winning of national independence, administrative centralization, attempts at social and political reform, and all the other potential accelerators of revolution discussed in this chapter are very unlikely, by themselves, to lead to revolution. Just as we can find many instances of economic crisis that do not coincide with the outbreak of revolution, we also can find many instances of government violence and elite fragmentation that merit only passing reference in the history of an otherwise stable political system.

Accelerators, then, are a necessary and immediate cause of revolution, but they are not a sufficient cause. And, in fact, even in this brief survey of accelerators I have been unable to avoid reference to some of the more fundamental causes of revolution that are discussed in the following chapter as "preconditions." But a final entry must first be added to our list of accelerators, and it concerns a characteristic of the revolutionary process that is not easily classified and that has received less attention in the literature on revolution than the accelerators identified above.

THE DEMONSTRATION EFFECT

"The demonstration effect" is a term from economic theory. It describes the tendency of consumers to alter their patterns of consumption as they observe changes in the consumption patterns of their neighbors or acquaintances. The alteration is typically in the direction of higher living standards.[27]

The term also seems appropriate to the study of revolution.[28] This is because revolutionary movements initiated by republicans, workers, peasants, nationalists, fascists, cultural separatists, as well as guerrilla warfare, coups d'état, even campus disorders, are not distributed randomly through history. They tend to cluster in time, suggesting that a revolutionary event in one place may act as an accelerator of the revolutionary process in another place at approximately the same point in time. An alternative label for this phenomenon might be "concurrent revolutions."

The success of the American Revolution, for example, is often cited as contributing to the outbreak of the French Revolution. And the initiation of the French Revolution in 1789 was immediately followed by revolutionary activity in Silesia, Hamburg, Belgium, Ireland, and elsewhere in central and northern Europe. The French Revolution and the Napoleonic wars in turn laid the basis for the independence movements in Latin America between 1810 and 1830. The successful Paris Revolution of July 1830 against the restored Bourbon monarchy touched off nationalist movements in Poland (against Russian domination), in Belgium (against Dutch domination), and appears to have been the accelerator of largely liberal revolutionary movements in Italy, Switzerland, Germany, Spain, and Portugal. In 1848 Paris was again the powder keg for revolutionary explosions throughout Europe, from Copenhagen through Berlin to Vienna, Budapest, Lombardy, and Palermo.[29]

Japan's military victory over Russia in 1905 suggested that the European powers were not so invincible after all, and the lesson appeared to accelerate the mobilization of nationalist movements in Persia in 1905, in Turkey in 1908, and in China in 1911. A study of the writings of the early Chinese radical intellectuals concludes that they "knew about other revolutions, they seemed to know a good deal about the French; they also observed the rise of the Young Turks and the Russian Revolution of 1905 very closely and excitedly, and referred to these and other revolutions frequently."[30]

News of the Bolshevik Revolution in 1917 revived anarchist movements in southern Spain and inspired communist revolts in Central Europe. Soviet-type governments were temporarily established in Hungary and Bavaria. Major communist parties were organized in France in 1920 and in Italy in 1921, and a communist uprising took place in Saxony in 1923. It was the apparently mounting menace on the left that, in a dialectic of political extremes, reinforced the growth of fascism. The Bolshevik coup engineered by Trotsky in 1917 served as a model for Mussolini in 1922. Mussolini's tactics inspired Hitler's attempted coup in Munich in 1923. The victory of the Nazis in Germany in January 1933 was quickly followed by a series of fascist and semifascist coups from Finland to Greece; in Austria in March 1933 and in Bulgaria in early 1934 tentative democratic institutions were replaced by fascist-type dictatorships.[31]

"Historical coincidence" would seem to be a wholly inadequate explanation for the timing of the outbreak of the Algerian revolution in October-November 1954. French colonialism in Indochina had received a major setback at Dienbienphu in May and an independent North Vietnam had been established in July. Anti-French independence movements in Algeria, Tunisia, and Morocco in the mid-1950s also seem to have been mutually reinforcing. And Ghana's independence from Great Britain in 1957 intensified anticolonial agitation in the Belgian Congo and in Portuguese Angola in the late 1950s and early 1960s. Race riots in the United States, military coups d'état in the Middle East, in Black Africa, and in Latin America also seem to be nonrandomly distributed through time. Following the overthrow of the Somoza dictatorship in Nicaragua in 1979, for example, the government of nearby El Salvador was forced from power by a military-civilian junta. The junta itself was then brought under pressure by mass demonstrations and street battles that took hundreds of lives. The actions of leftists provoked the mobilization of rightists who vowed to meet violence with violence and terror with terror. It was difficult to ignore the timing of these events—which seemed in the early 1980s to be as closely related to the Nicaraguan revolution of 1979 as Latin American instability in the 1960s was to the Cuban revolution of 1959.

The very listing of these examples suggests that the demonstration effect is largely in terms of analogous types of political movements. Antimonarchical movements or guerrilla insurgencies accelerate antimonarchical movements or guerrilla insurgencies, not military coups d'état. And military coups d'état accelerate military coups d'état, not anticolonial movements or industrial general strikes. Workers occupying a factory or peasants burning a manor incite other workers or other peasants to perform similar acts. Especially for these last types of collective violence, the demonstration effect helps to explain how largely spontaneous movements are generated. And the more telescoped in time the sequence of revolutionary events, the more prominent the role of spontaneity in revolutionary mobilization.

The extent to which a revolutionary event functions as an accelerator for analogous revolutionary activity elsewhere thus depends on (1) the effectiveness of communications networks, (2) the apparent success of the initial revolutionary event, (3) the cross-cultural relevance of the techniques and ideology characterizing the initial revolutionary event, and (4) the cross-cultural comparability of the "preconditions" for revolution. The attentive reader will note that this last variable again announces the subject matter of the following chapter.

FOR FURTHER TESTING

Some Propositions:

1. The majority of those who support or participate in revolutionary movements are mobilized initially by their self-interest and by their immediate concerns for personal well-being.
2. High revolutionary potential is likely to be raised even higher when the existing government initiates reform or seeks to change established patterns of politics—even when reform and change promise to work to the advantage of the underprivileged and those who may be sympathetic to revolution.
3. Analogous revolutionary events within geographic regions tend to be concentrated in time.

Some Hypotheses:

1. A society's revolutionary potential is directly related to the severity of,
   a. military defeat,
   b. economic crisis,
   c. fragmentation of the ruling elite.
2. There is a curvilinear relationship between the society's revolutionary potential and the extent of government violence.
3. There is an inverse relationship between the society's revolutionary potential and the regime's political legitimacy.

NOTES

[1] C. Johnson, 1966, p. 91.

[2] Hunter, 1940, p. 126.

[3] Sorokin, 1970, pp. 137-39. See Skocpol, 1979, for a variation on the theme sounded here: revolution may follow the administrative crises that are provoked by a strong challenge to the state's military capabilities.

[4] Gurr, 1970, pp. 183-85, summarizes some of the relevant literature and various interpretations of legitimacy.

[5] Needler, 1966.

[6] Rudé, 1959, pp. 196-200; Palmer, 1956, pp. 341, 472, and 493.

[7] Smelser, 1963, p. 373; Linz, 1968, table following p. 109; Woolf, 1969, pp. 123-29; Converse, 1964, p. 253.

[8] Smelser, 1963, p. 246.

[9] Gurr, 1970, p. 131.

[10] Olson, 1963; Geschwender, 1968.

[11] Berelson and Steiner, 1964, pp. 503 and 513; Melson and Wolpe, 1970; Lemarchand, 1968.

[12] Davies, 1962.

[13] Tanter and Midlarsky, 1967, p. 272 and Table 6, p. 273. The relationship, however, does not hold in the case of Latin America, which the authors explain in terms of the frequency of Latin American coups d'état.

[14] Levy, 1970.

[15] Kataoka, 1972, p. 426.

[16] Gurr, 1970, p. 249.

[17] Feierabend and Feierabend, 1966, Table 2, p. 255.

[18] Kecskemeti, 1961, p. 111.

[19] Bwy, 1968; Gurr, 1970, pp. 239-40; Markus and Nesvold, 1972.

[20] Richter, 1966, p. 107. Also see C. Johnson, 1966, p. 103; Pettee, 1966, pp. 16-17; Edwards, 1971, p. 84; Brinton, 1965, pp. 51-55; Gottschalk, 1971, pp. 107-8.

[21] Kecskemeti, 1961, pp. 118-22; Dallin and Breslauer, 1970, pp. 205-6. Meyer, 1971, esp. pp. 146-47, discusses the relationship of elite fragmentation and political crisis to a broader range of events in European Communist states since the Second World War.

[22] Wolf, 1969, p. 272; Beals, 1970, p. 248.

[23] Again, we here are interpolating the Feierabends' data into time-series variables.

[24] Bwy, 1968, p. 236. Italics in the original. Bwy's data also show that elite *stability* and the subsequent occurrence of "turmoil" are inversely related (−0.435).

[25] Quoted in Richter, 1966, p. 119.

[26] Lemarchand, 1968.

[27] See the discussion of "the demonstration effect," as initially formulated by James S. Duesenberry in 1949, by Olson, 1963, p. 538, and by Ridker, 1962, p. 5.

[28] For example, see Deutsch, 1964, p. 100.

[29] See Palmer, 1956, pp. 353, 456-58, and Chap. 12; and for a more detailed study of these events, Palmer, 1959-64. On the relationship between the frequent urban riots in Palermo, Catania, and Messina and the endemic peasant upheavals in Sicily in the nineteenth century, see Hobsbawm, 1959, p. 96.

[30] Gasster, 1969, p. xxv.

[31] Borkenau, 1962, pp. 380-81. For the influence of German National Socialism on fascism in Japan, see Scalapino, 1964, p. 117.

THE
SETTING
Preconditions

GEOGRAPHY

Troubled by complex questions, we naturally search for simple answers. But we must resist the temptation to explain the more basic causes of revolution—or of any social phenomenon—in terms of a single variable, however objectively self-evident its explanatory value. Human consciousness interacts with the conditions of human existence, and men and women can alter their social environment and develop different patterns of behavior even when their objective circumstances are similar or the same.

This first precondition, then, is not meant to imply a geographic determinism at work in the revolutionary process. But enough has been said already about the role of geography in guerrilla warfare and external support to make the point that geographic conditions are frequently determining in the success or failure of revolutionary movements. The same may be said of the preconditions essential to their appearance.

Geography, for example, plays an important role in structuring the communications network which, in turn, helps to determine the cross-cultural extent of the demonstration effect. It was not coincidental that revolutionary events in France from 1789 through 1848 had a much greater impact in the geographic areas adjoining France (the Lowlands, Switzerland, Italy, the Rhineland) than in Scandinavia, Great Britain, the Iberian Peninsula, Eastern Europe, or Russia. Thus the relative geographic isolation of a country can reduce or eliminate the impact of the demonstration effect.

Geographic isolation can work in other ways, too. The political and social structure of Sweden paralleled that of Germany before the First World War, especially in terms of a highly class-conscious aristocracy and middle class that resisted political democratization and the upward mobility of the Swedish lower classes. Its geographic isolation, however, enabled Sweden to escape the wars and consequent political and social crises that ravaged Germany and the Continent and to evolve in the direction of social democracy without the historical disjunctures represented by revolution.[1]

The geographic isolation of Ireland and Malaya meant the failure of revolutionary movements insofar as they depended on external support for success. But in Great Britain, the protection afforded by the sea meant a comparatively minor role for the military in British society and politics and the growth of an enterprising middle class along with burgeoning commerce and maritime trade. These in turn contributed in England to capitalism and, after 1689, to the evolution of a relatively stable and democratic political system.[2]

Geographic isolation and economic self-sufficiency also help to explain the relative political stability of the United States, Canada, Australia, and New Zealand. Along with other factors, the geographic remoteness of these countries meant that their colonization by Europeans was too late for the transplanting of a feudal social structure that, in Europe, laid the basis for a history marked by class conflict. In this sense, the international diffusion of social structure, as well as political culture, is in part a function of physical geography.

The economic geography of a country also helps to determine its revolutionary potential and the characteristics of revolutionary movements that do appear. In China from the mid-nineteenth through the mid-twentieth centuries, those areas susceptible to frequent flood and famine, especially in the Yangtze Valley, provided China's periodic upheavals with a disproportionate number of revolutionary leaders and followers.[3] Where transportation routes develop is also where economic change is most rapid. Differential rates of economic development in turn heighten the hostility between different ethnic groups and socioeconomic strata. And "the availability of mineral resources, the fertility of the soils, the export value of indigenous agricultural commodities, the proximity of a transportation crossroads—all condition the pace of social change" and, consequently, the characteristics of social conflict and revolutionary potential.[4]

The relationship of a country's economic geography to its political geography can affect the rate and nature of political change. Where industry and universities are located in or near the capital of a centralized state (as in France, but not in England), the agitation of workers and students is more likely to have significant political impact. In Egypt, political centralization and the narrow geographic boundaries of Egypt's principal economic resource–the Nile River Valley–have made impossible the organization of revolutionary movements based on the peasantry. Anticolonial movements against Great Britain thus were weak and political violence in Egypt has invariably taken the form of urban riots and coups d'état.[5] The economic, political, and physical geography of a country may in turn play a determining role in the distribution and mobility of its population.

DEMOGRAPHY

Between 1715 and the French Revolution of 1789, the population of France increased by almost half, from 18 to 25 million, and the rate of population growth was especially high between 1758 and 1770. Those born during this latter period had reached their maturity by 1789.[6] The population of China actually declined in the first part of the seventeenth century, but nearly tripled between 1700 and 1850. The Taiping Rebellion in China may be dated from 1848 to 1865. And for the sixty years preceding China's first upheavals in the twentieth century, the Chinese population grew at a rate that was probably unprecedented since at least the fourteenth century.[7]

By itself, however, a sudden increase in the size of a country's population is not a good predictor of revolution. Between 1850 and 1900 the population of most European countries grew rapidly, but this also was a period of relative social and political tranquillity. Several intervening variables, including the capacity of a country's economic resources, must play a role in elevating revolutionary potential along with population growth. The pressures of increasing population on limited agricultural resources have been cited as an important precondition for agrarian radicalism in China, the Philippines, Mexico, Algeria, Peru, Bolivia, Vietnam (especially in the North), India, and in many other countries.[8] The rate at which population growth exceeds agricultural resources can be accelerated by inheritance norms that require the father's land to be distributed equally among all his heirs (as in prerevolutionary China). And the potential for agrarian violence is especially high where the effects of too many people on too little land are reinforced by a highly unequal distribution of land among the various strata of the peasantry.

Overpopulation in rural areas in turn usually leads to rapid population growth in the cities, primarily through rural-urban migration. Especially where industrial development and employment opportunities fail to keep pace with urban population growth, the potential for urban violence is high. The population of Paris grew rapidly between 1800 and 1850 and thereby laid the basis for the mass participation that marked the revolutions of 1830 and 1848.[9] Between 1800 and 1900 the population of Moscow increased by 400 percent and the population of St. Petersburg increased by 500 percent.[10] Even for those who have jobs, however, employment in large factories along with thousands of other workers (as in Moscow and St. Petersburg) raises the potential for politicization and participation in mass-based movements. In large factories the worker is subordinated to a more impersonal management bureaucracy, communication between workers is facilitated, and their political consciousness is more easily raised by radical agitation and propaganda.[11]

But even for those urban residents who are unemployed or on the margins of the economy and newly arrived from rural areas, urban life means the disintegration of traditional norms and the welfare provisions and authority structures represented by family, tribe, religion, caste, and village. The urban citizen's susceptibility to mass violence and revolutionary mobilization is thus increased, although revolutionary movements of long duration and with institutionalized structures are highly unlikely in an urban setting. The rise of fascism in Germany and Italy, however, has been explained as partly a function of rural-urban migration (impelled by high birth rates before 1914) that vastly enlarged the lower classes of the cities and heightened the sensitivities of the urban middle classes to their threatened social status. And, in fact, the German Nazis and Italian Fascists, once in power, not only subordinated trade unions to the power of the state but halted the urban influx of rural dwellers.[12]

Where many of the preconditions for revolution exist but where revolutionary movements are weak or nonexistent, the out-migration of large numbers of citizens often seems to be a major explanatory variable. Those who emigrate to unsettled territory or to foreign countries are those who, in terms of youth, social mobility, and political activism, are the more likely prospects for revolutionary leadership and participation if constrained to remain at home. Their departure for promising horizons reduces the society's revolutionary potential or the chances of success in the event of revolutionary activity. These demographic dynamics appear to have been at work in Ireland in the nineteenth and early twentieth centuries, in England after the Puritan Revolution and the labor agitation associated with Chartism in the mid-nineteenth century, and in southern Italy around the turn of the twentieth century. In each case, emigration to the United States (or Australia) reduced the demographic pressures on economic resources and contributed to a reduction in the incidence of violence in the home country. The same phenomenon has been cited in the case of Algerians emigrating to Tunisia under the impact of French colonialism, British Loyalists leaving the American colonies for Canada after 1775, workers and farmers forsaking the eastern United States for the western frontier in the latter half of the nineteenth century, Catholics in North Vietnam fleeing to South Vietnam after 1954, East Germans moving to West Germany before 1961, anti-Castroites leaving Cuba after 1959, and Sicilians migrating to the Italian north in the 1950s and 1960s. In each instance, those who emigrated left behind a more politically passive population, often because it was more socially homogeneous, which worked to the advantage of the existing regime.

CULTURAL CLEAVAGE

Especially when immigrants are culturally distinguished from the majority of the indigenous population, in-migration can reinforce existing hostilities or introduce new cleavages into the society, raising its potential for collective violence. Citizens of the United States should not have to be reminded that racial or ethnic divisions are frequently associated with social conflict and political instability. Americans of Slavic, Germanic, Chinese, Japanese, Latin American, and Italian origin, and American Indians, Jews, and blacks have all been the targets of collective violence in various periods of United States history. Even before the urban upheavals of 1965 to 1968, the record of at least seventy-six race riots between 1913 and 1963 suggested some major failures in the realization of the American ideals of stability, equality, and democracy.[13]

In China, the Taiping Rebellion was based primarily on the hostility of Chinese ethnic minorities in South China for the "foreign" Manchu dynasty and resistance to the encroachments of migrant Chinese from the North. The Communist insurgency in Malaya after the Second World War, and the reconstituted guerrilla movement in Malaysia after 1971, recruited followers almost exclusively from the indigenous ethnic minorities, especially the Malayan Chinese. Communists in Vietnam also received strong support from the non-Vietnamese ethnic groups, including the Tho minority. Guerrilla activity in Thailand after 1965 was based largely on nonethnic Thais, including Malays and Chinese. In the 1960s and early 1970s, Arabs were aligned against blacks in Zanzibar and in the Sudan, blacks against East Indians in Trinidad, Hausa and Yoruba tribes against Ibos in Nigeria, and the Hutu against the Tutsi tribes in Burundi. The coups d'état that took place in Sierra Leone in 1967, 1968, and 1971 reflected the antagonisms between the Limba and Temne tribes. And Jews and Russian-oriented Slavic minorities in Eastern Europe between the First and Second World Wars were overrepresented in the electoral and membership ranks of the East European Communist parties.[14]

Political independence from a colonial power, economic development, population growth, or any of the accelerators of revolution discussed in the preceding chapter are likely to broaden the cleavage lines traced by race or ethnicity and thereby raise the society's revolutionary potential. Whether the society's cultural cleavages are manifested in urban turmoil, rural violence, civil war, guerrilla warfare, or coups d'état depends on many factors and is not always easy to predict. We must content ourselves for the moment, then, with trying to understand the preconditions of political violence and the revolutionary process in terms of cultural cleavage.

But racial or ethnic cleavage is not the only cultural basis for political conflict. *Linguistic* cleavage also has been the cause of confrontation and instability, and not only in many of the underdeveloped countries of Asia and Africa. German-speaking minorities among eastern Europe's Slavic peoples, Basques and

Catalonians in Spain, Flemish-speaking and French-speaking Belgians, have all been a source of conflicting interests and nonnegotiable demands that have placed severe strains on the fabric of government. In France, Breton-speaking separatists (from Brittany, or Bretagne) claiming to represent the aspirations for cultural independence of 3.3 million Bretons exploded more than 200 bombs in French government installations between 1966 and 1978, including a bomb that caused more than $1 million in damage to the palace of Versailles.

And wherever racial and linguistic cleavages are *reinforced* by each other, or by other cleavages—including those that are religious, economic, or ideological—the preconditions are in place for an especially explosive style of politics. The nationalist sentiments of Lithuanians subordinated to Moscow, of Croatians hostile to Belgrade, of Basques fighting Madrid, of Armenians in Turkey, and of Kurds in Iraq are intensified by religious, linguistic, *and* economic differences that complicate the cultural maps of these societies and that frequently have surfaced in various forms of political violence.

Before the creation of Bangladesh in 1971, for example, most West Pakistanis were Muslim and spoke Urdu. Most East Pakistanis also were Muslim, but they spoke Bengali and had closer cultural ties to the Hindu Bengalis in India. And while 60 percent of the Pakistani population lived in the East, the Western Parkistanis were politically and economically dominant. The Catholic minority in Northern Ireland, compared to the Protestant majority, is underprivileged economically and underrepresented politically. French-speaking separatists among the Catholic population of Quebec have received their strongest support where English-speaking Canadians of Protestant origin are the most economically prominent—in Montreal rather than in Quebec City or the Quebec countryside.

Federalism in Canada, India, and in Switzerland, however, appears to have reduced overt social conflict between cultural groups by limiting their social and economic interaction. And where religious and linguistic cleavages do not reinforce each other but instead overlap (as in Switzerland), or where the development of economic classes with industrialization cuts across lines of cultural cleavage (as in Holland), the society's chances for avoiding fratricidal strife are increased.

Religion deserves special attention because it can both raise and lower a society's potential for violence. Trotsky correctly understood that the "Old Believers"—one-fourth of Russia's Christian population in 1914—were an important source of revolutionary support because their hostility for the Russian Orthodox Church coincided with an intense opposition to the Russian state. In the early 1970s, increased migration of Christian Filipinos to the outer islands of the Philippines provoked the resident Muslims into acts of guerrilla warfare; by the early 1980s, the Muslim separatists had extended their struggle to the main islands and the capital where assassinations of government officials and other acts of terrorism demonstrated the Muslims' commitment to cultural (and so political) independence from the Christian government in Manila. The establishment of Pakistan in 1947 reflected the apparently irreconcilable conflicts between Muslims and Hindus in the Indian subcontinent after independence from Great Britain. And the frequently violent struggles between Catholics and Protestants since the Reformation make it clear that religious cleavages, by themselves, can be a volatile source of social conflict, especially where each of the competing religions considers itself the only true way to divine enlightenment and spiritual salvation.

Where there are no religious cleavages, however, a society's religion may reinforce prevailing authority norms and thereby reduce the potential for conflict along other lines of cleavage. This is especially true of Confucianism and Hinduism, which include elaborate codes prescribing the appropriate organization of social life and human conduct. Extreme differences in social status and wealth are thus legitimated by religious sanction, and it probably is no coincidence that peasant communism in India is strongest precisely where the Hindu caste system has broken down.[15] The individual's subordination to established authority, which is also explicit in Protestant Christianity, helps to explain the relative passivity of lower social classes, particularly of blacks in the southern United States. The traditional distrust of Catholicism for secular political authority and republican institutions, however, appears to have raised the potential for extremist political movements, especially of the fascist variety, even where the society's religious culture is relatively homogeneous (as in Italy). On the other hand, the Catholic Church in Ireland strongly resisted the organization of political movements, including those opposed to British control, fearing a reduction in the Church's influence over the Irish population. And part of the explanation for Castro's success was the relative weakness of the Catholic Church in Cuba, which traditionally has been less susceptible to the Church's authority than other Latin American countries, including those in which Castroite movements have failed.

Religion also may function as a stabilizing social force by providing alternative channels for the expression of discontent. The growth of Methodism and Protestant Nonconformity coincided with advancing industrialization in England (between 1790 and 1850) and converts were recruited primarily from among those lower classes most susceptible to radical political organization. Lay-preaching and membership in community churches provided status and social solidarity for individuals who had been uprooted by industrialism from traditional and more agrarian life-styles. The obvious precondition for religious nonconformity is a secular state that tolerates religious diversity, but new belief systems and cults lower the chances of their toleration as they deviate more widely from prevailing religious beliefs and practices.[16]

The intensification of France's economic exploitation of Algeria in the 1920s and 1930s also coincided with Islamic revivalism, deliberately encouraged by the French as an alternative to political unrest among the Muslim population. Following colonization of the western frontier by white settlers and military repression, American Indians turned to new forms of religious experience, including the use of peyote as a hallucinogenic drug. Religious revivalism and cultism in the United States declined after the First World War, grew rapidly during the Depression, and declined once again only to find new expression in the late 1960s. Particularly for American youths disenchanted with United States domestic and foreign policies and lacking political efficacy, the appeal of religious cultism and communal social organization appears to have been part of a time-honored response to periodic social strains. In this sense, religion serves as a surrogate or functional alternative to political involvement, and yesterday's revolutionary may be easily transformed into today's "Jesus-freak." We may hypothesize, then, that the appearance of religious revivalism and cultism suggests the existence of revolutionary preconditions, but actually lowers the society's revolutionary potential. The religious movement is also likely to be stronger as the forces of repression are understood to be in a largely unassailable position of authority. Instead of attempting to change the society, the religious enthusiast chooses to abandon society for an apparently more pure and uncorrupted life-style.[17]

A final note should be added to this section on the relationship between culture and revolutionary potential, and it is based on the premise that frequent violence in a society over extended periods of time represents a cultural or subcultural characteristic in and of itself. Just as coups d'état in Latin America are not randomly distributed in time (suggesting "the demonstration effect"), they are not randomly distributed according to political geography. Of the ninety-five successful coups in twenty Latin American countries between 1907 and 1966, almost half (48 percent) were concentrated in only five countries: Argentina, Bolivia, Ecuador, Haiti, and Peru.[18] Long before the twentieth century and revolutions in Russia, China, Vietnam, Cuba, and Mexico, the established patterns of political life in these countries included assassination, clandestine organization, peasant rebellion, and other forms of political violence. Frequent violence in the past, especially when it produced apparently positive results, tends to legitimate violence in the present and in the future. And people accustomed to political change through violence and unconstitutional procedures are unlikely to have a high regard for the norms of bargaining and compromise essential to democracy and political stability.[19]

LAND TENURE

Part of the definition of an agricultural society is that most people in the society depend directly on the land for their livelihood. Because the ownership of land is the primary measure of wealth and status, socioeconomic differences are much more visible in an agricultural society than in an industrial society. It certainly is no accident, then, that almost all of the revolutionary movements recorded by modern history have occurred in agricultural societies characterized by an extremely unequal distribution of land.

Interviews with 400 former Huk guerrillas in the Philippines in the 1950s found that the majority had joined the insurgency because they did not have sufficient land for their family's needs. Huk ideology induced the guerrillas to generalize from their personal circumstances, and 95 percent declared that "their main reason for fighting was to gain land for the peasants." Most of those who were interviewed cited the Philippine government's promise of free land as their primary motivation for defecting from the guerrillas.[20] The intensifying struggle between Muslims and Christians in the southern islands of the Philippines, throughout the 1970s and into the 1980s, was defined by a religious cleavage, but the underlying cause of the conflict may well have been the scarcity of land—which was made all the more scarce by the migration of Christian settlers from the north to the south.

Aggregate data from many countries also confirm the positive relationship between land inequality and revolutionary potential. In France before 1789, 80 percent of the population were peasants, and while the peasantry owned 40 percent of the land so did less than 2 percent of the population (including the nobility, monarchy, and the Church). As in Russia, peasants in France also felt that they should receive legal title to the land they worked, which far exceeded the 40 percent in their possession. Contrary to what had happened in England, however, the enclosure of common lands in Russia did not lead to the disappearance of the peasantry through rural-urban migration and industrialization. Eighty percent of the Russian population remained on the land as serfs or, after 1861, as legally free but heavily indebted peasants. And before the 1905 Russian Revolution, the poorest 10 million peasant families together held no more land than did the 30,000 largest proprietors—excluding the tsar, Church, and monasteries, whose disproportionate share of the land was even greater.

In Mexico in 1900, 1 percent of the total population owned 97 percent of the land. In the northern state of Chihuahua, where Pancho Villa's armies were active, seventeen families. owned 40 percent of the state's entire territory. In North China in the 1930s, one-third of the population owned more than two-thirds of the land; in the South, less than 5 percent of the population owned between 30 and 50 percent of the land. Prior to the Chinese Communist revolution, 80 percent of China's population were peasants, but only 20 percent of the total population were landowners.

In the Tonkin area of North Vietnam before the Second World War, 500 large landowners held 20 percent of the land. French colonists owned 20 percent of all the cultivated land in Vietnam, and 60 percent of all Vietnamese families owned no land at all. In South Vietnam, land reforms initiated by the Communists during their struggle with the French were cancelled by the Diem government after 1954. In Bolivia before the revolution of 1952, 10 percent of the agricultural population owned nearly 95 percent of the land. In Cuba before

1959, 10 percent of the total population owned two-thirds of the land, while two-thirds of the population were landless tenants, sharecroppers, or squatters without any legal claims to the land they worked. Ethiopia's revolution in 1974 may have been touched off by soaring inflation, rioting students, and a military astonished by its own audacity; but the preconditions for the revolution included a time-worn system of feudalism and serfdom in which 90 percent of the land was owned by 10 percent of the population—and many of the owners were absentees (including Ethiopia's emperor and the Orthodox Church).[21]

Inequality, however, is the socioeconomic condition of most of mankind and of all societies, and again it is important to test our hypotheses with reference to varying levels of political violence and in societies that have not undergone revolution. Raymond Tanter and Manus Midlarsky have compared the extent of land inequality for ten countries that experienced revolution between 1955 and 1960 with the same measure of land inequality for forty stable countries over the same time period. They concluded that "revolutions occurred in those societies with a higher degree of land inequality."[22] Their statistical measures of difference would have demonstrated an even higher association between land inequality and revolution if France, with a relatively low degree of land inequality, had not been included in the revolutionary category (few are likely to agree that the events of 1958 in Algiers and Paris represented a "revolution"). Comparing the extent of land inequality with interval data on political instability (deaths resulting from political violence), Bruce Russett found a correlation coefficient of .46 for forty-seven countries between 1945 and 1962. Controlling for the level of economic development, however, would have produced results explaining a greater percentage of the variance: of the eighteen noncommunist countries with more than 50 percent of their work force in agricultural employment, thirteen experienced at least one major instability event in the postwar period, and eight of these countries are very high on Russett's scale of land inequality.[23]

A highly unequal distribution of land, then, is most likely to raise a society's revolutionary potential under the conditions of a preindustrial economy. We may add some other intervening variables that reinforce the social and political impact of land inequality in an agricultural society. Where foreign interests play a major economic role, whether through international investment (as in China, Mexico, and Cuba) or through outright political control (as in Vietnam and Algeria), the hostilities generated by land inequality can be tied to the issue of anticolonialism, thereby raising to a very high point the society's revolutionary potential.

Inequalities of land distribution can also be exacerbated by absentee ownership, whether by foreigners or by the indigenous landed oligarchy. It is frequently pointed out that peasants in France before 1789 were better off than their counterparts in most of the rest of Europe, but the incidence of absenteeism was also higher in France than elsewhere. Absenteeism also has been associated with a rebellious peasantry in China (especially after the Revolution of 1911, and again in the 1930s with the Japanese occupation), in Vietnam (especially in the Mekong Delta region), in Russia, Ethiopia, Cuba, and in Bolivia prior to 1952.

The issue, however, is not so much the absence of the landlord from his estate as it is *the social solidarity and the strength of authority patterns cutting across the various social strata of the countryside.* Despite their impoverishment, peasants in India and Japan were relatively well integrated in the rural social structures of their societies—in India through the system of caste, which made the priest and landlord an important functional part of village life.[24] German peasants on the estates of the Prussian Junkers were no less anxious for land than peasants in prerevolutionary France and Russia. But the Junkers lived on their land and maintained a relatively close relationship with their peasants, who consequently shared their conservative outlook. Many Russian nobles, on the other hand, considered their country estates a vacation retreat from their houses in the towns and cities, and even when in the country they exhibited different manners, frequently spoke a different language (French), and lived according to styles that set them apart from the peasants who worked their land. The centralization of political and social life in the French court at Versailles meant a relatively high percentage of absentee landlords in most of provincial France and a heavier economic burden on the nobles. The nobility's resolve to reinstate the collection of feudal dues only intensified the peasants' sense of inequity. And the "feudal reaction" in France in the eighteenth century was all the more intolerable because the nobility no longer performed those political and economic functions that had once justified its claims on the peasantry.[25]

ECONOMIC DEVELOPMENT

The nobility's efforts to squeeze more out of the peasantry is also likely to coincide with basic economic change that the nobility—more so on the Continent than in England—is ill-equipped to cope with. The nobility in turn is typically responding to the development of capitalist agriculture and to the increased tax levies imposed by a centralizing monarch, whose demands for more money from the nobility end up on the doorstep of the peasantry. The major classes of feudal society thus are caught in the grip of a fundamental socioeconomic transformation that is perhaps best described as the growth of a market economy, and a market economy that has its most immediate impact on the production and distribution of agricultural commodities.

The end of subsistence-oriented agriculture also signals a major change in the socioeconomic structure of underdeveloped and colonial societies, regardless of the extent to which their histories have been marked by the more formal characteristics of feudalism. The common lands that may have been available to the peasant at an earlier time are incorporated into a system of private property. Road construction that serves an expanding regional market is supported by peasant labor and new taxes that are charged to local peasants. An economy based on money replaces the more traditional system of exchange through the barter of commodities, primarily agricultural produce. Taxes are assessed on the individual peasant instead of on the peasant village. For most peasants, a moneyed economy and the concentration of property ownership mean eventual borrowing at high interest rates and mounting indebtedness. The communal structure of peasant society breaks down as the peasantry is stratified into a minority of rich peasants, a larger minority of "middle" peasants, and a growing majority of "small" peasants, many of whom are transformed into agricultural day laborers or urban migrants as their land is absorbed by the new and wealthier peasant classes. In this sense, the economic progress imputed to capitalist development means increasing social and economic inequality. The growth of a market economy in agriculture thus entails the destruction of the traditional social values and authority patterns that characterized the earlier relationships between peasant and lord, man and society. The political authority of traditional elites and the ethics of social obligation decline as the peasant community gives way to a commercial society and as individual worth comes to be measured by money.

One of the fundamental preconditions for revolution, then, is not so much the poverty of peasants (or workers), but economic change that threatens the relative security and traditional status of men and women living according to norms and habits that are rapidly becoming anachronistic. The flash points of revolutionary activity in China were near Canton and Shanghai, and in Vietnam near Hanoi and Saigon, where peasants were either numbered among the new industrial proletariat or were most exposed to the new market mechanisms of capitalist agriculture.[26] Revolutionary peasants in France in 1789 were concentrated in those regions where the disintegration of feudal institutions was most advanced, while counterrevolution in the Vendée in 1793 reflected the apprehensions of those peasants who felt most threatened by the revolutionary government's actions on behalf of private property and commercialized agriculture.[27] The guerrilla activity and terrorism of the Mau Mau in Kenya after 1952 have been described as an "atavistic, tribe-based reaction" to the threat of modernization.[28] The immense loss of life and destruction of property in Colombia from 1946 through the 1950s, a period known simply as *la violencia,* has been explained as primarily "the defense of a traditional sacred order against secular modernizing tendencies undermining that order."[29] Summarizing his detailed studies of peasant-based revolution in Mexico, Russia, China, Vietnam, Algeria, and Cuba, the anthropologist Eric Wolf concludes that the precondition underlying all these revolutions was "the world-wide spread and diffusion of a particular cultural system, that of North Altantic capitalism."[30]

Higher revolutionary potential, however, also may result from the conscious political choices of ruling elites, whose passions for modern economic and military capabilities blind them to the social and psychological consequences of modernization. In Iran, for example, the Shah's "white revolution" launched "from the throne" in the 1950s and intensified in the early 1960s was designed to neutralize or eliminate the traditional landed elites who opposed the Shah's modernizing programs. This was the real objective behind the Shah's loudly proclaimed commitment to redistributing land to Iran's peasants. But certainly no more than 15 percent of Iran's peasants received land through the program, while the traditional patterns of farming and agrarian social organization were seriously disrupted. By the mid-1970s, Iran's total agricultural production had declined, the parcel system of annually allotting land to teams of villagers had been eliminated, the communal land belonging in common to all the peasants of the village had been absorbed into the newly expanded system of private farming, a new middle class of landlords and money-lenders had emerged, many of Iran's peasants lived in economic circumstances more precarious than before, and the traditional patterns of loyalties, dependencies, and responsibilities had been severely weakened or destroyed. Those most forceful in their opposition to these trends, most ideologically committed to rolling back the evils of modernization, and best prepared to fill the power vacuum created by the fall of the Shah, were Iran's clerical elites. Economic change initiated by the Shah had worked to the advantage of a reactionary clergy resolutely opposed to the Shah.

Where the market economy for agricultural exchange is well established *before* decolonization or the onset of modernization, however, the revolutionary potential of the peasantry is relatively low. The society's chances of making the transition from a traditional to an economically developed society with a minimum of social conflict are even greater if the process of agrarian modernization and industrialization is extended over a relatively long period of time. The institutions of the state thus have an opportunity to develop the welfare and integrative functions performed by the more traditional structures of an earlier day (family, village, tribe, caste, church, and nobility). The chances for stability are especially good if a majority of the citizens feels threatened by a foreign state during the critical stages of economic transformation: the danger to Great Britain posed by Napoleonic Europe, for example, helped to impart cohesion to British society during the relatively unsettled years of industrialization at the turn of the nineteenth century.[31] We might also hypothesize that the perceived threat of Israel has contributed to greater stability in the Middle East, particularly in Egypt, than might otherwise have been expected, given the major socioeconomic changes in Arab societies since the early 1950s.

On the other hand, revolutionary potential increases as the commercialization of agriculture coincides with industrialization, as urbanization proceeds at a faster rate than industrial development, and as industrialization is relatively rapid and telescoped in time. The more radical left-wing working-class movements in Europe developed precisely where industrialization was late and, once begun, where it moved forward at an accelerated pace.[32] Where industrialization was well underway but where substantial enclaves of a traditional agrarian society remained, the basis was laid for strong fascist movements, most obviously in Germany and Italy, but also in Spain, Austria, and in the more industrially developed countries of Latin America.[33]

The potential for major social and political instability is especially high where "developmental crises" overlap instead of occurring sequentially in time: basic land reform that breaks up the landed estates to the advantage of a growing middle peasantry; the replacement of subsistence farming with a market economy in agriculture; industrialization along with urbanization; national integration of previously parochial subcultures or relatively autonomous political regions; the secularization of the society through the separation of church and state and a reduction in the social and political roles of religion; political organization and integration of the newly mobilized masses of the modernizing society. In Spain in the 1930s, all these developmental crises occurred at the same time, laying the basis for an extremely destructive civil war.[34]

This is to suggest a curvilinear relationship between revolutionary potential and economic development or—in all its social and political ramifications— "modernization." (See Figure 11-1.) Revolutionary potential is low in traditional societies because of the low incidence of economic change that consequently exerts minimal pressures for adaptation on established political and social institutions. Revolutionary potential increases with the development of a market economy in agricultural production, with urbanization and industrialization, and according to the rate of economic change, the extent of foreign control, and the coincidence of the developmental crises associated with modernization. Revolutionary potential then declines as new authority patterns,

FIGURE 11-1   Revolutionary Potential and Modernization: A Curvilinear Relationship

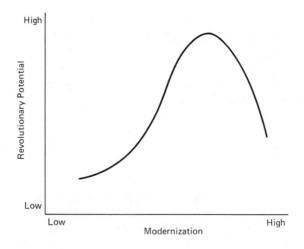

welfare institutions, and the social norms related to modernization are firmly established at an advanced stage of economic development.[35]

The most systematic testing of this hypothesis has been performed with cross-sectional data from a large number of countries. In one study, nine indices of change in the material conditions of life were correlated with a variety of instability events in sixty-nine countries, showing that "the higher the rate of change on the indices, the greater the increase in instability." Using national income to control for the level of economic development, the same study also found that the higher the rate of growth in national income for economically advanced societies, the greater their political stability.[36]

These findings lend support to my earlier suggestion that the classic period of revolutionary movements comes to an end with decolonization and advanced economic development. But war, depression, the unanticipated consequences of technological innovation, sudden alterations in demographic trends, or changing social values may once again raise the possibilities of revolution in many societies throughout the world. There still is much to learn about revolutionary potential, then, and in terms of some fundamental *non*economic variables, including the adaptative capability of governments confronted with major alterations in their societies. The alert reader will have noted already that it is less economic development per se that affects revolutionary potential than it is the ways in which the society's political and social structures respond to the challenge of economic development. The concluding sections of this chapter on revolutionary preconditions focus on these critical variables.

POLITICAL ADAPTATION

The closed authority structure of the Catholic Church proved unresponsive to demands for institutional reform, and the defeat of the reform-oriented Conciliarists in the mid-fifteenth century opened the way for the Protestant Reformation beginning in the early sixteenth century. Had the Church been able to reform itself, there might never have been a religious revolution or civil wars in Europe based on religious differences.

Sun Yat-sen in China, Fidel Castro in Cuba, Francisco Madero in Mexico, Ferhat Abbas in Algeria, and the eventual leaders of the Huk guerrillas in the Philippines all attempted to wring basic reforms through constitutional channels from the narrow oligarchies dominating their respective societies in the twentieth century. They ran for political office, encouraged the development of opposition parties, lobbied for basic change through the legislative and judicial process, or exhorted ruling elites to introduce needed reform. Like the Conciliarists, their efforts failed and each of them turned from constitutional politics to revolutionary action.

A low regard for the adaptive potential of political institutions is also likely to characterize newly emergent middle classes (Stuart England or Bourbon France) or military elites (the contemporary Middle East) confronted with royal autocracies opposed to modernization and based on the ascriptive norms of a traditional society. Many other examples may be cited to suggest that revolutionary potential is inversely related to the adaptive capability of government. Few studies of revolution, or of the characteristics of political stability in general, have missed an opportunity to elaborate on this obvious generalization.[37]

Its obvious quality, however, suggests that the generalization is dangerously close to being a tautology instead of a hypothesis. If religious schism in Christianity or revolution in France, Russia, China, or in any other country is the index of the low adaptive capability of authoritative institutions, the inverse relationship of the two variables is true by definition. If revolution fails or if no revolutionary movement appears, we must conclude that government institutions were eventually responsive to demands placed upon the system. But this does not extend our understanding of the revolutionary process either, and we clearly need some indices of political adaptation that are independent of the various manifestations of political violence.

Economic development means social mobilization—the elevation of political and social consciousness among new strata of the population whose increased dependency on the market heightens their demands for political representation and participation.[38] The old political structures based on a narrow oligarchy in the society must be made to accommodate the interests of the newly mobilized social classes, and among the best indicators of adaptive capability are suffrage reform, the legalization of trade-union activities, and the state's provision of welfare services.

Revolutionary potential is low not only where industrial development is relatively slow, but where the right to vote is *gradually* extended to all citizens. The reform of political representation thus has an opportunity to precede or coincide with economic change, social mobilization, and the development of new institutions (namely political parties) within the legitimating context of the broader political system (for example, monarchy and parliament). In Great Britain in 1820, fewer than 500 men, most of them peers in the House of Lords, elected the majority of members in the House of Commons. The Reform Bill of 1832 extended the suffrage to 12 percent of all adult males. In 1867, 30 percent of all adult males were enfranchised; in 1884, 75 percent; and in 1918 all adult males and women over 30 years of age were given the right to vote. But where the suffrage has been extended rapidly, as in France in 1848 and in Weimar Germany, the result has been political instability and authoritarian politics: the introduction of democratic political institutions outpaced the development of a political culture supportive of democratic and participatory norms.[39]

There was mounting labor violence in the United States after 1870, with fluctuations in the level of violence, which nonetheless remained relatively high until the 1930s. The New Deal of the Roosevelt Administration, however, gave government sanction to trade-union organization and collective bargaining and broadened the welfare services provided by the state. Labor violence declined as trade-union membership increased along with the workers' sense of national political representation.

In England, the socially troubled first decades of the nineteenth century contributed not only to Parliament's extension of the suffrage in 1832: trade-union organization was also permitted beginning in 1825; restrictions on the emigration of skilled workers were eliminated; the worst abuses of labor in factories and mines were curtailed; tariffs were lowered to reduce food costs; and capital punishment for more than 100 minor offenses (typically charged to the lower classes) was abolished.

In France, on the other hand, trade unions were not legally recognized until 1884. But liberalization of restrictions on trade-union organization and the introduction of collective bargaining between labor and management did not receive government sanction until after the election victory of the Popular Front in 1936. Trade-union membership in France immediately grew from 1 million to 5 million in 1937, reflecting the potential for unionization that earlier governments had succeeded in suppressing. In England, the responsibility of the state for administering public welfare was acknowledged in 1601 (1893 in France), and welfare services have been consistently more liberal in England than in France.[40]

Working-class politics in France, Italy, and Spain have always been more extreme than in England, the Lowlands, and Scandinavia, and in the former countries the working class (and intellectuals) have traditionally enjoyed less access to political institutions and less influence on public policy. In Germany, Bismarck's restrictions on working-class organization were coupled with extensive social welfare reforms, which helped to make German Social Democracy a moderate, even conservative, political force. But it was no coincidence that the more extreme expression of German socialism was in Prussia, where (unlike southern Germany) the working classes were excluded from the suffrage until 1918. And before the revolutions of the twentieth century in Russia, the suffrage was extremely limited, industrial strikes were prohibited, trade unions were illegal, and the welfare services of the state were almost nonexistent.

Other measures of the adaptive capability of political institutions include the variety of associational groupings in the society, the percentage of the population belonging to organizations, and the extent to which existing political parties, trade unions, and other groups recruit members from across the several lines of cleavage in the society. Each of these variables is inversely related to revolutionary potential. The development of intermediary groups between citizens and elites helps to reduce social conflict by integrating citizens into the existing social structure and political system, thereby encouraging the settlement of conflict through bargaining and compromise.[41]

But most of the countries of the underdeveloped world, including Bolivia both before and after the revolution of 1952, Nigeria before the civil war of 1966, and Colombia during the period of *la violencia,* have lacked associational structures that cut across the different cultural and economic strata of their societies. In Malaya after the Second World War, however, Great Britain encouraged the development of trade unions, political parties, and representative institutions of government that included all of Malaya's ethnic groups. The modernization of India's political institutions, both before and after independence from Great Britain, contributed to the recruitment of citizens from various strata of a highly segmented society; it also *preceded* the relatively slow social mobilization stimulated by India's equally slow economic development. The happy but unanticipated result has been a relatively stable political system, whose legitimacy has been further enhanced by the continuity of political authority provided by the ruling Congress party and by the long tenure of Nehru's charismatic leadership.[42]

In dramatic contrast to India is Iran, where the accelerated rate of modernization after the 1950s far outpaced the adaptation of the political system to new social forces, *and* to old social forces that were newly mobilized (the clergy). (See Table 11-1.) Early development of Iran's oil deposits began in the 1930s, but a government controlling at least 10 percent of the world's proven petroleum reserves was bound to intensify its exploitation of an increasingly profitable natural resource. By the early 1970s, 75 percent of Iran's population still lived by agriculture, while 80 percent of Iran's national income came from petroleum revenues. The clash between the traditional and the modern also was underlined by changes in Iran's countryside (see above under "economic development"), by changes in the life styles of Iran's urban citizens, and by the Shah's steadfast refusal to relinquish any political power. On the contrary, gestures in the direction of reform only confirmed the autocracy of the regime.

On the Shah's initiative, for example, a national political party had been organized and candidates had been elected to a two-house parliament. But the party's candidates had to be approved by the Shah; half of the 60-member Senate was directly appointed by the Shah; and members of the lower house (the *Majlis*) were granted only consultative authority. The government, or executive branch, was accountable to the Shah (not to parliament), and the Shah could dismiss the government and dissolve one or both houses of parliament at will. Organized political opposition was illegal. Suspected opponents of the Shah's regime—perhaps as many as 100,000 by the mid-1970s—were arrested, imprisoned, tortured, and often executed without chance of judicial remedy. The families of victims also had no right of legal appeal. The only law was the Shah's law.

Thus the Shah's variation on centralized and absolute monarchy came into irreconcilable conflict with the forces that were mobilized by socioeconomic change. The conflict between Iran's society and the Shah's state was all the more predictable given the power of Iran's national religion (Shi'ite Islam) and the

TABLE 11-1 Revolutionary Preconditions in Iran: Indicators of Social and Economic Change in Iran, Iraq, Syria, and Egypt

	IRAN	IRAQ	SYRIA	EGYPT
% increase, industrial production, 1960-1975	1,373	n.a.	177	352
% increase, per capita income	(1960–1974) 636	(1960–1973) 144	(1963–1970) 28	(1960–1973) 99
% average annual rate of inflation, 1970-1976	25.2	17.5	18.8	5.2
% increase, passenger cars in use, 1966-1974	315	38	32	76
% increase, television sets per 1000 population, 1964-1975	920	(1964–1970) 76	275	89

Sources: For the annual rate of inflation, see *Information Please Almanac, 1979* (New York: Information Please Publishing, Inc., 1978). All other data are calculated from *United Nations Statistical Yearbook, 1970, 1976, 1977,* and from *United Nations Compendium of Social Statistics, 1967.*

clergy's resolute hostility to the consequences of modernization. Had the Shah permitted a legal opposition, curtailed the powers of his secret police, delegated effective authority to governing institutions below the level of the monarchy, and encouraged the development of political parties that aggregated interests from across the spectrum of Iranian society, then the Shah might have neutralized the power of the clergy and saved his throne. But then the Shah would have been someone other than the Shah.

And in the more politically and industrially developed countries of the world, institutions that aggregate interests appear to be especially effective where elections between competing parties are organized according to single-member districts, thereby forcing the parties and the groups associated with them to appeal to diverse social strata in order to win an electoral plurality. By contrast, elections based on proportional representation tend to reinforce existing cleavages in the society. They also can proliferate political representation so that governing institutions, as in Weimar Germany, are rendered incapable of responding to either old problems or new crises (including economic depression). Fascism, in fact, has been interpreted as largely an attempt to continue economic development while maintaining social stability by reducing the effective political participation of the society's newly mobilized classes.[43]

The state's political institutions also improve their adaptive capability as opposition groups are well organized and are able to alternate with other political elites in the exercise of power. In Mexico, it may well be that the most enduring legacy of the Revolution has been the limitation on presidential tenure (six years), which has contributed to political stability by at least creating the illusion of a circulation of elites in the Mexican political process.

These findings help to explain the relative stability of advanced industrial states. Their high level of economic development is likely to coincide with a well-established system of groups and political institutions that facilitate the resolution of social and economic conflict according to the norms of peaceful political competition. But even in highly industrialized states the incidence of nonviolent political protest is likely to correlate with the open or closed characteristics of the particular political system. A study of demonstrations and other forms of collective protest in forty-three United States cities in 1968 found that the frequency of protest was lowest in cities of both low and high "opportunity structures" (measured by institutional and sociological variables), and highest in cities with a mix of open and closed characteristics.[44] These findings suggest the by now familiar curvilinear relationship between political stability and measures of the structural characteristics of politics and society: instability increases as the demands stimulated by economic development and social mobilization exceed the response capabilities of existing institutions, and declines only as the more activist citizens are organized and as political institutions prove responsive to their needs.

SOCIAL STATUS

The low adaptive capability of political institutions is almost invariably associated with rigidly stratified social structures. What raises revolutionary potential is economic change that complicates social stratification in the society, placing new demands on old institutions more suitable to the social structure of an earlier era. The characteristics of status distribution are thus a convenient summary of many of the more particular variables related to revolutionary potential.

"Status" refers to the honor or prestige accorded individuals or groups in terms of the positions they occupy or the roles they play in society. If everyone were equal in prestige or honor to everyone else in all social relationships, there would be no "status." The term, then, implies inequality in one or several dimensions of social life, and status hierarchies are a fundamental characteristic of all human social organization and have been identified even among many animals below the intelligence level of the human species.[45]

There are two attributes of social status that concern us here: status discrepancy and status mobility. "Status discrepancy" (sometimes called status "inconsistency" or "incongruity") denotes a conceptual division of the entire society into several categories: political, economic, and social. Status discrepancy in our present context usually means a relatively high status in the economic relationships of society but a relatively low status in its political and social subsystems. "Status mobility" refers to either increasing or declining status in any or all of the social subsystems. Clarification of these sometimes puzzling abstractions and of their close functional relationships in social reality is the objective of what follows.

We may begin with an ideal-type feudal society in which there is no status discrepancy or status mobility. The nobility enjoys high status in all the social subsystems, while the peasantry has neither wealth, aristocratic title, nor political influence. This is likely to be a highly stable society as fathers bequeath their status intact and unchallenged to their sons: status is inherited, or acquired by "ascription."

The potential for status discrepancy increases as a formerly elective monarchy becomes hereditary and as the monarch attempts to centralize political authority at the expense of the nobility. The status of the nobility is further compromised as a growing commercial class—a bourgeoisie recruited from urban artisans, from the more enterprising peasants, and perhaps from some of the nobility—increases its wealth along with the development of monetary exchange and a market economy. While the nobility's status remains high in the social subsystem, its status is declining both economically and politically. Status discrepancy also characterizes the growing bourgeoisie, whose increasing wealth is not matched by either its social status or its political influence. The bourgeoisie typically stands for the distribution of status in terms of "achievement" rather than ascriptive norms.[46]

At some point in this process the society's political institutions and social classes must confront two critical problems. To what extent will political influence be extended to the bourgeoisie (and after the bourgeoisie, as we have seen above, to the proletariat)? And to what extent will the nobility attempt to retain its traditional status by resisting both political change and the transformation of the society's bases of wealth?

In England, the nobility proved more "incorporative" than "insulative." Primogeniture meant that the father's aristocratic title and land were inherited only by the first-born male. There consequently were many sons of aristocratic English families who held neither title nor inherited wealth, and they frequently made quick social (through marriage) and economic (through business) alliances with the growing bourgeoisie. The closer relationship between England's social classes was also facilitated by the landed oligarchy's conversion to pasturage, sheep raising, and the production of wool, which made the landowners partners in England's commercial revolution. They thus proved more amenable to the introduction of achievement norms, particularly in the economic and political subsystems of the society. And where aristocratic classes have not been swept away by revolution or by their own refusal to adapt to economic change, they have been an important force for moderating the effects of industrial capitalism on a growing proletariat. By mediating between a rapacious bourgeoisie and a welfare-oriented working class, the aristocracy also has helped to inculcate in the workers a sense of the legitimacy of existing institutions.[47]

In Russia, France, Prussia, and in most of the other continental European countries, however, aristocratic titles were passed on to all the family's heirs, and aristocratic wealth continued to be measured by ownership in land—land almost invariably devoted to the production of cereal crops. This in turn often contributed to serfdom, and after the legal abolition of serfdom to the rigid stratification of social classes even in the context of the mobility pressures stimulated by economic development. Political conflict was more ideologically intense and characterized more by social cleavage than by consensus. And where an entrenched aristocracy resisted the upward mobility of an enterprising bourgeoisie, the aristocracy was swept aside (as in France), or the bourgeoisie remained a relatively weak social class, upwardly mobile in economic status but low in political and social status. Thus in the more industrialized societies the basis was laid for fascism, and German National Socialism may be credited with democratizing Germany's social structure through accelerated industrialization (for war), military defeat, and the consequent elimination of those social classes most resistant to the democracy represented by the Weimar and Bonn republics.[48]

But where the society's principal social class was a land-hungry peasantry, and where a weak middle class was also confronted by an entrenched landed oligarchy, the basis was laid for revolutionary movements on the left. This has been especially true of colonial societies where indigenous educated elites have been prevented from securing the political and economic status appropriate to their educational or social accomplishments. The politics of many states throughout the world have been agitated by students and educated minorities whose status discrepancy is indicated by their underemployment in low-status manual or clerical jobs. It was precisely these Western-oriented (meaning "modernization"-oriented) intellectuals who, in Russia and in parts of Asia and Latin America, identified the peasantry as an explosive force for revolutionary change.

The revolutionary undertaking has been even easier where a foreign elite monopolized the society's higher-status positions, making anticolonialism an argument not only for national self-determination but for status mobility according to egalitarian and achievement norms. In Vietnam, for example, a fledgling Vietnamese bourgeoisie was discriminated against in commercial trade, banking, and manufacturing, and the intelligentsia was denied access to the higher-status positions in the French colonial hierarchy. In 1943, approximately 40,000 Vietnamese had received higher education, but only 1 percent of this educated elite held a post in the civil administration. And before the Second

World War, 50 percent of the membership of the revolutionary Vietnam Nationalist party (the VNQDD) was drawn from this small minority of Vietnamese civil servants. The Japanese occupation opened the Vietnamese civil-service system and created political organizations to the advantage of upwardly mobile Vietnamese citizens, but the reimposition of French colonial authority after the war once again blocked their status mobility in the political, social, and economic hierarchies. In 1945 there were 640,000 educated Vietnamese, but only 2,550 had received French citizenship—an important measure of social status in Vietnam.[49]

A weak middle class in the context of an economically developing but largely agrarian society has also been cited as a major precondition for revolution in Russia, China, Mexico, and Cuba. In this sense, more recent political and social phenomena have confirmed Aristotle's judgment on the necessity of a large middle class for both political stability and relatively democratic institutions.[50]

In the context of status discrepancy, then, upward mobility raises a society's revolutionary potential on the left. The threat of downward mobility, on the other hand, is closely associated with increasing revolutionary potential on the right. Fascist movements receive their strongest support from those social classes that feel threatened by the upward mobility of workers or underprivileged ethnic minorities. The Nazis in Germany, the Fascists in Italy, Spain, Austria, and in other European countries during the interwar period, the *samurai* in Japan in the 1870s and 1880s, the Poujadists in France in the mid-1950s, French settlers in Algeria between 1956 and 1962, and the Ku Klux Klan and elements of the "Radical Right" in the United States have all been identified as representing the status anxieties of citizens threatened by downward mobility. Old wealth apprehensive of social and economic change, new wealth fearful of the implications of the lower classes' social mobilization, and the traditionally liberal sectors of an enterprising petite bourgeoisie may all prove susceptible to demagogic appeals that emphasize social order, political authority, and national unity against a foreign enemy or an indigenous ethnic minority.[51]

But for followers of revolutionary movements on both the left and right, participation and organizational membership in the movement can provide the status that is lacking in the established social order. Even the architects of a nonrevolutionary coup d'état in Latin America, Africa, or the Middle East are usually drawn from the middle-officer ranks where a sense of status immobility is likely to be greater than in the case of the highest-ranking officers who have a stake in the status quo. Guerrilla movements in China and Southeast Asia also have been noted for their superior mobility potential in comparison to existing political and social structures. And the peasant or urban intellectual who is denied a social ranking commensurate with his apparent abilities is likely to be a ready supporter of revolutionary movements that promise the elimination of elitism and the introduction of achievement norms for the allocation of status.[52]

Revolutionary potential, then, increases with economic development, social mobilization, and the low adaptive capability of political institutions because of the development of new status hierarchies: these latter increase the probability of status discrepancy and heighten the individual's or group's concern for status mobility. Revolutionary potential declines, however, as upper- and middle-class citizens cease to feel threatened by the lower classes, as the lower classes receive the material benefits of advanced industrialization, as the symbols of status differences decline in visibility, and as most citizens perceive the established order as providing them with economic security, political representation, and opportunities for status mobility.

The emphasis here on *perceptions,* however, suggests some very broad-range hypothesizing that is more appropriately treated in the context of theory development in the study of revolutionary movements—an underlying theme throughout this book and one we now must confront head on.

FOR FURTHER TESTING

Some Propositions:

Revolutionary potential is low in those societies,

1. that are geographically isolated;
2. that are politically independent;
3. that are economically developed;
4. that are racially, religiously, and linguistically homogeneous;
5. where geographic centers of education, economic power, and government do not coincide;
6. where new frontiers and/or out-migration open new opportunities to the more enterprising and activist members of the society;
7. where religion, nationalist identities, and popular culture (including sport) divert public attention from political and socioeconomic issues;
8. where the commercialization of agriculture precedes industrialization;
9. where developmental crises do not overlap in time but, instead, occur sequentially;
10. where democratic government and participatory norms are established patterns of political organization and behavior.

Some Hypotheses:

Revolutionary potential increases,

1. as population growth exceeds material resources;
2. as population growth aggravates existing inequalities in the distribution of wealth (including, especially, land);

3. as the ownership of land (in agrarian societies) is concentrated in the hands of elites who do not balance their exploitation of peasant labor with the provision of basic services to the peasantry;

4. as the rates of economic development and, in general, modernization exceed the adaptive capabilities of the political system;

5. as the society's status rankings across social class are discrepant (instead of congruent);

6. as mobility opportunities are low (instead of high);

7. as the middle classes feel threatened by the upward mobility of the lower classes.

NOTES

[1] Lipset, 1967, p. 270.

[2] Moore, 1966, p. 444.

[3] North and Pool, 1965, p. 404.

[4] Melson and Wolpe, 1970, p. 1116.

[5] Leiden and Schmitt, 1968, pp. 160 and 165.

[6] Melotti, 1965, pp. 156-57.

[7] Gasster, 1969, p. 4; Wolf, 1969, pp. 127-28.

[8] For a summary of some of the relevant bibliography and findings, see Zagoria, 1971.

[9] Pinkney, 1964, p. 2.

[10] Davies, 1963, p. 351.

[11] Trotsky, 1957, Vol. I, pp. 9-10; Hamilton, 1967, p. 134; Zeitlin, 1967, pp. 168-79; Wolf, 1969, pp. 74-75.

[12] Organski, 1969, pp. 23-38. For bibliography and findings on the relationship between urban population density and aggressive behavior, see Galle et al., 1972. The same study finds a high correlation between juvenile delinquency and four measures of population density for seventy-five communities in Chicago between 1958 and 1961 ($R = 0.917$).

[13] Lieberson and Silverman, 1965. Baskin et al., 1972, identified 578 events of "race-related civil disorders" in the United States between 1967 and 1971.

[14] On this last point, see Burks, 1961. The author extends his analysis beyond Eastern Europe, however, and interprets communism as primarily a vehicle for ethnic minority protest.

[15] See Zagoria, 1971. On the stabilizing role of Confucianism in Japan, see Scalapino, 1964, pp. 94-95.

[16] The classic study on the political and social relevance of Methodism in England is by the French scholar Élie Halévy, whose six volumes on *A History of the English Peoples in the Nineteenth Century* first appeared in English translation between 1912 and 1930. See especially Vol. I of the 1960 London edition.

[17] On the close functional relationship between religious cultism and radical political movements, see Hobsbawm, 1959, pp. 128-30; Smelser, 1963, pp. 15-16, 198, and 326-28; Gusfield, 1968; and Lipset, 1970, pp. 218-19.

[18] Gurr, 1970, p. 219. Also see pp. 176-77 where Gurr reports findings from his 114-nation study and concludes that "collective violence breeds collective violence."

[19] LaPalombara and Weiner, 1966, p. 420.

[20] Molnar, 1965, pp. 78-85.

[21] The data reported here are taken from several sources, including Palmer, 1956; Russett, 1964; Melotti, 1965; Wolf, 1969; and Beals, 1970. Also see Hobsbawm, 1959, p. 75, where he notes that the strength of Spanish anarchism was concentrated in Andalusia where "80 percent of the rural population owned no land at all."

[22] Tanter and Midlarsky, 1967, p. 277.

[23] Russett, 1964. See Table 1.

[24] Moore, 1966, pp. 469-70.

[25] On this point, see especially Richter, 1966, p. 108, and Moore, 1966, p. 63. Moore, 1978, represents an elaboration of the argument: "Anger at the failure of authority to live up to its obligations, to keep its word and faith with the subjects, can be among the most potent of human emotions and topple thrones" (p. 510).

[26] McColl, 1967.

[27] Smelser, 1963, p. 61, summarizes de Tocqueville on this first point; regarding the Vendée, see Moore, 1966, pp. 92-101.

[28] Davies, 1963, p. 354.

[29] Weinert, 1966, p. 340. Booth, 1974, adds to the economic variable the intensity of electoral competition between Colombia's Liberal and Conservative parties.

[30] Wolf, 1969, p. 276. For another broad range perspective on socioeconomic change and peasant politics, see Migdal, 1974. Additional support for Wolf's hypothesis and documentation drawn from specific countries may be found in Hobsbawm, 1959, pp. 2, 67-68, and 80; Birnie, 1962, Chap. 2; Landsberger, 1968; Lemarchand, 1968; Huntington, 1968, p. 296; with specific reference to parts of Burma and Vietnam, see Scott, 1976.

[31] Palmer, 1956, p. 401.

[32] Lipset, 1963, pp. 53-57; Kornhauser, 1959, p. 154. For Marx's understanding of the relationship between the rate of industrialization and revolutionary potential, see Avineri, 1969, p. 151.

[33] Schoenbaum, 1967, pp. 28 and 34; Moore, 1966, p. 445; Organski, 1969, pp. 19-25.

[34] Linz, 1968, pp. 5–6. Also see Huntington, 1968, p. 399.

[35] Further analysis and supporting data on the high instability associated with transitional societies, as compared to traditional and modern societies, may be found in Alker and Russett, 1964, pp. 306–7; Pye, 1964, pp. 163–64; Olson, 1963; and Lerner, 1958. Also see Huntington, 1968, p. 41, where the author concludes that "modernity breeds stability, but modernization breeds instability."

[36] Feierabend and Feierabend, 1966, pp. 263–68. Also see Banks and Textor, 1963, where the variables associated with twenty-two stable and ninety-three less stable countries confirm the findings reported here.

[37] For example, C. Johnson, 1966, esp. Chap. 4; Almond and Powell, 1966, p. 234; Brinton, 1965, pp. 36–39 and 51–64; Smelser, 1963, pp. 240 and 330; and Pettee, 1966, and Friedrich, 1966. The most systematic treatment of the principal variables discussed in this section is in Eisenstadt, 1966, and in Huntington, 1968. See Huntington's summaries of his argument on pp. 4, 79, and 266.

[38] Deutsch, 1961, defines "social mobilization" as "the process in which major clusters of old social, economic and psychological commitments are eroded or broken and people become available for new patterns of socialization and behavior."

[39] The relationship between the pace of suffrage reform and political stability is discussed in LaPalombara and Weiner, 1966, pp. 430–31, and in Lipset, 1963, pp. 227–28. On the characteristics of political culture appropriate to stable democracy, see Almond and Verba, 1965, esp. Chap. 13. Eckstein, 1966, studies Norway to document his thesis that stable democracy depends on the congruity of authority patterns in government and in the associational structures of the society, including the family.

[40] Birnie, 1962, Chaps. 9 and 12–14, documents the disparities between England and France in these categories of political adaptation.

[41] See Kornhauser, 1959, and especially the concluding chapters of Dahrendorf, 1959. The real issue here, however, may be in terms of the patterns of interaction between political elites and counterelites, whose tendencies toward compromise or confrontation may be structured only nominally by the society's intermediary associations. The characteristics of a society's associational structure, then, are perhaps only an indirect measure of its potential for stability (or instability).

[42] Huntington, 1968, p. 84.

[43] This interpretation of fascism, in both Europe and Latin America, is perhaps best developed by Silvert, 1970. The same generalizations also may be applied to Japan in the 1930s: see Halpern, 1966.

[44] Eisinger, 1973.

[45] Berelson and Steiner, 1964, p. 253. Among the nonhuman animal species known to have status hierarchies functional to their social organization are primates, dogs, wolves, goats, hens, walrus, and several varieties of water fowl.

[46] See especially Bendix, 1970.

[47] Schumpeter, 1947, pp. 134–39; Birnie, 1962, p. 186; Lipset, 1967, pp. 279–81.

[48] Schoenbaum, 1967, Chap. 8, esp. pp. 239–43. Barrington Moore, Jr., summarizes

his arguments on the political effects of various relationships between nobility, bourgeoisie, and peasantry in his landmark study (Moore, 1966, pp. xv–xvi).

[49]McAlister, 1971, pp. 74–75; Wolf, 1969, p. 180.

[50]See Book V, 1221–22, of Aristotle's *Politics;* also see Lipset, 1970, p. 170; and, on Aristotle, especially Kort, 1952. Moore, 1966, p. 418, writes succinctly, "No bourgeois, no democracy." James Harrington's "law of balance"–formulated in his *Commonwealth of Oceana* in 1656–also anticipates some of the more contemporary observations regarding status discrepancy: for Harrington, the Puritan Revolution was caused by the imbalance between property distribution (increasingly diffused) and the distribution of political power (relatively concentrated) in England prior to 1640. Similar hypotheses may be found in the writings of Machiavelli, Saint-Simon, and–of course–Marx.

[51]Among the relevant literature, see Lipset, 1970, pp. 274–75; Carsten, 1967, p. 232; Berelson and Steiner, 1964, pp. 487–88; Iglitzin, 1972, pp. 59–60; and Bell, 1963. On the antimodernization sentiments represented by the *samurai* revolts in Japan, see Scalapino, 1964, pp. 98 and 106.

[52]See Huntington, 1968, pp. 198–208; Pye, 1956, pp. 128–35; Molnar, 1965, pp. 5, 78, 274, and 116 where Mao is reported to have urged recruitment of unsuccessful politicians, doctors, and lawyers in the lower echelons of their professions. Rolph, 1971, p. 21, writes that "Social and professional mobility within the Viet Cong movement, as compared with the static elitism of the GVN's hierarchy, has always been a strong incentive for the poor but ambitious young peasant. Indeed, the Viet Cong cadres have come to constitute a new professional and social class in the countryside. Rapid promotion upward for the able party official has also been a hallmark of the movement."

IN SEARCH
OF A THEORY
OF REVOLUTION

THEORY[1]

Conventional wisdom regards "theory" and "theoretical" as the opposite of "fact" and "practical." Someone who dabbles in theory is lost in abstractions and probably finds it difficult to tie a shoestring or turn a door knob. The problem with conventional wisdom is that it is long on convention and short on wisdom.

Strictly speaking, "theory" is *theory* only if it refers to the real world. Theories must be susceptible to empirical testing. Ironically, however, theories cannot be tested, at least not directly tested. Only hypotheses (and propositions) can be tested. And a theory stands or falls according to the validity of the hypotheses subsumed and implied by the theory.

Theories, then, are generalizations based on particulars. Theories explain and predict. ("Models" only predict, and their predictions may be right but for the wrong reasons.) Theories are summaries of facts, summaries that impart logical coherence to the facts. Formally, a "theory" is a generalization from which a series of logically related and testable hypotheses can be deduced. Clearly, then, "theory" is not the opposite of "fact"; theories make facts meaningful.

FROM FACT TO HYPOTHESIS

Consider the "facts" of revolution as these facts have been organized and presented in the preceding chapters of this book. The chronologies of revolutionary events in six countries presented in Chapter 3 include hundreds of facts about revolution. More facts have been added in subsequent chapters, facts drawn from many societies over an extended period of time, facts that relate to societies with high and low revolutionary potential and to successful and unsuccessful revolutionary movements.

The first problem is how to classify these facts. The titles of Chapters 4 through 11 and the topical headings of these chapters clearly indicate the classification scheme adopted for the book's subject matter.

The next step is to interpolate the facts into variables, and then to relate two or more variables to each other in terms of their apparent causal relationships. The resulting propositions and hypotheses, including those listed at the conclusions of Chapters 4 through 11, are a concise summary of the book's tentative findings about the characteristics of the revolutionary process. Even if we *dis*confirm a proposition or an hypothesis, we have learned something important (i.e., that the predicted relationship of the variables does *not* exist). Thinking in terms of propositions and hypotheses is a convenient way of sharpening the conceptual apparatus of the mind and of compacting a lot of material into a small space. From studying the propositions and hypotheses appended to the preceding chapters, the astute reader also will have understood the difference between propositions and hypotheses: hypotheses have variables that vary by degree and that are measured in terms of more-or-less; the variables of propositions are measured in terms of either-or.

The question we confront now, then, asks about the possibility of tying several or many of these propositions and hypotheses together in order to generate a theory of revolution.

THEORY OR TAUTOLOGY?

Not coincidentally, the variables identified in the preceding chapters have become ever more difficult to operationalize and to test, even as we seem to have moved toward a more complete understanding of the causes and characteristics of revolution. The more "broad-range" our conceptual organization of the data, the greater the difficulty of testing our hypotheses (and propositions). Their acceptability becomes more a matter of self-evidence, even aesthetic appeal, than a question of their fit with reality. The dangers of tautology are especially obvious when we discuss revolutionary potential in terms of *perceptions* of status discrepancy and mobility opportunity (the variables identified at the conclusion of the preceding chapter).

How do we know, for example, that the French bourgeoisie in 1789, or that Chinese and Vietnamese peasants and intellectuals in the twentieth century, revolted because their upward mobility in one or more of the subsystems of their society was blocked? Or that the lower-middle and working classes in England and the United States did not revolt in the twentieth century because they perceived sufficient opportunities for economic security, political representation, and upward social mobility?

Presumably we know by the very fact of their revolutionary or nonrevolutionary behavior. But this is not an explanation of the variations in revolutionary potential, which must be evaluated by indicators that are independent of the incidence of revolution or political violence. The apparent hypothesis actually is a tautology, because both variables are measured by the same phenomenon.

Tautology is a logical problem especially characteristic of "systems theory," or the equilibrium model of politics and society. The conceptual weaknesses of this approach are all the more apparent when it is applied to the study of revolution. The assumption is that the various structures, processes, and beliefs that make up a society fit together in a logical or functional way, and that revolution is the result of a breakdown somewhere in the system. The resulting logic based on this first premise is embarrassingly self-evident. For example:

Rebellions . . . signify failures, small or large, of the political system.[2]

Revolutions result from unsuccessful tension-management; peaceful politics result from successful tension-management.[3]

No government is likely to be overthrown from within its territory until it loses the ability to make adequate use of its military and police powers.[4]

. . . revolution is always avoidable if only the creative potentialities of political organization can be realized.

So long as a society's values and the realities with which it must deal in order to exist are in harmony with each other, the society is immune from revolution.

If a system is basically functional . . . , efforts at artificial mobilization will fall on barren soil and be rejected.[5]

Each of these apparently earth-shaking statements is true by definition. Although the characteristics of the independent variable (for example, the functional balance or equilibrium of the society) are supposed to explain and predict variations in the dependent variable (revolution), the former in fact is measured by the latter. The tendency toward tautology in "systems theory" is so obvious that Chalmers Johnson, its leading exponent in the study of revolution, admits "the tendency toward tautology in practical applications of systems theory."[6] If "practical applications" means "hypothesis testing," "systems theory" then fails on the basis of its own internal contradictions and conceptual inadequacy. In the face of such disarming candor, however, it may be discourteous to ask, "So why get trapped in the first place?" Perhaps our urge to be theoretical is, ultimately, a comment on our need for aesthetic balance and harmony. "Systems theory," like Greek architecture, may be structurally magnificent, but it is functionally limited (very limited).[7]

If we are to develop a theory of revolution, then, we must be certain to separate our indicators of revolutionary potential from the actual incidence of revolution; and we also must remember to test our hypotheses in societies where revolutions have succeeded, where they have failed, and where they have not appeared at all. I am pleased to be the first to point out that the findings and interpretations presented in this book do not always meet these demanding criteria for theory development in the study of revolution. But this is also, I think, a sobering comment on the problems of developing a theory of revolution.

NONFALSIFIABILITY

Tautological statements, by their very nature, are nonfalsifiable. They thus fail to meet a critical test of the scientific quality of theoretical formulation: a theory has scientific standing—not by virtue of its apparent confirmation through empirical testing—but only if we can conceive of findings that would *dis*confirm the theory. Nonfalsifiable propositions have the appearance of scientific theory, but they are conceptually organized (more by inadvertence than design) to explain any variation in the data. Not being susceptible to disconfirmation, they are nonfalsifiable and thus lack scientific standing.[8]

The tendency toward nonfalsifiable propositions is especially characteristic of the attempt to explain revolution in terms of the psychological dimensions of human behavior. The assumption here is that no theory of revolution is complete unless it takes into account human motivation—which, in fact, is another indicator of an attempt at broad-range (as opposed to middle- or narrow-range) theory development. The "range" of theory often is misunderstood as a reference to the number of cases, or geographic extent, posed by the research problem. Theoretical "range" instead refers to the distance between the theory and the data essential to testing the theory (or its derivative hypotheses and propositions). And when the data are inferential instead of directly observable, the argument is almost certainly an assault on the broad-range battlements of theory-building. This is especially obvious in the case of those students of revolution who seek to explain revolution with reference to human motivation.

James C. Davies, for example, a leading contributor to this field of study and avowedly in search of the "natural laws" of revolutionary behavior, has concluded that "eventually the study of the revolutionary state of mind, where it all begins anyhow, will lead directly to the fascinating study of the brain . . . ."[9]

David Schwartz has argued that "the psycho-political disturbances which end in revolution begin in the psyche . . . ."[10] These and similar statements on the basic causes of revolution typically find their theoretical expression in the contention that "aggression is always a consequence of frustration," and that "aggressive behavior of the usually recognized varieties is always traceable to and produced by some form of frustration."[11]

These statements, by themselves, also are true by definition. Their tendency toward nonfalsifiability is in their methodology of testing, which is almost invariably in the form of inferential logic. How can we determine human motivation except by inferring it from observable behavior? A revolutionary act, then, implies frustration, while political passivity in the face of all the more objective indicators of revolution suggests insufficient frustration: by attempting to explain everything, we end by explaining nothing. But we can presumably solve the ambiguities of political sociology by plunging into the depths of political psychology. This also may be described as the "macro-micro" leap, or the inference of individual psychological characteristics from observed social phenomena.

Samuel Huntington, for example, notes the frequent revolutionary activity of students, intellectuals, and the middle classes of modernizing societies, and concludes:

> This opposition does not stem, in most cases, from any material insufficiency. It is an opposition which stems instead from psychological insecurity, personal alienation and guilt, and an overriding need for a secure sense of identity.[12]

Other theorists have sought to locate the source of revolutionary behavior in the psychological disturbance that results from Oedipal guilt or the repressed sexual behavior associated with authoritarian family norms.[13]

As in the case of systems theory, confirmation of these propositions and others that are derived from psychological premises requires the development of indicators that are independent of aggressive behavior. It also requires clarification of the circumstances in which frustration does induce aggression, because aggressive behavior is only one of many possible expressions of frustration: others include religious zeal, artistic creation, athletic competition, criminal activity, drug or alcoholic addiction, and even psychological withdrawal and passivity (the very opposite of aggression)—which have been associated with prolonged or intense frustration.[14]

But even if these theoretical demands should be met successfully, there are no grounds for assuming that human consciousness (or the unconscious?) and the motivations that derive from it operate independently of biology or even of the physical environment: there is no way of demonstrating that an apparent cause is an *ultimate* cause. If our penchant for total explanation leads us into psychological reductionism, it also may lead us to an unending circularity of causal relationships.[15]

Where should we draw the line? Probably at the point where the measurement of our variables is based less on observable behavior than on inferential logic. This will not satisfy those who think that little can be accomplished outside the framework of broad-range theory. The substance and theoretical style of this book, however, are an attempt to demonstrate that hypotheses of the middle range can substantially advance our understanding of a complex political and social process. And the more alert reader will already have noted that I have attempted (not always with success) to avoid psychological imputation, precisely because of its inferential quality, and the consequent tendencies toward tautology and nonfalsifiability.

RELATIVE DEPRIVATION

By far the most commonly cited broad-range theory of revolutionary behavior is that of "relative deprivation" (RD). This theory also has pronounced tendencies toward tautology and nonfalsifiability. But in the hands of a few skillful scholars it has proved to be more capable than systems theory of generating hypotheses and more adroit in attempting to bridge the macro-micro gap—if in fact it is possible to infer collective behavioral patterns from the psychological and behavioral characteristics of individuals.

The leading theorist in this category of theory development is Ted Robert Gurr, whose work represents a remarkable synthesis of many of the hypotheses on political violence, integrated into the framework of relative deprivation. Indeed, one of Gurr's major objectives is to show how almost all hypotheses and theories related to political violence can be subsumed under relative deprivation. His principal variables in this undertaking include: (1) the extent to which the individual perceives deprivation in the categories of his or her social or psychological life, and (2) the individual's attitudes toward the appropriateness and efficacy of political violence.[16]

Much of the value of Gurr's study, however, is in the data he generates and the hypotheses that he tests—invariably at the *middle-range level* of theory: for example, the relationship between wages expected and wages received by workers (as determined by survey research in Italy and France) as a partial measure of their potential for violence.[17] This also helps to make the point that inference from aggregate data does not directly test the relative deprivation hypothesis.[18]

We must rely, then, on survey data—direct interviews of citizens—in order to avoid the nonfalsifiability inherent in inferential argument, especially at the level of psychological analysis. Understandably, this has not been extensively attempted, and even carrying out the necessary survey research does not mean that a citizen's sentiments of relative deprivation can be correlated with the actual incidence of violent behavior.

One study that does meet these requirements, however, is by Harlan Hahn (1970), who conducted a modified quota sample survey of 270 black residents in a riot area of Detroit shortly after the 1967 Detroit riots. Two categories of respondents were identified, those favoring racial integration in the United States and those supporting black separatism. The latter group (22 percent of the sample) also was identified as much more ideologically militant and far more active during the 1967 riots. What can we learn from Hahn's findings about the relationship of relative deprivation to political violence?

It is the adjective "relative" that complicates the task of confirming the falsifiability of relative deprivation concepts and, consequently, of establishing RD's scientific standing as theory. For example, black separatists in the Detroit sample, compared with the less violent integrationists, had a lower average income and were less likely to own property.[19] Thus we could conclude that, because they had less, the separatists' sense of deprivation was greater than that of the integrationists. And this finding explains why the separatists were more active in the 1967 Detroit riots. Relative deprivation.

Hahn's findings also include the following: the black separatists, compared with the integrationists, had a higher level of educational attainment. Thus we could conclude that, compared with the integrationists, the separatists' sense of deprivation was greater because their more advanced education had raised their expectations higher. Relative deprivation. In fact, this particular interpretation is characteristic of the literature on modernization that integrates its findings into the conceptual categories of RD.

But what if the data showed that, compared with the integrationists, the separatists, (1) had a *higher* average income, owned *more* property, and (2) had a *lower* level of educational attainment? In other words, what if the data painted a picture that was exactly opposite to the picture the data did paint?

We still could argue the validity of RD—as follows: (1) the higher economic standing of the black separatists brought them closer to the living standards of Detroit's *white* community, and so intensified the separatists' sense of deprivation (or their sense of inequality and injustice as a function of racial identity); and (2) the *integrationists'* higher level of educational attainment enhanced their potential for identifying with the values and norms of white society, and so the integrationists were less active in the 1967 riots. Relative deprivation. What's the point? Relative deprivation can be used to explain *any configuration of the findings*. It explains the passivity or activism of the impoverished or the privileged. It consequently is nonfalsifiable.

The particular merit of Hahn's study, however, is that it also asked respondents to locate themselves on the "Cantril Self-Anchoring Striving Scale," which is probably the most direct test of an individual's sense of relative deprivation.[20] But Hahn was unable to find any significant difference between integrationists and separatists (and so ideological militancy and violence proneness) in terms of this direct measure of relative deprivation. The author concludes that "approval of black separatism has been inspired less by frustrations concerning the present status of black men in a white society than by an idealistic vision of the future." [21]

Much the same point can be made with reference to concepts of alienation and communist voting. Unable to explain the persistence of communist voting *and* improving conditions of life, many social scientists have taken refuge in the "black box" of psychological imputation. Communist voters might be better off than they were twenty, ten, even two years ago, but their sense of alienation (or relative deprivation?) is still high and that explains their continued communist orientation. This variation on RD theory apparently is able to explain why, in some cases, better paid workers vote communist while less skilled and lower paid workers vote for socialist or bourgeois parties. The communists' sense of relative deprivation is higher. (In fact, the same black box plunge is made by Marxists when they are constrained to explain why the predicted socialist revolution has failed to occur in advanced capitalist countries: "false consciousness.")

Samuel Eldersveld's 1967 postelection survey research in India represents, in part, a direct and sophisticated test of the alienation hypothesis. [22] The extent of a voter's alienation is measured in Eldersveld's study by responses to questions related to political efficacy, attitudes toward government, and the respondent's perceptions of improvement or deterioration in his or her economic situation. These variables in turn are correlated with the voter's partisan preferences. The important point is this: there is absolutely no correlation between partisan orientations and sentiments of alienation. For example, those who were the most consistent supporters of the ruling Congress party (the government party) also were more alienated from government than were those voters who supported the principal opposition parties. And of the three principal opposition parties, the Indian Communists had the highest percentage of voters who acknowledged an improvement in their economic conditions. As in the case of black separatists in Detroit, India's communist voters (and communist voters in many countries) apparently are understood better in terms of what they want instead of what they oppose. Or what social scientists *think* they oppose.

CONCEPTUAL UTILITY

This underlines a major conceptual weakness in the interpretation of political extremism or violence that argues in terms of alienation, frustration-aggression, or relative deprivation. The emphasis is on the negative and the positive is either underestimated or ignored altogether. Revolutionaries are understood to be rebelling *against* instead of rebelling *for*. The society that undergoes revolution is thought to have a surplus of deprivation, to be unhealthy (in Crane Brinton's metaphor), or to be dysfunctional (for the systems theorist). Revolutionaries consequently are labeled social misfits, psychologically disabled, as somehow out of joint with their time and place. (Perhaps they are, but only by definition.) Revolutionary behavior that is motivated by ideological conviction, by a commitment to justice and to a more equitable distribution of wealth and opportunity, is neglected to the advantage of equally value-laden interpretations that, however, imply a preference for the status quo and political stability.

In fact, without reference to the positive dimension of revolutionary behavior we cannot fully explain the tenacity of revolutionary leaders and followers who persisted in pursuing their programs for revolutionary change in the face of almost insurmountable odds. It seems more than a little one-sided to differentiate privileged and rebellious intellectuals from passive slum-dwellers by identifying the former as more *relatively* deprived; or to describe militant students from bourgeois families as more *relatively* deprived than their nonactivist counterparts who are from working-class families and whose education depends on their own manual or clerical labor.

There also is declining conceptual utility as we ascend the ladder of broad-range theory in search of an ever more inclusive generalization that can account for all the variations in revolutionary potential. Is our understanding of a particular revolutionary movement enhanced by aggregating all the revolutionary participants into a single conceptual category—for example, that of relative deprivation: peasants who want land, workers who want job security, bourgeois who want a free market, students who want assured status, and revolutionary leaders who want power in order to correct existing abuses or who simply want power? As the hypothesis or theory becomes more general, it becomes more difficult to test empirically and it also loses its capacity to identify and clarify the more discrete and meaningful characteristics of the revolutionary process.[23]

This is in part because of the difficulty of assigning appropriate values to the many variables that are necessarily included in broad-range theory. How should we "weight" the variables of status discrepancy, population density, the rate of industrialization, the presence of a colonial power, the role of government violence, the extent of land inequality, and all the other variables discussed in this study, when we attempt to explain or predict the appearance, success, or failure of revolution? It is true that we may be aided in this particular effort by some sophisticated statistical techniques (for example, path analysis, multiple regression, or, to a lesser extent, factor analysis). But these techniques depend on quantification, and how do we quantify the qualities of leadership, the strength of organization, or the effectiveness of cross-cutting alliances among revolutionary followers? Even an impressionistic weighting of specific variables is likely to vary from one society to another and over time for any given society, as well as from one researcher to another. We are constantly troubled, then, by the ambiguity and inferential quality of those apparently more meaningful variables that moved us in the direction of broad-range theory in the first place. This is especially true when, at the broad-range level, we attempt to differentiate the role of economic from noneconomic factors in human motivation.[24]

Another problem of broad-range theory is its assumption of causal relationships between events or processes extended through time. Given the difficulty of demonstrating causality even in the context of events almost immediately associated in time and space, it would seem especially difficult to demonstrate (for example) that the Mexican Revolution of 1910 was "the ultimate result" of the introduction in Mexico of a market economy in agriculture in the mid-nineteenth century.[25] And yet these kinds of generalizations are among the more conceptually useful insights available from the literature on revolution, despite their relatively low standing as theory. It probably is no coincidence that the most sophisticated broad-range theory of revolutionary behavior—that of relative deprivation—is extremely narrow in the time-span of its variable construction and hypothesis testing. It also is probably most appropriate for societies at those stages of development where material concerns represent the dominant social values.

Neither broad-range theory nor hypotheses of the middle range, however, can surmount the theoretical problem of "threshold." Precisely at what point in the escalation of government violence is revolutionary activity suppressed rather than provoked? Just how "closed" must a society's opportunity structure be before social mobilization results in collective violence? What is the rate of industrialization that stimulates working-class radicalism, and how fast can voting rights be extended without exceeding institutional capabilities?

Simply enumerating these questions helps to explain why theory development in the study of revolution should not be expected to attain the levels of sophistication that characterize many other fields of study in the social sciences. Students of revolution must typically deal with tendency statements and never with measures that express absolute certainty and only rarely with propositions or hypotheses based on statistical probability. These limitations, by themselves, make impossible the development of a theory of revolution—because, formally speaking, theory is necessarily deductive (and it is impossible to deduce propositions or hypotheses from statements of tendency or probability).

Nor do students of revolution have a conceptual counterpart to the economists' quantifiable measures of gross national product or monetary exchange. We do not have the controlled laboratory environment of the psychologists who work with a small number of subjects. Nor do we have the closed-option parameters that have aided political scientists in the study of the behavior of voters, legislators, and judges. Revolutionary behavior takes place outside of an established institutional context. It is open-optioned in the sense that each individual has many choices to make as he or she considers the political alternatives. And the behavioral process of revolution is essentially nonrepetitive. The study of revolution consequently differs markedly from (for example) the study of voting behavior, where the voting process is repeated frequently over a limited period of time with relatively few changes in the principal variables, and where the voter's options are clearly delineated in an established institutional setting.

If by "theory," then, we mean an empirically testable series of hypotheses and propositions that are logically deduced from a broad-range and falsifiable generalization, there is no theory of revolution. Nor is there ever likely to be one. But if by "theory" we mean a conceptual paradigm (or framework) that is sufficiently abstract to include within its purview many essentially independent and middle-range hypotheses, there are several theories of revolution. And there are likely to be more of them as the study of revolution continues. But their respective advantages and disadvantages are a function of self-evidence rather than "empirical validity," and their conceptual utility is likely to vary according to the values of the researcher and the particular society under study.[26]

We thus should not expect to answer all the questions that an insatiable curiosity raises to our level of consciousness. We instead should commit ourselves to plodding along at a middle-range level of hypothesis formulation and testing, avoiding insofar as possible a reliance on inferential data, scrupulous in our disdain of tautological expression. We should seek to identify and clarify the apparent patterns of regularity and continuity that are associated with revolution and not expect to explain fully or to predict accurately any or all of the phenomena associated with the revolutionary process. There is no flash of insight that will unlock the mysteries of revolution. If the study of revolution were as susceptible to scientific analysis as is the physical environment, we long ago would have produced our Isaac Newton.

This is not to deny that mankind naturally desires to know, or to think it knows. Theory satisfies the mind, as justice satisfies the soul. But the search for theory and justice is endless, and neither the thinker nor the revolutionary is likely to find what he or she is searching for. It is the searching, however, that gives meaning to life.

NOTES

[1] Here the thoughtful reader is urged to ponder the quotations that preface this book, especially the quotation from Emerson.

[2] Kornhauser, 1964, p. 142.

[3] Feldman, 1964, p. 117.

[4] Brinton, 1965, p. 253. One of the obvious indicators of tautological expression, whether or not the intent is to contribute to "systems theory," is the appearance in the statement of qualifying adjectives or adverbs: in this case, "adequate."

[5] These last three examples of tautology are from C. Johnson, 1966, pp. xiv, 60, and 162. Other examples of tautology in Johnson's book may be found on pp. 22, 94, 96–98, and 102.

[6] C. Johnson, 1966, p. 120.

[7] Cohan, 1975, Chap. 6, also is skeptical of the conceptual utility of systems and functionalist approaches to the study of revolution.

[8] The classic statement of "falsifiability as a criterion of demarcation" between scientific and nonscientific propositions is by Karl R. Popper, *The Logic of Scientific Inquiry* (New York: Science Editions, 1961), esp. pp. 40–43.

[9] Davies, 1971, pp. 4 and 317.

[10] D. Schwartz, 1971, p. 113.

[11] Dollard et al., 1971, p. 166.

[12] Huntington, 1968, p. 371. Similar inferences may be found on pp. 47, 54–55, 57, and 276. See Pye, 1962, for an explanation of the relationship between modernization and political instability which is expressed in terms of "identity crisis": political instability in developing nations is the individual's psychological insecurity writ large (very large).

[13] See the arguments of Wolfenstein and Hoffer, as summarized by Gurr, 1970, pp. 163–64; and Reich, 1946, with specific regard to German National Socialism.

[14] See the summaries of the relevant literature by Corning, 1971, pp. 346–49; Stone, 1966, p. 169; Berelson and Steiner, 1964, p. 271.

[15] To put the issue in propositional form: The impulse to lift one's hand (or to start a revolution) originates in, (1) the brain, (2) the stomach, (3) one's back yard. (Prove it.)

[16] Gurr, 1970, pp. 12–14 and Chap. 2. Gurr defines relative deprivation as "a perceived discrepancy between men's value expectations and their value capabilities" (p. 13). Also see the Appendix, pp. 360–67, where Gurr summarizes the hypotheses and corollaries discussed in his book.

[17] Gurr, 1970, pp. 64–65. But see p. 81 where the author *infers* both the increasing effectiveness of government repression and declining "participatory and status values" from the declining incidence of violence among South African blacks.

[18] For example, Feierabend and Feierabend, 1966, present some useful findings derived from cross-national testing of aggregate data, but their attempt to link their middle-range findings with the broad-range theory of relative deprivation results in tautology. See their article on p. 250, and Table 2, p. 255, where the highest variable loading on the "revolt" factor is, not surprisingly, "revolts."

[19] The findings reported here are summarized in Hahn, 1970, Table 1, p. 42.

[20] See Cantril, 1965. The "Self-Anchoring Striving Scale" asks respondents to locate themselves at one point along a continuum with ten positions, the two extremes representing the best and the worst possible life that respondents could experience.

[21] Hahn, 1970, p. 43. See Tilly, 1978, for a political-conflict approach to the study of revolution that is consciously designed to avoid the conceptual weaknesses of frustration-aggression and RD theories.

[22] Samuel J. Eldersveld, *The 1967 Indian Elections: Patterns of Party Regularity and Defection*. Paper presented to the annual meeting of the American Political Science Association, New York City, Sept. 2–6, 1969. Eldersveld's research is part of the ambitious cross-national study of voting behavior carried out by social scientists at the University of Michigan. A more complete summary of Eldersveld's findings and of other research on alienation, protest voting, and communist electorates is in Greene, 1971.

[23]Or, in hypothetical form, the broader the range of theory, (1) the more that the researcher's personal values are likely to influence the research and analysis, (2) the further removed the argument is from observable patterns of organization and behavior (and so the more difficult it is to operationalize and to test), and (3) the more ambiguous the explanations and predictions implicit in the theory.

[24]For example, see Gurr, 1970, p. 148.

[25]Wolf, 1969, p. 13; or the argument that the Chinese Communist revolution was the logical result of a series of upheavals beginning in China in the eighteenth century (Schurmann, 1967, p. xxxi).

[26]"The proponents of competing paradigms are always at least slightly at crosspurposes. Neither side will grant all the non-empirical assumptions that the other needs in order to make its case . . . . The competition between paradigms is not the sort of battle that can be resolved by proofs." Thomas S. Kuhn, *The Structure of Scientific Revolutions* (Chicago: University of Chicago Press, 1962), p. 147. Kuhn's point may be illustrated in our present context: Gurr subsumes frustration-aggression and status discrepancy theories within relative deprivation; Huntington, however, uses frustration-aggression and relative deprivation interchangeably, although frequently within the framework of systems analysis; while C. Johnson (1966, p. 63) subsumes relative deprivation within his own systems-oriented concept of "value disequilibrium." On the other hand, Geschwender, 1968, subsumes theories of relative deprivation, social mobility, and status discrepancy within a variant of Festinger's theory of cognitive dissonance.

SELECTED BIBLIOGRAPHY

ALKER, HAYWARD R., JR., and BRUCE M. RUSSETT. 1964. "The Analysis of Trends and Patterns," in Bruce M. Russett et al., *World Handbook of Political and Social Indicators.* New Haven: Yale University Press.

ALMOND, GABRIEL A., and G. BINGHAM POWELL, Jr. 1966. *Comparative Politics: A Developmental Approach.* Boston and Toronto: Little, Brown and Company.

———, and SIDNEY VERBA. 1965. *The Civic Culture: Political Attitudes and Democracy in Five Nations.* Boston and Toronto: Little, Brown and Company.

ANDRESKI, S. L. 1969. "Some Sociological Considerations on Fascism and Class," in S. L. Woolf, ed., *The Nature of Fascism.* New York: Vintage Books.

ARENDT, HANNAH. 1965. *On Revolution.* New York: The Viking Press, Inc. First published in 1963.

AVINERI, SHLOMO. 1969. *The Social and Political Thought of Karl Marx.* Cambridge, England: Cambridge University Press.

BAIRD, LEONARD. 1970. "Who Protests: The Social Base of the Student Movement," in Julian Foster and Durward Long, eds., *Protest: Student Activism in America.* New York: William Morrow & Co., Inc.

BANKS, ARTHUR S., and ROBERT TEXTOR. 1963. *The Cross-Polity Survey.* Cambridge: The M.I.T. Press.

BASKIN, JANE A. et al. 1972. "The Long, Hot Summer?" *Justice Magazine,* I (Feb.), 6–21.

BEALS, CARLETON. 1970. *The Nature of Revolution.* New York: Thomas Y. Crowell Company.

BELING, WILLARD A. 1970. "Mobilization of Human Resources in Developing Nations," in Willard A. Beling and George O. Totten, eds., *Developing Nations: Quest for a Model.* New York: Van Nostrand and Co.

BELL, DANIEL, ed. 1963. *The Radical Right.* Garden City, N.Y.: Doubleday & Company, Inc.

BENDIX, REINHARD. 1970. "What is Modernization?" in Willard A. Beling and George O. Totten, eds., *Developing Nations: Quest for a Model.* New York: Van Nostrand and Co.

BERELSON, BERNARD, and GARY A. STEINER. 1964. *Human Behavior: An Inventory of Scientific Findings.* New York: Harcourt, Brace & World, Inc.

BERGER, PETER L., and RICHARD JOHN NEUHAUS. 1970. *Movement and Revolution.* Garden City, N.Y.: Anchor Books, Doubleday & Company, Inc.

BILLIAS, GEORGE A., ed. 1970. *The American Revolution: How Revolutionary Was It?* New York: Holt, Rinehart & Winston.

BIRNIE, ARTHUR. 1962. *An Economic History of Europe, 1760-1939.* London: Methuen and Co., Ltd. First published in 1930. Seventh and revised edition published in 1957.

BLANKSTEN, GEORGE. 1958. "Revolutions," in H. E. Davis, ed., *Government and Politics in Latin America.* New York: The Ronald Press Company.

BLUMER, HERBERT. 1939. "Collective Behavior," in R. E. Park, ed., *An Outline of the Principles of Sociology.* New York: Barnes & Noble, Inc.

BOOTH, JOHN A. 1974. "Rural Violence in Colombia, 1948-1963," *The Western Political Quarterly,* 27(Dec.), 657-79.

BORKENAU, FRANZ. 1962. *World Communism: A History of the Communist International.* Ann Arbor: Ann Arbor Paperbacks, The University of Michigan Press. First published in 1939.

BOUDON, RAYMOND. 1971. "Sources of Student Protest in France," *The Annals of the American Academy of Political and Social Science* (May).

BOWDLER, GEORGE A. 1981. "The Downfall of Somoza, 1978-1979," *South Eastern Latin Americanist,* XXV (Dec.).

BRINTON, CRANE. 1965. *The Anatomy of Revolution.* New York: Vintage Books. First published in 1938.

BROGAN, D. W. 1966. *The Price of Revolution.* New York: Grosset and Dunlap, Inc., Universal Library Edition. First published in 1951.

BURKS, R. V. 1961. *The Dynamics of Communism in Eastern Europe.* Princeton: Princeton University Press.

BURTON, ANTHONY. 1976. *Urban Terrorism: Theory, Practice and Response.* New York: The Free Press.

BWY, DOUGLAS. 1968. "Dimensions of Social Conflict in Latin America," in Louis H. Masotti and Don R. Bowen, eds., *Riots and Rebellions: Civil Violence in the Urban Community.* Beverly Hills: Sage Publications, Inc.

CANTRIL, HADLEY. 1965. *The Pattern of Human Concerns.* New Brunswick, N.J.: Rutgers University Press.

CARSTEN, F. L. 1967. *The Rise of Fascism.* Berkeley and Los Angeles: University of California Press.

CARTWRIGHT, DORWIN. 1971. "Risk Taking by Individuals and Groups: An

Assessment of Research Employing Choice Dilemmas," *Journal of Personality and Social Psychology,* XX(Dec.), 361-78.

CASSINELLI, C. W. 1976. *Total Revolution: A Comparative Study of Germany under Hitler, the Soviet Union under Stalin, and China under Mao.* Santa Barbara, Calif. and Oxford, England: Clio Books.

COHAN, A. S. 1975. *Theories of Revolution: An Introduction.* New York: Halsted, Wiley.

COMPARATIVE POLITICS. 1976. "Special Issue on Peasants and Revolution," 8(April), 321-478.

CONVERSE, PHILIP E. 1964. "The Nature of Belief Systems in Mass Publics," in David E. Apter, ed., *Ideology and Discontent.* New York: The Free Press of Glencoe.

CORNING, PETER A. 1971. "The Biological Bases of Behavior and Some Implications for Political Science," *World Politics,* XXIII(April), 321-70.

DAHRENDORF, RALF. 1959. *Class and Class Conflict in Industrial Society.* Stanford: Stanford University Press.

DALLIN, ALEXANDER, and GEORGE W. BRESLAUER. 1970. "Political Terror in the Post-Mobilization Stage," in Chalmers Johnson, ed., *Change in Communist Systems.* Stanford: Stanford University Press.

DAVIES, JAMES C. 1962. "Toward a Theory of Revolution," *American Sociological Review,* XXVII(Feb.), 5-19.

———. 1963. *Human Nature in Politics: The Dynamics of Political Behavior.* New York: John Wiley & Sons, Inc.

———, ed. 1971. *When Men Revolt and Why: A Reader in Political Violence and Revolution.* New York: The Free Press.

DEBRAY, RÉGIS. 1970. "Castroism: The Long March in Latin America," in George A. Kelly and Clifford W. Brown, Jr., eds., *Struggles in the State: Sources and Patterns of World Revolution.* New York: John Wiley & Sons, Inc. First published in 1965.

DEGALO, SAMUEL. 1976. *Coups and Army Rule in Africa.* New Haven: Yale University Press.

DEUTSCH, KARL W. 1961. "Social Mobilization and Political Development," *American Political Science Review,* LV(Sept.), 493-514.

———. 1964. "External Involvement in Internal War," in Harry Eckstein, ed., *Internal War: Problems and Approaches.* New York: The Free Press of Glencoe.

DOLLARD, JOHN, et al. 1971. "Frustration and Aggression: Definitions," in James C. Davies, ed., *When Men Revolt and Why: A Reader in Political Violence and Revolution.* New York: The Free Press. First published in 1939.

DOWNTON, JAMES V., JR. 1973. *Rebel Leadership: Commitment and Charisma in the Revolutionary Process.* New York: The Free Press.

DUFF, ERNEST, and JOHN McCAMANT. 1976. *Violence and Repression in Latin America.* New York: The Free Press.

ECKSTEIN, HARRY, ed. 1964. *Internal War: Problems and Approaches.* New York: The Free Press of Glencoe.

———. 1965. "On the Etiology of Internal Wars," *History and Theory,* IV, 133-63.

———. 1966. *Division and Cohesion in Democracy: A Study of Norway.* Princeton: Princeton University Press.

EDWARDS, LYFORD P. 1971. "Advanced Symptoms of Revolution," in

Clifford T. Paynton and Robert Blackey, eds., *Why Revolution? Theories and Analyses*. Cambridge: Schenkman Publishing Co., Inc. First published in 1927 and in Edward's *The Natural History of Revolution*.

EISENSTADT, S. N. 1966. *Modernization: Protest and Change*. Englewood Cliffs, N.J.: Prentice-Hall, Inc.

EISINGER, PETER K. 1973. "The Conditions of Protest Behavior in American Cities," *American Political Science Review*, LXVII (March), 11–28.

ELKINS, STANLEY M. 1971. "Slavery and Personality," in James C. Davies, ed., *When Men Revolt and Why: A Reader in Political Violence and Revolution*. New York: The Free Press.

ELLUL, JACQUES. 1970. "The Psychology of A Rebellion: May–June 1968," in George A. Kelly and Clifford W. Brown, Jr., eds., *Struggles in the State: Sources and Patterns of World Revolution*. New York: John Wiley & Sons, Inc.

ELTON, GODFREY. 1923. *The Revolutionary Idea in France, 1789–1871*. New York: Longmans, Green & Co., Inc.

ENGELS, FRIEDRICH. 1971. "The Peasant War in Germany," in James C. Davies, ed., *When Men Revolt and Why: A Reader in Political Violence and Revolution*. New York: The Free Press. Excerpted from Engels's *The Peasant War in Germany*, 1850.

FALL, BERNARD. 1965. "The Viet-Cong—Unseen Enemy," *New Society Magazine* (London), April 22.

FEIERABEND, IVO K., and ROSALIND L. FEIERABEND. 1966. "Aggressive Behaviors within Polities, 1948–1962: A Cross-National Study," *Journal of Conflict Resolution*, X(Sept.), 249–71.

FELDMAN, ARNOLD S. 1964. "Violence and Volatility: The Likelihood of Revolution," in Harry Eckstein, ed., *Internal War: Problems and Approaches*. New York: The Free Press of Glencoe.

FISCHER-GALATI, STEPHEN. 1963. "The Peasantry as a Revolutionary Force in the Balkans," *Journal of Central European Affairs*, XXIII (March), 12–22.

FLACKS, RICHARD. 1970. "Who Protests: A Study of Student Activists," in Julian Foster and Durward Long, eds., *Protest: Student Activism in America*. New York: William Morrow & Co., Inc.

FRIEDRICH, CARL J. 1966. "An Introductory Note on Revolution," in Carl J. Friedrich, ed., *Revolution*. New York: Atherton Press.

GALLE, OMER R., WALTER R. GOVE, and J. MILLER McPHERSON. 1972. "Population Density and Pathology," *Science*, CLXXVI(April), 23–30.

GANN, LEWIS H. 1971. *Guerrillas in History*. Stanford: Hoover Institute Press.

GASSTER, MICHAEL. 1969. *Chinese Intellectuals and the Revolution of 1911: The Birth of Modern Chinese Radicalism*. Seattle and London: University of Washington Press.

GESCHWENDER, JAMES A. 1968. "Explorations in the Theory of Social Movements and Revolutions," *Social Forces*, XLII(No. 2), 127–35.

GIAP, VO NGUYEN. 1964. *People's War, People's Army*. New York: Frederick A. Praeger, Inc.

GIBB, CECIL A. 1966. "The Principles and Traits of Leadership," in A. Paul Hare, Edgar F. Borgata, and Robert F. Bales, eds., *Small Groups: Studies in Social Interaction*. New York: Alfred A. Knopf, Inc.

GOODSPEED, DONALD J. 1962. *The Conspirators: A Study of the Coup d'Etat*. New York: The Viking Press, Inc.

GOTTSCHALK, LOUIS. 1971. "Causes of Revolution," in Clifford T. Paynton and Robert Blackey, eds., *Why Revolution? Theories and Analyses.* Cambridge: Schenkman Publishing Co., Inc. First published in 1944.

GREENE, THOMAS H. 1971. "The Electorates of Nonruling Communist Parties," *Studies in Comparative Communism,* IV (July–Oct.), 68–103.

GURR, TED ROBERT. 1970. *Why Men Rebel.* Princeton: Princeton University Press.

GUSFIELD, JOSEPH R. 1968. "The Study of Social Movements," *International Encyclopedia of the Social Sciences,* Vol. 14, 445–52. New York: Crowell Collier and Macmillan, Inc.

HAGOPIAN, MARK N. 1974. *The Phenomenon of Revolution.* New York: Dodd, Mead & Company.

HAHN, HARLAN. 1970. "Black Separatists: Attitudes and Objectives in a Riot-torn Ghetto," *Journal of Black Studies,* I (Sept.), 35–53.

HALPERIN, S. WILLIAM. 1964. *Mussolini and Italian Fascism.* Princeton: An Anvil Original, D. Van Nostrand Co., Inc.

HALPERN, MANFRED. 1966. "The Revolution of Modernization in National and International Society," in Carl J. Friedrich, ed., *Revolution.* New York: Atherton Press.

HAMILTON, RICHARD F. 1967. *Affluence and the French Worker in the Fourth Republic.* Princeton: Princeton University Press.

HAYDEN, TOM. 1966. "The Politics of 'The Movement,' " *Dissent,* XIII (Jan.–Feb.), 75–87.

HOBSBAWM, E. J. 1959. *Primitive Rebels: Studies in Archaic Forms of Social Movement in the 19th and 20th Centuries.* New York: W. W. Norton & Company, Inc.

HOFFER, ERIC. 1951. *The True Believer: Thoughts on the Nature of Mass Movements.* New York: Harper and Brothers.

HOPPER, REX D. 1950. "The Revolutionary Process," *Social Forces,* XXVIII (March), 270–79.

HUIZER, GERRIT. 1972. *The Revolutionary Potential of Peasants in Latin America.* Lexington, Mass.: Lexington Books.

HUNTER, ROBERT. 1940. *Revolution: Why, How, When?* New York: Harper and Brothers.

HUNTINGTON, SAMUEL P. 1962. "Patterns of Violence in World Politics," in Samuel P. Huntington, ed., *Changing Patterns of Military Politics.* New York: The Free Press of Glencoe.

———. 1968. *Political Order in Changing Societies.* New Haven: Yale University Press.

IGLITZIN, LYNNE B. 1972. *Violent Conflict in American Society.* San Francisco: Chandler Publishing Co.

JAMESON, J. FRANKLIN. 1956. *The American Revolution Considered as a Social Movement.* Boston: Beacon Press. First published in 1926.

JANOS, ANDREW C. 1964. "Authority and Violence: The Political Framework of Internal War," in Harry Eckstein, ed., *Internal War: Problems and Approaches.* New York: The Free Press of Glencoe.

JOHNSON, CHALMERS. 1966. *Revolutionary Change.* Boston: Little, Brown and Company.

JOHNSON, RICHARD. 1972. *The French Communist Party versus the Students.* New Haven: Yale University Press.

KAMENKA, EUGENE. 1966. "The Concept of a Political Revolution," in Carl J. Friedrich, ed., *Revolution.* New York: Atherton Press.

KATAOKA, TETSUYA. 1972. "Communist Power in a War of National Liberation: The Case of China," *World Politics,* XXIV (April), 410–27.

KAUTSKY, JOHN H. 1969. "Revolutionary and Managerial Elites in Modernizing Regimes," *Comparative Politics,* I (July), 441–67.

KECSKEMETI, PAUL. 1961. *The Unexpected Revolution: Social Forces in the Hungarian Uprising.* Stanford: Stanford University Press.

KELLY, GEORGE A. 1970. "The Contemporary French Doctrine of 'La Guerre Révolutionnaire,' " in George A. Kelly and Clifford W. Brown, Jr., eds., *Struggles in the State: Sources and Patterns of World Revolution.* New York: John Wiley & Sons, Inc.

———, and LINDA B. MILLER. 1970. "Internal War and International Systems: Perspectives on Method," in George A. Kelly and Clifford W. Brown, Jr., eds., *Struggles in the State: Sources and Patterns of World Revolution.* New York: John Wiley & Sons, Inc.

KENNER, MARTIN, and JAMES PETRAS, eds. 1969. *Fidel Castro Speaks.* New York: Grove Press.

KLING, MERLE. 1956. "Toward a Theory of Power and Political Instability in Latin America," *Western Political Quarterly,* IX (March), 21–35.

KOHL, AMES, and JOHN LITT. 1974. *Urban Guerrilla Warfare in Latin America.* Cambridge, Mass.: The M.I.T. Press.

KORNHAUSER, WILLIAM. 1959. *The Politics of Mass Society.* Glencoe, Illinois: The Free Press.

———. 1964. "Rebellion and Political Development," in Harry Eckstein, ed., *Internal War: Problems and Approaches.* New York: The Free Press of Glencoe.

KORT, FRED. 1952. "The Quantification of Aristotle's Theory of Revolution," *American Political Science Review,* XLVI (June), 486–93.

KROEBER, ALFRED L., and CLYDE KLUCKHOHN. 1952. "Culture: A Critical review of Concepts and Definitions," *Papers of the Peabody Museum,* XLVII (No. 1a).

LANDSBERGER, HENRY. 1968. "The Role of Peasant Movements and Revolts in Development: An Analytical Framework." Ithaca, N.Y.: New York State School of Industrial and Labor Relations, Cornell University. Reprint Series No. 236.

LANE, DAVID. 1969. *The Roots of Russian Communism: A Social and Historical Study of Russian Social-Democracy, 1898–1907.* New York: Humanities Press, Inc.

———. 1971. *Politics and Society in the USSR.* New York: Random House.

LA PALOMBARA, JOSEPH, and MYRON WEINER, eds. 1966. *Political Parties and Political Development.* Princeton: Princeton University Press.

LASSWELL, HAROLD D., with RENZO SERENO. 1965. "The Fascists: The Changing Elite," in Harold D. Lasswell and Daniel Lerner, eds., *World Revolutionary Elites: Studies in Coercive Ideological Movements.* Cambridge: The M.I.T. Press.

LAWRENCE, T. E. 1962. *Seven Pillars of Wisdom.* New York: Dell Publishing Co., Inc. First published in 1926.

LE BON, GUSTAVE. 1971. "The Psychology of Revolutions," in Clifford T. Paynton and Robert Blackey, eds., *Why Revolution? Theories and Analyses.* Cambridge: Schenkman Publishing Co. Excerpted from Le Bon's book of the same title, first published in 1913.

LEGUM, COLIN, and MARGARET LEGUM. 1964. *South Africa: Crisis for the West.* New York: Frederick A. Praeger, Inc.

LEIDEN, CARL, and KARL M. SCHMITT. 1968. *The Politics of Violence: Revolution in the Modern World.* Englewood Cliffs, N.J.: Prentice-Hall, Inc.

LEMARCHAND, RENÉ. 1968. "Revolutionary Phenomena in Stratified Societies: Rwanda and Zanzibar," *Civilisation,* XVIII(No. 1), 16–51.

LERNER, DANIEL. 1958. *The Passing of Traditional Society.* Glencoe, Illinois: The Free Press.

———, with ITHIEL DE SOLA POOL, and GEORGE K. SCHUELLER. 1965. "The Nazi Elite," in Harold D. Lasswell and Daniel Lerner, eds., *World Revolutionary Elites: Studies in Coercive Ideological Movements.* Cambridge: The M.I.T. Press.

LEVY, SHELDON G. 1970. "Attitudes Toward Political Violence," in J. F. Kirkham, S. G. Levy, and W. J. Crotty, eds., *Assassination and Political Violence.* New York: Frederick A. Praeger, Inc.

LEWIS, JOHN W., ed. 1970. *Party Leadership and Revolutionary Power in China.* London: Cambridge University Press.

———, ed. 1974. *Peasant Rebellion and Communist Revolution in Asia.* Stanford: Stanford University Press.

LEWIS, OSCAR. 1965. *La Vida.* New York: Vintage Books.

LIEBERSON, STANLEY, and ARNOLD R. SILVERMAN. 1965. "Precipitants and Conditions of Race Riots," *American Sociological Review,* XXX (Dec.), 887–98.

LINZ, JUAN J. 1968. *From Falange to Movimiento-Organización: The Spanish Single Party and the Franco Regime (1936–1968).* Mimeograph.

LIPSET, SEYMOUR MARTIN. 1963. *Political Man: The Social Bases of Politics.* Garden City, N.Y.: Anchor Books, Doubleday & Company, Inc. First published in 1960.

———. 1967. *The First New Nation: The United States in Historical and Comparative Perspective.* Garden City, N.Y.: Anchor Books, Doubleday & Company, Inc. First published in 1963.

———. 1970. *Revolution and Counter-Revolution: Change and Persistence in Social Structures.* Garden City, N.Y.: Anchor Books, Doubleday & Company, Inc.

LLERENA, MARIO. 1978. *The Unsuspected Revolution: The Birth and Rise of Castroism.* Ithaca: Cornell University Press.

LUNACHARSKY, ANATOLY VASILIEVICH. 1968. *Revolutionary Silhouettes.* New York: Hill and Wang. Translanted by Michael Glenny. First published in 1923.

LUTTWAK, EDWARD. 1969. *Coup d'Etat: A Practical Handbook.* Greenwich, Conn.: Fawcett Publications, Inc.

LUXEMBURG, ROSA. 1967. *The Russian Revolution.* Ann Arbor: University of Michigan Press.

McALISTER, JOHN T., Jr. 1971. *Vietnam: The Origins of Revolution.* New York: Doubleday & Company, Inc.

McCOLL, ROBERT W. 1967. "A Political Geography of Revolution: China, Vietnam, and Thailand," *Journal of Conflict Resolution,* XI(No. 2), 153–67.

MALAPARTE, CURZIO. 1932. *Coup d'Etat: The Technique of Revolution.* New York: E. P. Dutton & Co., Inc. Translated by Sylvia Saunders.

MALLIN, JAY. 1966. *Terror in Vietnam.* Princeton: D. Van Nostrand Co., Inc.

MAO TSE-TUNG. 1970. "Problems of Strategy in China's Revolutionary War," in George A. Kelly and Clifford W. Brown, Jr., eds., *Struggles in the State: Sources and Patterns of World Revolution.* New York: John Wiley & Sons, Inc. First published in 1936.

MARCUM, JOHN A. 1969 and 1978. *The Angolan Revolution.* In two volumes. Cambridge, Mass. and London: The M.I.T. Press.

MARKUS, DAVID, and BETTY NESVOLD. 1972. "Governmental Coerciveness and Political Instability: An Exploratory Analysis," *Comparative Political Studies,* V(July), 231–42.

MELOTTI, UMBERTO. 1965. *Rivoluzione e Società.* Milan: Ed. La Culturale.

MELSON, ROBERT, and HOWARD WOLPE. 1970. "Modernization and the Politics of Communalism: A Theoretical Perspective," *American Political Science Review,* LXIV(Dec.), 1112–30.

MEYER, ALFRED G. 1971. "Political Change through Civil Disobedience in the USSR and Eastern Europe," in Edward Kent, ed., *Revolution and the Rule of Law.* Englewood Cliffs, N.J.: Prentice-Hall, Inc.

MIDLARSKY, MANUS, and RAYMOND TANTER. 1967. "Toward A Theory of Political Instability in Latin America," *Journal of Peace Research,* IV, 290–327.

MIGDAL, JOEL S. 1974. *Peasants, Politics, and Revolution: Pressures toward Political and Social Change in the Third World.* Princeton, N.J.: Princeton University Press.

MILLER, NORMAN N. 1971. *Military Coup in Uganda.* Hanover, N.H.: American Universities Field Staff, Inc. East Africa Series, X(No. 3).

MILLS, C. WRIGHT. 1960. *Listen Yankee: The Revolution in Cuba.* New York: McGraw-Hill Book Company.

MOLNAR, ANDREW R. 1965. *Human Factors Considerations of Undergrounds in Insurgencies.* Washington, D.C.: Special Operations Research Office, The American University.

MOORE, BARRINGTON, Jr. 1966. *Social Origins of Dictatorship and Democracy: Lord and Peasant in the Making of the Modern World.* Boston: Beacon Press.

——. 1978. *Injustice: The Social Bases of Obedience and Revolt.* White Plains, N.Y.: M. E. Sharpe, Inc.

MURRAY, ROGER, and TOM WENGRAF. 1963. "The Algerian Revolution," *New Left Review,* No. 22, 14–65.

MYERS, DAVID G., and GEORGE D. BISHOP. 1970. "Discussion Effects on Racial Attitudes," *Science,* CLXIX(August), 778–79.

NEEDLER, MARTIN C. 1966. "Political Development and Military Intervention in Latin America," *American Political Science Review,* LX(Sept.), 616–26.

NEUMANN, SIGMUND. 1949. "The International Civil War," *World Politics,* I (April), 333–50.

NORDLINGER, ERIC A. 1977. *Soldiers in Politics: Military Coups and Governments.* Englewood Cliffs, N.J.: Prentice-Hall, Inc.

NORTH, ROBERT C., with ITHIEL DE SOLA POOL. 1965. "Kuomintang and Chinese Communist Elites," in Harold D. Lasswell and Daniel Lerner, eds., *World Revolutionary Elites: Studies in Coercive Ideological Movements.* Cambridge: The M.I.T. Press.

OLSON, MANCUR, JR. 1963. "Rapid Growth as a Destabilizing Force," *Journal of Economic History,* XXIII(Dec.), 529–52.

ORGANSKI, A. F. K. 1969. "Fascism and Modernization," in S. J. Woolf, ed., *The Nature of Fascism.* New York: Vintage Books.

PAIGE, JEFFREY M. 1975. *Agrarian Revolution: Social Movements and Export Agriculture in the Underdeveloped World.* New York: The Free Press.

PALMER, ROBERT R. 1956. *A History of the Modern World.* New York: Alfred A. Knopf, Inc.

———. 1959-64. *The Age of the Democratic Revolution.* (In 2 volumes.) Princeton: Princeton University Press.

PARSONS, TALCOTT. 1951. "Personality and Social Structure," in Alfred H. Stanton and Stewart E. Percy, eds., *Personality and Political Crisis.* Glencoe, Ill.: The Free Press.

———. 1964. "Some Reflections on the Place of Force in Social Process," in Harry Eckstein, ed., *Internal War: Problems and Approaches.* New York: The Free Press of Glencoe.

PEARSON, NEALE J., and RICHARD PERES. 1971. *The Failure of Cuban Revolutionary Strategy in Latin America.* A paper presented to the Annual Meeting of the Western Political Science Association, Albuquerque, New Mexico, April 8-10, 1971.

PETTEE, GEORGE. 1966. "Revolution: Typology and Process," in Carl J. Friedrich, ed., *Revolution.* New York: Atherton Press.

PICKLES, DOROTHY. 1947. *France Between the Republics.* London: Love and Malcomson.

PIKE, DOUGLAS. 1966. *Viet Cong.* Cambridge: The M.I.T. Press.

PINKNEY, DAVID H. 1964. "The Crowd in the French Revolution of 1830." *American Historical Review,* LXX(Oct.), 1-17.

PUTNAM, ROBERT D. 1967. "Toward Explaining Military Intervention in Latin American Politics," *World Politics,* XX(Oct.), 83-110.

PYE, LUCIAN W. 1956. *Guerrilla Communism in Malaya: Its Social and Political Meaning.* Princeton, N.J.: Princeton University Press.

———. 1962. *Politics, Personality, and Nation-Building: Burma's Search for Identity.* New Haven: Yale University Press.

———. 1964. "The Roots of Insurgency and the Commencement of Rebellions," in Harry Eckstein, ed., *Internal War: Problems and Approaches.* New York: The Free Press of Glencoe.

RACE, JEFFREY. 1972. *War Comes to Long An.* Los Angeles and Berkeley: University of California Press.

RAPOPORT, DAVID C. 1966. *"Coup d'état:* The View of the Men Firing Pistols," in Carl J. Friedrich, ed., *Revolution.* New York: Atherton Press.

REDL, FRITZ. 1966. "Group Emotion and Leadership," in A. Paul Hare et al., *Small Groups: Studies in Social Interaction.* New York: Alfred A. Knopf, Inc. First published in 1942.

REICH, WILHELM. 1946. *The Mass Psychology of Fascism.* New York: Orgone Institute Press. Translated by Theodore P. Wolfe. First published in 1933.

RICHTER, MELVIN. 1966. "Tocqueville's Contributions to the Theory of Revolution," in Carl J. Friedrich, ed., *Revolution.* New York: Atherton Press.

RIDKER, RONALD G. 1962. "Discontent and Economic Growth," *Economic Development and Cultural Change,* XI(Oct.), 1-15.

RIVERO, NICOLAS. 1962. *Castro's Cuba: An American Dilemma.* Washington, D.C.: Luce.

ROLPH, HAMMOND. 1971. *Vietnamese Communism and the Protracted War.* American Bar Association.

ROSENAU, JAMES N. 1964. "Internal War as an International Event," in

James N. Rosenau, ed., *International Aspects of Civil Strife.* Princeton: Princeton University Press.

RUDÉ, GEORGE. 1959. *The Crowd in the French Revolution.* Oxford, England: The Clarendon Press.

RUMMEL, R. J. 1966. "Dimensions of Conflict Behavior Within Nations, 1946-1959," *Journal of Conflict Resolution,* X(March), 64-73.

RUSSELL, D. E. H. 1974. *Rebellion, Revolution, and Armed Force.* New York: The Academic Press.

RUSSETT, BRUCE M. 1964. "Inequality and Instability: The Relation of Land Tenure to Politics," *World Politics,* XVI(April), 442-54.

SANDERS, THOMAS G. 1970. *Rojismo: The Resurgence of Colombian Populism.* Hanover, N.H.: American Universities Field Staff, Inc. West Coast South America Series, XVII(No. 8).

SCALAPINO, ROBERT A. 1964. "Ideology and Modernization: The Japanese Case," in David E. Apter, ed., *Ideology and Discontent.* New York: The Free Press of Glencoe.

SCHOENBAUM, DAVID. 1967. *Hitler's Social Revolution: Class and Status in Nazi Germany, 1933-1939.* Garden City, N.Y.: Anchor Books, Doubleday & Company, Inc.

SCHRECKER, PAUL. 1966. "Revolution as a Problem in the Philosophy of History," in Carl J. Friedrich, ed., *Revolution.* New York: Atherton Press.

SCHUELLER, GEORGE K. 1965. "The Politburo," in Harold D. Lasswell and Daniel Lerner, eds., *World Revolutionary Elites: Studies in Coercive Ideological Movements.* Cambridge: The M.I.T. Press.

SCHUMPETER, JOSEPH. 1947. *Capitalism, Socialism and Democracy.* New York: Harper and Brothers. First published in 1942.

SCHURMANN, FRANZ. 1967. *Ideology and Organization in Communist China.* Berkeley and Los Angeles: University of California Press.

SCHWARTZ, BENJAMIN I. 1958. *Chinese Communism and the Rise of Mao.* Cambridge: Harvard University Press. First published in 1951.

SCHWARTZ, DAVID C. 1971. "A Theory of Revolutionary Behavior," in James C. Davies, ed., *When Men Revolt and Why: A Reader in Political Violence and Revolution.* New York: The Free Press.

SCOTT, JAMES C. 1976. *The Moral Economy of the Peasant: Rebellion and Subsistence in Southeast Asia.* New Haven: Yale University Press.

SILVERT, KALMAN H. 1970. *Man's Power: A Biased Guide to Political Thought and Action.* New York: The Viking Press.

SIMMEL, GEORG. 1955. *Conflict and the Web of Group Affiliations.* Glencoe, Ill.: The Free Press. Translated by Kurt H. Wolff. First published in 1908.

SINGER, DAVID. 1970. *Prelude to Revolution: France in May 1968.* New York: Hill and Wang.

SKILLING, H. GORDON. 1970. "Group Conflict and Political Change," in Chalmers Johnson, ed., *Change in Communist Systems.* Stanford: Stanford University Press.

SKOCPOL, THEDA. 1979. *States and Social Revolutions: A Comparative Analysis of France, Russia, and China.* Cambridge, England: Cambridge University Press.

SMELSER, NEIL J. 1963. *Theory of Collective Behavior.* New York: The Free Press of Glencoe.

SNOW, EDGAR. 1971. "Genesis of a Communist: Childhood," in James C. Davies, ed., *When Men Revolt and Why: A Reader in Political Violence*

and Revolution. New York: The Free Press. Excerpted from *Red Star Over China,* first published in 1938.

SOROKIN, PITIRIM A. 1970. "Fluctuations of Internal Disturbances," in George A. Kelly and Clifford W. Brown, Jr., eds., *Struggles in the State: Sources and Patterns of World Revolution.* New York: John Wiley & Sons, Inc. Excerpted from *Social and Cultural Dynamics* (4 volumes), 1937–1941.

STEPAN, ALFRED. 1971. *The Military in Politics: Changing Patterns in Brazil.* Princeton, N.J.: Princeton University Press.

STONE, LAWRENCE. 1966. "Theories of Revolution," *World Politics,* XVIII (Jan.), 159–76.

TANTER, RAYMOND, and MANUS MIDLARSKY. 1967. "A Theory of Revolution," *Journal of Conflict Resolution,* XI(No. 3), 264–80.

TAYLOR, CHARLES LEWIS. 1970. "Turmoil, Economic Development and Organized Political Opposition as Predictors of Irregular Government Change." Paper presented to the Sixty-sixth Annual Meeting of the American Political Science Association, Los Angeles, September 8–12, 1970.

THOMPSON, SIR ROBERT. 1966. *Defeating Communist Insurgency.* New York: Frederick A. Praeger, Inc.

THORNTON, THOMAS PERRY. 1964. "Terror as a Weapon of Political Agitation," in Harry Eckstein, ed., *Internal War: Problems and Approaches.* New York: The Free Press of Glencoe.

TILLY, CHARLES. 1964. *The Vendée.* Cambridge: Harvard University Press.

———. 1978. *From Mobilization to Revolution.* Reading, Mass.: Addison-Wesley.

———, and JAMES RULE. 1965. *Measuring Political Upheaval.* Research Monograph No. 19, Center of International Studies, Woodrow Wilson School of Public and International Affairs, Princeton University.

TROTSKY, LEON. 1957. *The History of the Russian Revolution.* Ann Arbor: University of Michigan Press. Translated by Max Eastman. First published in 1932.

VON DER MEHDEN, FRED R. 1969. *Politics of the Developing Nations.* Englewood Cliffs, N.J.: Prentice-Hall, Inc.

———. 1973. *Comparative Political Violence.* Englewood Cliffs, N.J.: Prentice-Hall, Inc.

WEINERT, RICHARD S. 1966. "Violence in Pre-Modern Societies: Rural Colombia," *American Political Science Review,* LX(June), 340–47.

WOLF, ERIC R. 1969. *Peasant Wars of the Twentieth Century.* New York: Harper & Row, Publishers.

WOLFINGER, RAYMOND E., et al. 1964. "America's Radical Right: Politics and Ideology," in David E. Apter, ed., *Ideology and Discontent.* New York: The Free Press of Glencoe.

WOOLF, S. J. 1969. "Did A Fascist Economic System Exist?" in S. J. Woolf, ed., *The Nature of Fascism,* New York: Vintage Books.

ZAGORIA, DONALD S. 1971. "The Ecology of Peasant Communism in India," *American Political Science Review,* LXV(March), 144–60.

———. 1973. "Theories of Revolution in Contemporary Historiography," *Political Science Quarterly,* 88(March), 23–52.

ZEITLIN, MAURICE. 1967. *Revolutionary Politics and the Cuban Working Class.* Princeton: Princeton University Press.

ZINNER, PAUL E. 1962. *Revolution in Hungary.* New York: Columbia University Press.

INDEX